Open access edition supported by the National Endowment for the Humanities / Andrew W. Mellon Foundation Humanities Open Book Program.

© 2019 Johns Hopkins University Press
Published 2019

Johns Hopkins University Press
2715 North Charles Street
Baltimore, Maryland 21218-4363
www.press.jhu.edu

The text of this book is licensed under a Creative Commons Attribution-NonCommercial-NoDerivatives 4.0 International License: https://creativecommons.org/licenses/by-nc-nd/4.0/.
CC BY-NC-ND

ISBN-13: 978-1-4214-3018-8 (open access)
ISBN-10: 1-4214-3018-5 (open access)

ISBN-13: 978-1-4214-3117-8 (pbk. : alk. paper)
ISBN-10: 1-4214-3117-3 (pbk. : alk. paper)

ISBN-13: 978-1-4214-3116-1 (electronic)
ISBN-10: 1-4214-3116-5 (electronic)

This page supersedes the copyright page included in the original publication of this work.

THE PLAY AND PLACE OF CRITICISM

Other Books by Murray Krieger

The Problems of Aesthetics (*co-editor with Eliseo Vivas*)
The New Apologists for Poetry
The Tragic Vision: Variations on a Theme in Literary Interpretation
A Window to Criticism: Shakespeare's *Sonnets* and Modern Poetics
Northrop Frye in Modern Criticism (*editor*)

THE PLAY AND PLACE OF CRITICISM

by Murray Krieger

The Johns Hopkins Press, Baltimore

Copyright © 1967 by The Johns Hopkins Press
Baltimore, Maryland 21218

Library of Congress Catalog Card Number 66–24405

To M. O. Percival

PREFACE

Once I had decided to produce a volume of collected essays, I enjoyed the prospect of writing some shorter pieces which I had fallen into the habit of putting aside for my book-length projects. Thus almost half these essays have been written in the last two or three years; none was published before 1956, and only a few appeared before 1960. Further, I have not always been able to resist some reworking of older pieces. More than the scattered remnants of my history, then, this volume for the most part constitutes the most recent and considered statement of my critical position. This fact makes it easier for me to make the claim, all too conventional in books like this, that here is no random collection of essays but rather an organized grouping of them in accordance with a central plan. This claim receives support also from what I sadly acknowledged in an earlier Preface to be "my innate single-mindedness," so that "the more I work the more I find my various projects turning out to be aspects or developments of one project which I like to think of as a single body of theoretical and applied criticism." I fear, therefore, that no essay I would produce could be in any serious sense random or even occasional, though I have sometimes lamented this fact.

Consistent in these essays is the intimate relation of theoretical to applied criticism, of the "place" of criticism to the "play" of criticism. It is this relation which firmly unites the two sections of the book. The theoretical and the applied seemed so interchangeable to me at times that I was uncertain about whether to include some pieces in one or the other section, although the surrounding pieces usually helped me make up my mind. Running through both the theoretical and applied criticism is the doctrine which I earlier termed contextualism. Readers familiar with my work know that I refer to the context of the work rather than to the context of a social-historical moment or the context of a writer's body of work, of his "vision." At the same time they know that I do not mean to enclose the work within purely formalist considerations, that I am concerned largely—if not primarily—with the existential reflections of contextual relations.

The contextualist theme that organizes this body of essays necessarily leads to my recurrent concern with the limited possibilities of criticism as an open, non-poetic discourse that seeks to capture a closed poetic system. The necessity of critical modesty and the temptations of critical arrogance come to form a second unifying theme. It is thus a consequence of my aesthetic that I must organize this volume about the dual and opposed notions of the "play" and the "place" of criticism. And these in turn lead to what I hope is a healthy restraint upon temptations to critical dogmatics, a continuing argument for the critic's empirical as well as his theoretical impulse. His theory may put him firmly in his "place" but, insofar as it is possible, not by precluding the freedom of his "play."

The empirical impulse must keep the critic a player always, in the several senses of that splendid word *player*. During the years across which these essays span, I have learned that the task of the critic, as he matures and learns his task and from his task, is to play freely—but with his own theoretical assumptions as well as with the work to which he addresses himself. He must finally respect both his position and the current work, but only with the awareness that his position should be an incomplete, ultimately inconsistent, developing thing to be left open at the farther end for the impact of the new experience. At the same time he must have the companion awareness that what he calls "the work" is no more than his vision of the work, subject to change with his own change and with his assumption of new assumptions—which is to say, his assumption of new roles to play.

Thus this volume should become a medley of themes and counterthemes: the reader should find not only statements of a position and applications of it, but retreats from it, at moments even mockery of it in the awareness of other tentative roles to be played—both theoretical self-indulgence and theoretical self-criticism. I must hope that this attempt to express and explore my own freedom does not too seriously inhibit those theoretical contributions I for much of the time mean to make. It is the risk any critic must take to avoid the greater risk of dogma, of theoretical self-enclosure. And if I have doubts about wanting the poem to be an open system, I have no doubts about the desirable openness of the critical act.

But I must confess a single sense in which the critical mind revealed in these essays means to be less than wholly open or unlimitedly playful. For there is a single assumption without which I could pretend to no consistency of theoretical objective. The reader will note that the method, and even the recurrent metaphors and allusions, behind all I do in criticism or say about criticism in this volume springs from the notion that the literary work is, or at its best wants to be, a closed form, a tale forever retold, circular as well as progressive: its own urn. The tradition of literary aesthetics that took its various paths only after beginning with this assumption had little reason until lately to discover and to examine critically what it had been assuming. But the recent defenders of literary openness, romantically embattled and self-consciously undisciplined, have insisted on an alternative kind of voice for literature, the instinctual voice that had been automatically bypassed in the search for the refinements of form. In their anti-aesthetic, anti-critical posturings for the anti-poem, in their movements at once toward total speech and toward total silence, in their desire to replace art with life, the word with the naked act, the rebels against the major Western tradition in poetics may undo all that underlies the concerns of this book and the long line of books that stand behind it. I, too, am assuming, then, what most aesthetics in the West have since Aristotle assumed about the desirability of closedness, of integrity, without probing the claim at its foundation. To attempt a justification of what has seemed so obvious for so long, to meet head-on its recently arisen alternative, its restless, chaos-seeking, brawling antagonist, is beyond my interest as it is beyond my daring. The new day of the anti-poet, dedicated to an anti-aesthetic, is for me in my complacency just the latest disguise for Old Night.

Since these essays span ten years and a score of occasions, the personal debts I have incurred along the way are too numerous to list. There are all those who have shared in my development; there are the chairmen of symposia and the editors of journals who have created the occasions for which pieces were written; there are the colleagues who have patiently and helpfully read individual essays in manuscript. These and others form a group whose size is a humbling reminder of how profoundly the scholar's is a collaborative task. But my wife Joan must be mentioned and thanked singly as the one constant collaborator on every manuscript, on every occasion.

M. K.

Newport Beach, California
September, 1966

ACKNOWLEDGMENTS

The essay "The Innocent Insinuations of Wit: The Strategy of Language in Shakespeare's *Sonnets*" is published here for the first time. The other essays first appeared earlier and are reprinted here—occasionally in original form, sometimes slightly revised, sometimes considerably rewritten or supplemented—with permission as listed below. I am very grateful to all who, by generously granting their permission, have made this volume possible.

Part I of "The Play and Place of Criticism" is taken from "The Poet and His Work—and the Role of Criticism," *College English*, XXV (March, 1964) (by permission of The National Council of Teachers of English); the balance of the essay is previously unpublished. "The Dark Generations of *Richard III*" is reprinted from *Criticism*, I (Winter, 1959); "The 'Frail China Jar' and the Rude Hand of Chaos" is reprinted from *The Centennial Review*, V (Spring, 1961); " 'Dover Beach' and the Tragic Sense of Eternal Recurrence" is reprinted from *The University of Kansas City Review*, XXIII (Autumn, 1956). "*The Marble Faun* and the International Theme" first appeared as the Afterword to *The Marble Faun or The Romance of Monte Beni*, by Nathaniel Hawthorne, a Signet Classic, The New American Library, 1961. For "From *Youth* to *Lord Jim:* The Formal-Thematic Use of Marlow," I combined portions of "Conrad's *Youth:* A Naive Opening to Art and Life," *College English*, XX (March, 1959) (by permission of The National Council of Teachers of English), and the Afterword to *Lord Jim*, by Joseph Conrad, a Signet Classic, The New American Library, 1961. "The Ekphrastic Principle and the Still Movement of Poetry; or *Laokoön* Revisited" recently appeared in *The Poet as Critic*, ed. Frederick P. W. McDowell (Northwestern University Press, 1967).

"The Disciplines of Literary Criticism" is reprinted from *The College*

ACKNOWLEDGMENTS

Teaching of English, ed. John C. Gerber with John H. Fisher and Curt A. Zimansky, Appleton-Century-Crofts, 1965 (by permission of The National Council of Teachers of English); "Joseph Warren Beach's Modest Appraisal" is reprinted from my review of Joseph Warren Beach, *Obsessive Images: Symbolism in Poetry of the 1930's and 1940's,* ed. William Van O'Connor, *Journal of English and Germanic Philology,* LXI (April, 1962); "Contextualism Was Ambitious" is reprinted from *Journal of Aesthetics and Art Criticism,* XXI (Autumn, 1962); "Contextualism and the Relegation of Rhetoric" is reprinted from *Papers in Rhetoric and Poetic,* ed. Donald C. Bryant, University of Iowa Press, 1965; "Critical Dogma and the New Critical Historians" is reprinted from *The Sewanee Review,* LXVI (Winter, 1958); "Northrop Frye and Contemporary Criticism: Ariel and the Spirit of Gravity" is reprinted from *Northrop Frye in Modern Criticism: Selected Papers from the English Institute,* ed. Murray Krieger, Copyright © 1966 by Columbia University Press; "The Existential Basis of Contextual Criticism" is reprinted from *Criticism,* VIII (Autumn, 1966).

The materials assembled in "Platonism, Manichaeism, and the Resolution of Tension: A Dialogue" are reprinted with permission from the following sources: from W. K. Wimsatt, *Hateful Contraries: Studies in Literature and Criticism,* University of Kentucky Press, 1965; from *The Tragic Vision: Variations on a Theme in Literary Interpretation,* by Murray Krieger, Copyright © 1960 by Murray Krieger, by permission of Holt, Rinehart and Winston, Inc.; from W. K. Wimsatt, review of *The Tragic Vision* by Murray Krieger, *Journal of English and Germanic Philology,* LXI (January, 1962); from sections by W. K. Wimsatt, Hyatt H. Waggoner, Robert B. Heilman, Murray Krieger, of *What to Say About a Poem,* CEA Chap Book, Copyright © 1963 by the College English Association, Inc., Supplement to *The CEA Critic,* XXVI (December, 1963). Further permission for reprinting these materials has been granted by Professors Wimsatt, Waggoner, and Heilman.

TABLE OF CONTENTS

II. THE PLACE OF CRITICISM   129

   9. The Disciplines of Literary Criticism   131

   10. Joseph Warren Beach's Modest Appraisal   149

   11. Contextualism Was Ambitious   153

   12. Contextualism and the Relegation of Rhetoric   165

   13. Critical Dogma and the New Critical Historians   177

   14. Platonism, Manichaeism, and the Resolution of Tension: A Dialogue   195

   15. Northrop Frye and Contemporary Criticism: Ariel and the Spirit of Gravity   221

   16. The Existential Basis of Contextual Criticism   239

   Index   253

THE PLAY AND PLACE OF CRITICISM

The gift which you possess of speaking excellently about Homer is not an art, but . . . an inspiration; there is a divinity moving you, like that contained in the stone which Euripides calls a magnet, but which is commonly known as the stone of Heraclea. This stone not only attracts iron rings, but also imparts to them a similar power of attracting other rings; and sometimes you may see a number of pieces of iron and rings suspended from one another so as to form quite a long chain: and all of them derive their power of suspension from the original stone. In like manner the Muse first of all inspires men herself; and from these inspired persons a chain of other persons is suspended, who take the inspiration. For all good poets, epic as well as lyric, compose their beautiful poems not by art, but because they are inspired and possessed. . . . For the poet is a light and winged and holy thing, and there is no invention in him until he has been inspired and is out of his senses. . . . Do you know that the spectator is the last of the rings which, as I am saying, derive their power from the original magnet; and the rhapsode like yourself and the actors are intermediate links, and the poet himself is the first link of all?

(Plato, *Ion*)

I
The Play and Place of Criticism [1]

 It is clear enough, and generally acknowledged, that in recent years, with the growth of skepticism about the powers of criticism, the poem has been increasingly returned to its creator in ways that critical fashions of not long ago would hardly have led us to expect. Perhaps, however, this was a predictable reaction to those years in which literary criticism and the object on which it was exclusively to focus received more than their due of attention and justification. Hence the proliferation of phenomenological studies of poets, of studies of poets as myth-makers—a focusing on "vision" that has come to make up a serious critical and theoretical revision. It is as if we would no longer be content with middlemen in our desire to come as close as we can to the source of inspired vision, to the stone of Heraclea.

In the midst of this new swing, I must try to keep the wheel from turning too far in the descent in criticism's fortunes, to keep the critic's warning voice still with us as we return to the creator, who not only precedes him but in fact makes his existence possible. I must, in short, defend the play of criticism even as I acknowledge that criticism must know its place.

I

Let me take as my text and my definition of the critic's role, as it is juxtaposed to the poet's, this brilliantly concise statement by Leo Spitzer,

---

[1] A shorter version of Part I of this essay was delivered to the College Section of the NCTE at the 1963 meeting and published in *College English* XXV (March, 1964), 405–12, with the title "The Poet and His Work—and the Role of Criticism," under the general subject for the session, "The Poet's Voice and the Critic's Voice in the Teaching of Literature."

who here dignifies the critic with the name of "philologist": Poetry, he tells us,

> consists of *words,* with their meaning *preserved,* which, through the magic of the poet who works within a "prosodic" whole, arrive at a sense-beyond-sense; and . . . it is the task of the philologist to point out the manner in which the transfiguration just mentioned has been achieved. The irrationality of the poem need not lose anything at the hands of a discreet linguistic critic; on the contrary, he will work in accord with the poet (although with no regard to his approval), insofar as he will patiently and analytically retrace the way from the rational to the irrational: a distance which the poet may have covered in one bold leap.[2]

In this statement are all the issues concerning how the critic can try to raise his voice in unison with the poet's. Spitzer is here answering Karl Shapiro who, in his "A Farewell to Criticism" (*Poetry,* 1948), makes the language of poetry so totally *sui generis* that it comes to be made up of "not-words," utterly different from the same words used in prose. These not-words, according to Shapiro, "in their retreat from meaning, arrive at a prosodic sense-beyond-sense." Hence the impossibility of the very enterprise of criticism and the need for Shapiro's blithe farewell to it, in the interest of the uniqueness of each poem's language system.[3] From this position we can see the force of Spitzer's counterstatement: it insists upon *"words,* with their meaning *preserved,"* rather than "not-words" in a "retreat from meaning," as the materials of poetry; and it insists upon the tracing of the immediate "transfiguration" in the "prosodic" whole from words with their meaning preserved to the "sense-beyond-sense" as a feasible function of criticism instead of denying any proper function for criticism at all. Seeing the intimate relation between the materials of the poem and the surrounding world which provides them, Spitzer refuses to engage in the mystique that cuts them off as "not-words." He does acknowledge, with Shapiro, that the prosodic whole of the poem ends in a sense-beyond-sense; but he denies that it begins this way, claiming rather that the prosodic whole exercises a transfiguring force that allows what goes in as words with their meaning preserved to come out as sense-beyond-sense. So Spitzer may be claiming a mystique of his own, but—since it is a movement "from the rational to the irrational"—it is one which the critic is permitted to make it his business to trace.

The critic for Spitzer, then, is seen as a mediator between the unique

---

[2] Leo Spitzer, *Essays on English and American Literature,* ed. Anna Hatcher (Princeton, 1962), pp. 141–42.

[3] It is hardly necessary to mention that Shapiro has come a long—and I would say unfortunate—way from this position.

language of the poet and the common language of the rest of us. That is, he provides a mediate discourse that follows upon—indeed creeps after—the *im*mediate phenomenon of transfiguration. Spitzer falls between two extreme views of the relation of poetic discourse to non-poetic discourse. At the one extreme, as a kind of inevitable consequence of Crocean purity, is Shapiro's view of the poem's organization of "not-words"; but at the other extreme is the refusal to see anything at all unique about the poem, to see it as an untransfigured collection of words with their meanings preserved. The latter view sees poetry itself as mediate, so that criticism, finding the poem comfortably available, can end up just another form of philosophic discourse about a somewhat more disordered form of discourse no different in kind from itself or from any other discourse. Spitzer seeks to keep the workings of the poetic context (the prosodic whole) immediate while allowing it to remain available to the mediating discourse of the critic; indeed he seeks to keep the poem itself open at the front end (words with their meaning preserved) even as the system *qua* system miraculously transfigures its materials so as to seal itself off in its sense-beyond-sense. And the critic struggles in his painfully analytic way to account for the poet's linguistic leaps made by words that multiply their internal dimensions. But the critic can do it, according to Spitzer. A poet like St. John of the Cross, "content with the stock of words already given by the language, . . . multiplies, by repetition, variation, and syntactical disposition, the density of the web of semantic interrelations," until "these words have become endowed with a mystical depth which makes them appear as new words (though they *are*, *pace* Mr. Shapiro, the old words)" (p. 169). And Spitzer the philologist must help show us how this phenomenon can occur, moving step by perceptive step to trace a movement that no steps could have managed.

Although the critic in this manner dogs the poet's steps—imposing them even where the poet has leapt and not stepped—and will to this extent "work in accord with the poet," still Spitzer tells us he will do so with no regard for the poet's approval. The critic apparently can be true to the poem and not to the poet, indeed can be true to the poem by denying its parentage. Elsewhere Spitzer tells us a poem must have "vision" to be "poetic," and he concerns himself with the peculiarity of a poet's vision, the special way the poet conceives "a world radically different from our everyday and workaday world of ratiocination and practicality."[4] Indeed recent critics have become increasingly occupied with such visions and the poets they

[4] *Essays on English and American Literature*, pp. 218–19, for quotations and discussion in this paragraph.

characterize. But is this not a way of turning to the poet from his work? to the poet as seer from his work as object? to the human prime-mover from his artifact, which is only metaphorically his child? Not so for Spitzer, who, in the manner of the contextualist critic, is finally concerned, not with the vision behind the work, but with the vision that is formed *as* the work, is defined by the new word that is the work, is identical with the work as a prosodic whole. For beyond the need for a poetic vision, as a mere raw material, is the need for the work to transform the merely "poetic" to the "artistic," that is, to transform the different vision of a world to a "work of art . . . characterized by its self-sufficiency and organic perfection which allow it to stand out as an independent whole." So if the poet has vision, as critics we must center our interest on how it speaks, not *in* the poem but *as* the poem. As a poet speaking, he speaks the immediacy of his subjective vision in the immediate objectivity that the poetic system encloses. And his is the only discourse that can unite immediacy with objectivity—though at an enormous discursive price. In view of this unique conjunction, we can hardly restrict the poem in its workings to what the man or his life can tell us in languages other than that of this poem. Only it can allow us total access to the vision—and its world—which he *as poet* creates, and thereby objectively structures, for himself and for us all.

This view of the poem and its vision as irreducible to its author and his vision leads to our viewing literary criticism as a distinct, analytic, and thus rationally ordered set of disciplines, irreducible to the disciplines governing the use of biographical and other historical data. And we would accordingly justify the need to find a separate place for criticism in the training of the teacher of literature, who would necessarily find himself incurring the profound obligations and pleasures of the critic's role as Spitzer conceives of it. But we must not inflate our expectations about what even the best criticism can accomplish, if its primary objective is to make its voice a high-fidelity account of the poet's. In terming criticism a rational pursuit, we may, like Spitzer, too easily assume that its orderly manner will not inhibit it as it tries to trace the baffling machinations of the fully activated poetic context.

Spitzer, it will be remembered, saw that the critic must "patiently and analytically retrace the way from the rational to the irrational: a distance which the poet may have covered in one bold leap"—thus from sense (the old words with their meaning preserved) to the sense-beyond-sense of the transfigured new word. What precisely is irrational about the operation of poems, if *irrational* is really the proper word? Clearly what Spitzer must mean is that the multiple and simultaneous ways in which words—their sounds, their meanings, their extension into metaphor, archetype, character, and action—interact within the poetic context defy the rational operations of our critical discourse, which after all owes the same obligations to the semantic, syntactic, and logical operations of language as all other nonpoetic discourse does. But to claim that poetry has ways that resist any exhaustive explanation by more orderly discourse is not really to argue that poetry itself is either rational or irrational in its nature but that it is of another order to which the terms *rational* and *irrational* really do not apply, may even be irrelevant. As the system becomes fully empowered, as it explodes into life, all elements that began as mere references swell with the burden of associations absorbed from its neighbors. Or should I change the metaphor and mix alchemy with recent politics by saying that each element becomes gilt with the associations of all?

Language can be manipulated in our best poems in ways that do serious violence to the ways in which we are accustomed to find semantics, syntax, and logic operating. And yet, as the word *manipulated* suggests, it is language whose behavior is finally controlled and directed—perhaps more completely and efficiently so than in any other form of discourse. But it is an order of control utterly alien to what we expect to find except in poetry. It is language in rebellion against the ways in which we normally use it as a counter for things; it is language that subverts its normal auxiliary function of denying its own terminal existence in order, instrumentally, to lead us to the world; it is language that proclaims itself as substance and its own world of multiplying meanings as sovereign.[5] If we find that the law of non-

[5] I wish there were time on this occasion to observe more precisely this kind of operation in the poetic context. But examples of this sort of movement in language cannot be traced in a moment. My entire study of Shakespeare's *Sonnets* in *A Window to Criticism: Shakespeare's* Sonnets *and Modern Poetics* (Princeton, 1964) stems from just these miraculous manipulations of language. (See the following essay on the subject in this volume.) The *Sonnets*, of course, are full of them. To cite at random, one cannot try to justify the full sense of "image" in Sonnet 3 ("Look in thy glass and tell the face thou viewest") or the juxtaposition of "used" and "lives" in Sonnet 4 ("Unthrifty loveliness, why dost thou spend") or the rumination over the stately ruin that is "mortal" in Sonnet 64 ("When I have seen by Time's fell hand defaced") or the bitter "wise world" compounded of "vile world" and "vilest worms" in Sonnet 71 ("No longer mourn for me when I am dead") or the multiplication of those eloquent demonstrative pronouns in Sonnet 74 ("But be contented. When that fell arrest") or the magnificent "hugely politic" as the culmination of the anti-political imagery of Sonnet 124 ("If my dear love were but the child of state") without being astounded with all that seems to happen at a stroke. The way in which

contradiction does not appear to apply to this sovereign world of language, the fault is not with that world but with our too rational insistence upon being propositional about it, with our insistence upon measuring a unique discourse with the yardsticks of our common discourse, which we assume is the only kind going. And if we are sensitive enough to find that a discourse eludes these measuring instruments, we charge it with behaving "irrationally," although its behavior is proper, indeed is *perfectly* proper, to its poetic order as the behavior of our discourse probably never is to its non-poetic order.

But how, then, should the critic treat the meaning of this poetic context, provided he can think of the word *meaning* without automatically reducing it to the sort of meaning yielded by non-poetic discourse? He may see that, just as the language has interrelations within it that function in terms of a unique system of controls, so its world reflects unique interrelations among those tensions, even contradictions, that characterize our experience at its most immediate, felt level. This level we may term the existential in its unique fullness that denies those generalizing concepts and propositions that our limited discourse forces us to impose upon it. In its dynamics the existential must resist the fixity that all discourse requires as a condition for its very being. Only the poetic context can claim the dynamics, the multiple and contradictory tensions within its own interrelations, that match those of the existential level of our reality. Yet it also has those elements of order and control—its own elements, responsive to its own needs—that can fix this fluid existential level for the perception of us all, though without thinning its density. The poetic context can, however, claim freedom from any more generally imposed elements of order and thus from the frozen discourse of logically marshalled propositions which, however much they may intend to speak of the unique person in the uniqueness of his existence, can finally speak only a generic tongue addressed to universal instances, not to instantaneous ones. All this is to echo the earlier notion that only poetry can be a discourse that unites the immediate with the objective, that matches the immediacy of subjective experience with the objectivity of the fixed, formal precision that gives poetry its aesthetic

---

these movements are earned is hardly logical, though they are indeed earned. And the meanings finally arrived at can hardly be reduced to what biography or conventions can tell us any more than they can be reduced to what a dictionary can tell us, no matter how sound its historical principles. But neither, alas, can they even be reduced totally to what the language of a critic can tell us as he tries to keep up with all that happens to words as the context newly refines and defines itself.

nature. Other discourse, necessarily and purposefully mediate, must restrict itself only to the mediating rational framework imposed upon experience to rob it of its baffling immediacy that teases us and our discourse out of thought. But what, then, of the critic with his mediate discourse and his immediate poetic object—immediate precisely because it resists both translation and abstraction? Unless he wishes to compete with the poem by writing a poem of his own—which is probably a way only of producing second-rate criticism as well as second-rate poetry—how is he to frame his dialect even to approach his object?[6]

Perhaps the following oversimplified diagram will help frame his problem, even if it only shows his plight as the more desperate. (The philosopher and the poet both move straight across from left to right, so that the arrows apply only to the critic's movements.)

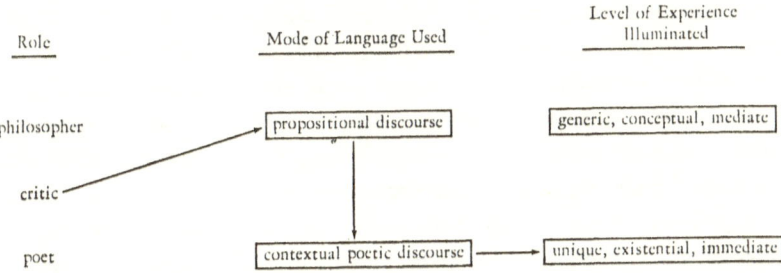

At least this diagram indicates what the critic may most want to do, though his materials prevent him from doing so. The critic, borrowing something from each, somehow is to work his way back and forth between the language used by the poet and that used by the philosopher and between the experiences each is to illuminate. Granted that the philosopher also may wish to illuminate the unique, existential level of experience; but his language, influenced as it is by its logical obligations, reduces whatever aspects of the existential he means to treat to the commonly universal level

---

[6] Throughout this essay I am of course assuming an ideal poem, that is, the perfection of the poetic context in its workings—a perfection that in fact rarely if ever occurs. To the extent that it does not occur, the critic's judgmental function requires him to point out as deficiencies in the poem those places where its unique language system fails, where it opens too easily and immediately to his common language, and ours. To the extent that the critic must struggle—as, in this essay, I have him struggling—with a unique language system in the totality of its operations, using only his own inadequate language, he is acknowledging the aesthetic perfection of the poem, so that his struggles carry an implied evaluation of the highest sort.

permitted—indeed invented—by the coherent organization of his propositional structure. What is being claimed, then, is that the pre-analytic level at which we most immediately exist can be fixed or objectified only in the self-complicating dynamics of the poetic context, and that any attempt to objectify it in a more common language, responsive to more general demands, will—as it trims away the many diverting dimensions of poetic discourse—lose the mysterious uniqueness at the heart of our existence. The critic must be aware of these dangers—and disheartened by them since his own language is so limited in its dimensions. He alone takes upon himself the futile, self-defeating task of using propositional discourse in order to reveal its limitations, to shame it before the poetic, exposing its utter inadequacy to the experience it claims to talk about. Still propositional discourse is all he has to use to grasp the uniqueness of contextual discourse, even as the latter is the only discourse that can grasp the uniquely existential. The critic must try to grasp the contextual within the terms of the propositional while trying to avoid the generic, conceptual world of experience to which this discourse, as propositional, must lead. Finally, of course, he can no more manage this feat than the philosopher can, so that the arrow toward the right of my diagram—suggesting that the critic can move, with his limited discourse, through the poetic context to the uniquely existential in experience—is misleading about his accomplishments even if it properly represents his ambition. He too finds himself, with all mediators, in the conceptual and generic. But there is always his primary act of faith toward the object as unique and the experience it illuminates as unique, even if his necessary obligation to his language makes the gesture somewhat quixotic. So the procedure is muddy and self-defeating; but it *does* proceed—doggedly and with a clumsy pragmatism that is his response to what is theoretically denied him. What he produces must, within its own orderly framework, be *rationally* clearer than the poem in order to justify its existence as criticism; yet it must be muddier than the conceptual order in order to justify the existence of poetry.

The critic must fail: he must end in a hopeless middle ground of a would-be existential philosophy even as he recognizes that very phrase as an oxymoron. He may have to sound like a philosopher obsessed with the unreconcilable contradictions in the human condition, with its irrationality, so that he would differ from the too rational philosophizer upon poetry only in that his paraphrases would be more tortuous, or more double-faced and resistant to system. Not that the world of the poem is really a chaotic, would-be propositional world that—through a strange combination of poetic economy and rational waywardness—manages to make several incompatible assertions at once. It merely *seems* contradictory—is made to stand forth stripped of its true nature—when the critic, using the only discourse at his disposal, tries to talk rationally about it. The poem, as contextual, no more asserts contradictions than it asserts anything else. But through its very *being* the poem provokes its enraptured critic to use his language of limited rapture to talk about the poem as if it were making such assertions, although its *meaning* cannot be reduced to them, as the critic well knows. As with its vision, the only assertion the poem makes is the one that all its aspects work together to make as together they make the poem by becoming the poem. In its wholeness this assertion, again like the vision, cannot be caught in the critic's language even as it catches him in the experience of itself. So, inadequate language or not, the critic is driven to try to catch for us all what it is that has caught him.

The contextualist view of poetry has always had to make the distinction we have seen in Spitzer between the old words, which the words of the poem were before this poem and which they seem to be in this poem until it works its systematic magic, and the new word which this poem becomes, with its system working to provide its unique definition. Accordingly, the contextualist has also had constantly to worry about how the mediating critic, with his old words, could hope to approach the new word that is the poem any more successfully than could any other non-poet. With this worry we are back to the post-Crocean *cul de sac* that we found with Shapiro leads to the temptation of purism: the declaration of the total inaccessibility of the poem to criticism. Of course, this is a more comforting view for poets than it is for critics, who must save what they can, turning from despair in their task even as they resist vainglorious pretensions for it.

So we may have to be less optimistic than Spitzer about the power of criticism, with its analytic, unilinear language creeping in its petty pace, to capture the multiple levels of simultaneity which the acrobatic poetic context displays. And these limitations of the power of criticism the critic and his readers must never forget: we must always remain aware of our need to turn again and again from the critic to the poet and his voice, since the critic's total faithfulness—let me repeat—must be to them, provided by the poet's voice we mean only the one that speaks in and through the work, *as* the work. The more remarkable the poetic context, the more marked the critic's limitations, but also the more privileged his task and the less he can resist it. Though he should know that a commonness of language dictates that only a difference of degree, sometimes barely measurable, separates the critical reductions of a crude message-hunter from his own attempts to wrestle with his terms to torture them *toward* a faithful rendering of the untranslatable, still he struggles to prove that failures can be partial and that proof of their partiality constitutes also a partial victory over the unavoidable incapacities of his materials. This gives him courage to be the pragmatist who can try to come closer rather than farther even as he sees the all-or-none in his situation: the theoretical impossibility of his forcing his discourse to be, like himself, more than the poem's victim. But he is a better, a more victorious critic as he understands that, by choosing his role and knowing his place, he chooses to be the victim of that role and that place even as he is the victim of the poem. He restricts himself to the propositional dialect to which all but the poets must finally restrict themselves. Yet he must seek to bring into that coarse medium—and in it display to the rest of us—that elusive dialect of the language system whose unique capacities derive from its power to slip from the grasp of the common tongue.

In the end it seems that I am calling for a rhapsodic criticism; that is, for echoes of the poem and commentaries on the poem by the critic as rhapsode in the Greek manner. We must remember how, according to Plato, Ion the rhapsode suffered—without defense—at the hands of Socrates. Yet we ask the critic to be rhapsode, his voice at once his own and moving in response to the poet's. Drawn into the poet's fine frenzy through the pull of the stone of Heraclea referred to in my epigraph from Plato, the critic is caught between Homer's irresistible and unreasoning frenzy and the ineluctable reasoning of the smirking Socrates. He cannot account for the former even as he is held accountable by the latter. So he feels inadequate to both.

Robert Penn Warren put the matter with incomparable brilliance in his improved version of the fable of Orillo at the opening of his well-known essay "Pure and Impure Poetry":

> . . . the poem is like the monstrous Orillo in Boiardo's *Orlando Innamorato*. When the sword lops off any member of the monster, that member is immediately rejoined to the body, and the monster is as formidable as ever. But the poem is even more formidable than the monster, for Orillo's adversary finally gained a victory by an astonishing feat of dexterity: he slashed off both the monster's arms and quick as a wink seized them and flung them into the river. The critic who vaingloriously trusts his method to account for the poem, to exhaust the poem, is trying to emulate this dexterity: he thinks that he, too, can

win by throwing the lopped-off arms into the river. But he is doomed to failure. Neither fire nor water will suffice to prevent the rejoining of the mutilated members to the monstrous torso. There is only one way to conquer the monster: you must eat it, bones, blood, skin, pelt, and gristle. And even then the monster is not dead, for it lives in you, is assimilated into you, and you are different, and somewhat monstrous yourself, for having eaten it.

So the monster will always win, and the critic knows this. He does not want to win. He knows that he must always play stooge to the monster. All he wants to do is to give the monster a chance to exhibit again its miraculous power.

The critic is a critic in that his activity puts the poem to a most severe test: it must work to make him fail. Conversely, he must knowingly fail to make it work. To the extent that he is a good critic and a faithful reader, that failure will be a significant measure of its success.

II

Let me add a confession to undercut the modest note with which the critic tries to disarm both reader and poet. I begin it with a frank question: How, in view of so restrained a statement of the place of criticism, can the critic manage the freedom for the play that makes his activity an enlarging one for himself and his culture? The double injunction—criticism must freely play but criticism must know its place—has conflicting demands in its two parts. If we have seen the more modest side of the critic in attitudes like that represented by the Warren quotation as a summary of all I have said so far, we now must confront the boldness—even arrogance—that lurks just beneath the mask of humility that leads the critic to pose as tragic hero, one who fails in order to guarantee the work's success. As the critic in one mood seeks his success in his small, purposeful, even sacrificial failure, so he can in another mood, as frustrated artist himself, become emboldened to seek in his criticism a free act that is his own triumph.

But is this not the very competing with the poet—the critic's creation of a pseudo-poetry—that we saw his fealty to his beloved object expressly proscribe? Undoubtedly so. And our critic in his more self-effacing mood must consistently proscribe it. In this mood we saw him view poetry as the sole form of discourse that manages to enclose *objective immediacy,* the fusion and transformation of that subjective *immediacy* which is one's unexpressed inward vision and that *objective* mediacy which is non-poetic discourse (including, alas, criticism properly restrained). As both objective and immediate, the poem becomes the sole form that is an altogether *realized* act of freedom, the capturing—the stilling, the embodiment—of movement that still moves.[7]

If, however, the critic can have *his* objective discourse only by foregoing immediacy for mediacy of discourse, he must choose to be bound by the limits of the poem that is his object even as he seeks to play freely within those bounds. But this is to make that adverb "freely" a deceit, contradicted at every moment by the bounds. The critic may declare his freedom by insisting on his play, but he will still marshal his justifying evidence from the poem as he goes. What this evidence will justly allow becomes, then, the boundary concept restricting the freedom of his play and keeping his activity in its place.

Nevertheless, the critic's defensive position will cause him to muster, and in part yield to, his arrogance. As we have seen in Plato's rhapsode trapped between Homer and Socrates, the critic must expect to be disliked by the poets for violating their systems with his discursive intrusions; and he must expect to be distrusted, if not scorned, by other systematic users of non-poetic discourse—scientific and philosophic—for struggling along with a bastard language not systematically propositional because of its borrowings from the poetic and not systematically poetic because of its dependence on propositional proprieties. Yet as middleman he must struggle along in just this way to serve the rest of us as the "rings" farther removed from the poetic source—that is, to serve culture in the historical march of its institutions and ideas. For to all these he must make discursively available a contextually-existentially unique system which, for all its words, is discursively as silent as a statue. Yet we need the grasp of all that it in its special way "says" in its propositional silence, although our own coarsely utilitarian habits of language put us in need of the critic's help.

Before the silent perfection of the poetic system, the critic, in his judgmental role, can grunt his own silent approval of the system. If he grunts his disapproval, he can manage to talk as well, to explain the incompleteness of the system, its control by other, extramural systems. But on the favorable side, beyond grunting his approval, he can—in hopes of leading us to "see" and then silently to grunt our own approval—point to the elusive internal relations that may until now have escaped our notice, can point to the magical and unpredictable accretions of meaning that have been set in motion.

---

[7] The essay "The Ekphrastic Principle and the Still Movement of Poetry," below, is devoted to the exploration of this definition of poetry.

The Play and Place of Criticism

So the critic can grunt and, to substantiate his grunts of approval, he can point. But can he speak? Well, as Benedetto Croce's negations have taught us, the critic can tell us all that the poem is *not* as he seeks to protect it from non-poetic systems. So he can speak negatively of what it is not and what it does not mean. But can he speak positively of what the poem is and means? Clearly, in spite of all that argues he cannot, he must speak to this purpose. And he must speak in a way that, cautious and distrustful of itself and its imprisonings, yet imposes discursive system, however tentatively, sporadically, sloppily. Otherwise, for all its superb functioning, the poem may have no more than aesthetic effects on us, may be prevented from shaping our vision of our world. Of course, the great poems have always managed to have more than aesthetic effects and to help shape the vision of their culture, but not so many as might have—and those not so profoundly and as immediately as they might have—if each had its critic, at once diffident and daring, at once imposing discursive categories and forcing these to vibrate to the poem's destruction of categories. The critic, then, must make the thematic plunge as he forces his fidelity to the poem to give way in part to his responsibility to history and his ambition for himself. His difficulties, however they alert his caution, can end only by feeding his daring.

The presumptuous critic can insist that his tentative superimposition of structure upon the poem—a structure at once discursively responsible and existentially immediate, at once referential and free, sanctioned by the work and sanctioned by his play—is an act of freedom possible and even promising to the writer. Here is a notion that can foster either self-deception or recklessness in him. The blank page in his typewriter is not open to the *totally* free creation, the utter self-realization, of poet or storyteller. Rather the critic's is a discourse that moves, however freely, in response to a story already told but silent—silent as Keats' urn—concerning its meaning and the meaning of its beauty. So the critic's discourse remains only variations on a theme, a "performance" of the poem, formed *through* the work, even as it dares, self-deceptively, for the occasion, pretend to be the poem's one discursive equivalent.

How can we call this a free act, then? How can we properly restrain the critic without at the same time curbing the presumption he needs if he is to muster the daring that can tame the poem to the discursive limits to which the perception of the rest of us is measured? How can he play within his place? How balance his strangely incomplete creative freedom with his responsibility? In short, to what extent is his voice his own, to what extent his poet's? To what extent must his energies be spent, and his freedom drained away, by his worrying about matching the two voices, reducing his own to echo?

As soon, then, as we move beyond the properly pious acknowledgment of the primacy of the poem to the inevitable presumption of its critic, we are confronted by the antithetical pulls of his play and his place: on the one hand the free, self-indulgent practice of criticism as a masterful enterprise, and on the other the restricting considerations—prompted by literary theory—of its role or function, and necessarily of its limits. The critic's antithetical pulls, insofar as he must act in response to them both, make his a paradoxical, if not impossible, movement. His position, then, is no less difficult than I earlier claimed it to be in describing the proper modesty of his place; but its difficulty is now more honestly seen to have its roots in his arrogance as well as in his humility. And we must measure the full resonance of the critic by his self-assertion as well as by his submission: by his satisfying the mutually incompatible demands of play and place, act and theory, freedom and bondage. He must, in short, be responsive to his roles as both maestro and second fiddle. This volume may be seen as yet another futile attempt to join the two demands and the two roles, or at least—if I may close this essay in the modest vein—to demonstrate them, side by side, momentarily in peaceful coexistence.

I
THE PLAY OF CRITICISM

2

The Innocent Insinuations of Wit:
The Strategy of Language in Shakespeare's *Sonnets*

This essay is intended as a postscript to my book *A Window to Criticism: Shakespeare's* Sonnets *and Modern Poetics* (Princeton, 1964). There I tried to maneuver Shakespeare's language in the *Sonnets* into a typological system of metaphor, a system that would express the substantive union of discrete entities made possible first by love and then by poetry as love's unique discourse. But in my pursuit of the direction and constellation of the metaphors, I did not generalize upon the strategy in accordance with which these manipulations of metaphor were managed, the method—the unique syntactical dispositions—which controlled their farthest reaches. I propose here to stand aside from my more substantive work and to try to do just this. In the course of this essay I shall occasionally have to echo a few observations on individual sonnets from my book and make some fresh ones. But here these observations are to serve a totally different purpose since, I repeat, it is the method or strategy, and not the substance or thematic range, of Shakespeare's language that concerns me.

If I were to use a single phrase to characterize Shakespeare's strategy at its best, I would term it "the innocent insinuations of wit"—and if "innocent insinuations" suggests an oxymoron, this is precisely to my purpose. The "innocent" is apparent only: on the face of it there is no guile in the words as they marshal themselves into syntax. But at their best the undercurrents in the sonnets seem to wind themselves about into unforeseen unions of meaning that create constant surprises for us and—we almost allow ourselves to believe—for their poet. What artfulness there is, is artless, though its subtlety demands our endless search—and admiration. For, as the word *wit* assures us, everything has been under a shrewd aesthetic control all along.

This strategy is perhaps best seen by contrast to another, and my use of

19

the overused term *wit* permits me to draw this contrast. Some time back my friend and former colleague Leonard Unger, borrowing terms from Freud, proposed to establish a scale along which poetry could be measured, a scale extending from the extreme of "dream-work" to the extreme of "wit-work."[1] As I understood it, at the "wit" end of the scale he would place the self-consciously metaphysical poem, whose metaphorical development is traceably explicit in a strategy that borders on the exhibitionist. Whatever unpredictable accretions the dialectic may achieve, it achieves through a mastery of manipulation that is everywhere observable—indeed that shouts to be observed. At the "dream" end of the scale he would place the poem that appears to be controlled by little more than random association. If a poem by John Donne reflects the "wit" strategy, the Shakespearean sonnet reflects the "dream" strategy. But the word *strategy* is all-important, as is the word *appears* in the claim that the "dream-work" "*appears* to be controlled by little more than random association." For surely Unger did not mean that the one kind had art while the other left all to chance. It is not a choice between strategy and no strategy but a choice between strategies, between a strategy of explicit wit and an apparent strategy of dream which, after all, has its own wit, however innocently it seems to insinuate it and, thus, to entwine and capture, as it enraptures, us.

This contrast between the strategies of Donne and Shakespeare is not dissimilar to an earlier one drawn by John Crowe Ransom, except that Ransom's was far less sympathetic—indeed it was positively disrespectful—to Shakespeare. In his by now nearly infamous "Shakespeare at Sonnets"[2] Ransom accuses Shakespeare of having, in effect, insufficient strategy, of failing to have what Ransom elsewhere terms "the courage of [his] metaphors"—which is the very courage that he sees Donne as having. For Ransom seems to have fallen into the error—which I have rejected—of claiming that the metaphysical is the only strategy that wit may employ, so that if the poet does not indulge it, he is turning from wit altogether: he is giving over the reins from the intellect, which critics in the line from Eliot have assured us is the ruling faculty for poetry as wit, to mere emotion ruled by little more than the rushes of chance. And heaven pity the clumsy, inconsistent structure of language, little better than careless prose, that arises

[1] To my knowledge he has never developed this proposal in his published writings beyond the epigraph to, and the hints lurking in the background of, his essay "Deception and Self-Deception in Shakespeare's *Henry IV*," *The Man in the Name* (Minneapolis, 1956), pp. 3–17.
[2] *The World's Body* (New York, 1938), pp. 270–303.

from such indulgence, such abdication of rule. Heaven pity it, for the Ransomian critic will not!

It is by reason of the multiple strategies allowed by the Unger formulation that I prefer it and see it as a capacious alternative to Ransom's. (So, I suspect, would Ransom for many years now—indeed from a period not long after his early and narrowly polemic, if then necessary, way of positing his doctrine.) It was in part for this reason also that I saw in the subtler, dreamlike play of wit of poems like Shakespeare's *Sonnets* challenges to critical method in the Renaissance lyric far more pressing than the intricate, but more clearly patterned, lines of the metaphysicals. Between the golden and the drab poets that C. S. Lewis too conveniently speaks of in his history of sixteenth-century literature in England are poets whose wit need not lead to the open skepticism, open paradox, and open cacophony that deny the golden voice of poetry, poets who produce not the shock of open clash, but the ever-renewed wonder at the surprises to which soft and cherished words can—almost on their own and by accident—lead us. But only *almost*, of course. And of no poet more than Shakespeare in his *Sonnets* can we make this claim. This is why he becomes the greatest challenge, and the delineation of his strategy the greatest necessity, to a disciplined criticism of the lyric.

I

I shall propose here just two of the ways in which Shakespeare produces his deceptive effects, ways in which a seeming looseness works its dialectical path into the tightest of aesthetic traps. The first I term association as dialectic. Instead of the common metaphysical tactic of working carefully through an image, allowing it to expand into the constitutive symbol that becomes the poem, the poet shifts rapidly and with a seeming abandon from image to image. Yet there seems to be no way of our justifying the selections and movements aesthetically; that is, we can neither claim a principle in terms of which they are exhaustive possibilities that together comprehend a whole, nor can we even justify a principle of inclusion for those we have or of exclusion for those we have not. The choice rather seems quite arbitrary: the poet seems to choose those that occur to him as they occur to him, and he stops when he has enough to satisfy the externally imposed limits of the sonnet form. The individual image is hardly developed but is mentioned and dropped, and the next one picked up with no sense of inevitability even tried for.

The Play of Criticism

We can relate this habit causally to the commonly acknowledged weakness of the Shakespearean sonnet form, in contrast to the Italian: that three prosodically independent quatrains and the epigrammatic couplet are too many semi-autonomous units for so brief and powerful a lyric as the sonnet. And in making this relation a general observation, we have further struck at the aesthetic firmness of Shakespeare's frequent practice. We seem to be taking dead aim at the "when . . . when . . . then" sonnet as typically unsatisfying. The poet chooses at random two or three examples—just about any two or three will do—in the natural and the human world of some universal process, say mutability, devoting a couple of lines or at most a quatrain, beginning with "When," to each example; he adds, for contrast, the painful consequence of these observations, prefixed by an expressed or implied "Then"; and he closes with a generalizing couplet that expresses the poet's sadness at, and struggle against, the inevitability as it touches him and his love. Here is hardly a formula that promises much more than the obvious, though prettily and wistfully dressed up, hardly a formula that can hope to transform conventional materials into a unique aesthetic form and symbolic statement. Nor was it, in the hands of many lesser poets.

How does Shakespeare, despite this seeming relaxedness of attitude toward his materials, subdue the passivity of dream through the strategy of wit? Sonnet 12 would seem to be a typically uncontrolled example of this flabby form—and typically devoted to the poet's sentimental regrets at the ruinous passage of time. Possible instances of the universal process are everywhere, to be found as soon as looked for; nor do the ones chosen at first appear especially ingenious in their selection or combination.

When I do count the clock that tells the time,
And see the brave day sunk in hideous night;
When I behold the violet past prime,
And sable curls all silver'd o'er with white;
When lofty trees I see barren of leaves
Which erst from heat did canopy the herd,
And summer's green, all girded up in sheaves,
Borne on the bier with white and bristly beard;
Then of thy beauty do I question make,
That thou among the wastes of time must go,
Since sweets and beauties do themselves forsake
And die as fast as they see others grow;
    And nothing 'gainst Time's scythe can make defence
    Save breed, to brave him when he takes thee hence.

The octave begins with the painfully simple reference to the clock, which is further weakened by the redundancy of the first line and the obvious opposition of "brave day" and "hideous night." Then the symbols of summer's death: the fading flower of line 3 juxtaposed to the fading hair of line 4, followed by the leafless trees of lines 5–6 and "summer's green" which has been cut down (lines 7–8). These are the random examples cited in the octave from which the personal application of the sestet is to follow.

But is there not a structure to these as Shakespeare deploys them? There is—and, as is often the case in these sonnets, it arises out of the way in which he builds, gradually and almost imperceptibly, to the finally total union of nature and man, out of the metaphorical reduction of the human world to the natural or rather the reading of the natural world in terms of its human consequences. The violets and the human hair are juxtaposed, as if by association; they are analogous coordinates, but only that, since no relation between them is suggested. But in the next two lines nature is brought into explicit relation with animal life. The trees are related to the herd as its former protector from summer's heat. Or is the herd human too by extension, the humanity of pastoral convention, humanity in its natural—its communal, its herd—aspect? And is this not the herd which *is* under nature's protection, the nature in whose fruitfulness, mirror of its own, it must trust? But this is only the merest suggestion, only the faint glimpse of possibility—we can hardly be sure. The two lines that follow make us certain, even as they make the union of man and nature total—which is to say, substantive: "And summer's green all girded up in sheaves/ Borne on the bier with white and bristly beard." The funeral of "summer's green" is transformed as we watch from merely personified nature to the literally human in nature. It is, of course, the "bier" and its crucial echo in "beard" which manage this utter transformation. Unquestionably "beard" is brilliant: in its vegetative meaning it is true to the grain, the now lifeless "green," even as, in combination with the almost homonymous "bier" which makes it possible for "beard" to work its double way, it humanizes the ritual procession. "Borne on the bier with white and bristly beard." *Exeunt* as natural man is inevitably borne from the stage.

In three two-line units, then, we have moved from analogy to relation to identity between nature and man. Although this poem, as a "when . . . when . . . then" sonnet, seems to promise only a series of undeveloped, alternative analogies drawn from an apparently random association and designed to illustrate a single general claim, it has gradually grown into a full, total, and even substantive union of its varied elements. For it has been a seemingly random movement from chance analogy to a two-faced, single-bodied metaphor.

The Play of Criticism

How proper that only now has Shakespeare earned his logical conclusion beginning on line 9; only now can he justly say that consequential word "then": "Then of thy beauty do I question make/That thou among the wastes of time must go." The vision to which he has built in the octave has been too inclusive and conclusive for anything less mandatory than "*must go*"—even for nature's fairest flower, the loveliest of men. And the generality with which the couplet begins ("And nothing 'gainst Time's scythe can make defence") is given fearful specificity as "Time's scythe" returns us to the earlier described harvest that awaits us all as we move toward the "white and bristly beard" that will place us, like spent grain, on the bier to be borne as all *exeunt*. "Time's scythe" cuts several precise ways by cutting its one universal way in line 13. How fully Shakespeare has refreshed, has given new substance to, the conceit of the grim reaper that grows naturally out of the analogy of the life of man to the seasons of vegetable life.

Still there is more than this. For the escape from the scythe that cuts at all levels must spring from the poem, whose materials seem to build toward a destruction that is escape-proof. And, as if by accident, these materials will provide the poet-Monte Cristo the tools he needs, even out of the carelessly weak opening two lines we have observed ("When I do count the clock that tells the time/And see the brave day sunk in hideous night"). For in the couplet the hopelessness of the penultimate line ("And nothing 'gainst Time's scythe can make defence") is taken back at the last moment by that remarkably polysemous word—here a mere preposition (or is it?)—"Save" ("Save breed, to brave him when he takes thee hence"). The way to resurrection is the universal way that is the way of "breed," always the answer to the "barren," the always newly won "canopy" for "the herd." But why, in terms of the poem? Because this way is the "brave" way. We recall that in line 2 it was the "brave day" that was lost as symbol for all that time destroys ("When I do count the clock that tells the time/And see the brave day sunk in hideous night"). This phrase, "brave day," reasserts itself in the "brave" of the last line ("Save breed, to brave him when he takes thee hence"). In this line "brave" is an echo, a reflection of the "breed" with which it alliterates: it is the breeding which is the braving of time. But as an echo also of line 2, "brave" is at the same time a kind of equivalent for day, that which the "hideous night" has replaced. By braving time through breed, the friend in effect restores the bravery which is day, overcoming night (and the destructive cycle of the natural process), which is hideous in the extinction it threatens.

In the octave, in the relation of the octave to the conclusive third quatrain, and in the relation of all these to the couplet, to the stopping short of total defeat, the naiveté of apparent association has become the witty strategy of dialectic. The poet has (I shall not say unwittingly) made available to himself the very materials he needs. The very process of the poem has seemed to be a dreamlike search that has led us (and, the illusion persuades us, has led the poet) to discover, to come upon, almost to trip upon an aesthetically sound resolution whose inevitability has been fed by all that he has uttered.

Let me cite more briefly several other examples of association become dialectic. We can observe a similar movement to a similar fusion of man and nature in the considerably more brilliant "when" sonnet, Sonnet 64:

When I have seen by Time's fell hand defaced
The rich proud cost of outworn buried age;
When sometime lofty towers I see down-razed,
And brass eternal slave to mortal rage:
When I have seen the hungry ocean gain
Advantage on the kingdom of the shore,
And the firm soil win of the watery main,
Increasing store with loss and loss with store:
When I have seen such interchange of state,
Or state itself confounded to decay;
Ruin hath taught me thus to ruminate—
That Time will come and take my love away.
    This thought is as a death, which cannot choose
    But weep to have that which it fears to lose.

In moving from the first to the second quatrain, we move from the world of man to the world of nature, from the succession of political states to the succession of unending cycles in the rhythmic heart of the universe. Shakespeare begins by observing the destruction of the noblest and most ambitious of human productions, with the ironic use of "eternal" ("brass eternal") the clue to his scornful view of human claims to immortality. Even more insulting to the "eternal" is its being at the mercy of a rage that is itself "mortal." Thus the contrast between these "mortal agents," in the first quatrain, who have undone their victims, the would-be "eternal" who are themselves to be undone in turn, and the natural, seemingly immortal agents who face a mutual undoing in the second quatrain. As if to prove the claim that the human political state is a microcosmic reflection of the universal state under time, the antagonists of the second quatrain, the ocean and the shore, are rendered totally in human terms, as they act in accordance with political motives. Thus the apparent distinction between the human and the natural in the two quatrains comes to be methodically blurred. All the realms of "state" have been identified and reduced to the extreme consequences of its narrowest meaning, that of human politics. The word "state," despite its range of meanings, from narrow to broad, from politics to the general condition of being (or rather of becoming), is shown to be a single reductive entity that can contain and unite them all even within its narrowest confines. For these confines can be extended unlimitedly without losing their more precise limitations. The ocean, seen as "hungry" for the acquisition of another's, reduces "the kingdom of the shore," only later to be forced to give back what it has gained along with some of its own. Thus the inconclusive (even as it is the most conclusive and inclusive) "interchange of state" or, in terms that suggest the first quatrain, "state itself confounded to decay," as the political sense of state achieves its universal sway under time, incorporating the other senses. The many politic antagonists can only interchange their states, as his metaphor enables Shakespeare's human and natural antagonists to interchange *their* states. And all, mutually aided or mutually impeded, must eventually face the reduction to identity, the obliteration which is the obliteration of "state" itself as an entity, as a static concept. (The redundancy is intended.)

A similar reduction to the indifferent sameness of mutability and decline is emphasized as the uniting force of yet another "when . . . when . . . then" sonnet, Sonnet 15.

When I consider everything that grows
Holds in perfection but a little moment,
That this huge stage presenteth naught but shows
Whereon the stars in secret influence comment;
When I perceive that men as plants increase,
Cheered and check'd even by the self-same sky,
Vaunt in their youthful sap, at height decrease,
And wear their brave state out of memory;
Then the conceit of this inconstant stay
Sets you most rich in youth before my sight,
Where wasteful Time debateth with Decay,
To change your day of youth to sullied night;
    And, all in war with Time for love of you,
    As he takes from you, I engraft you new.

The universality of time's process begins in the first line with the "everything" that permits of no exceptions. Its all-inclusiveness is echoed by the unqualified "naught but" of line 3, the "selfsame" of line 6; and as a most constant "conceit" it sharply underlines the "inconstant stay" (line 9) which characterizes man's feeble role in the natural process. It is the utterly contingent, "inconstant stay" of man, thrown against the "conceit" of the uncontingent single law of time, that justifies the use of the theatrical figure that reduces "everything" to helpless, insubstantial puppetry. An indifferent, pagan nature that is pure process and thus absolute in its transience controls completely. It is the nature of the influencing stars and the maddeningly "selfsame sky" that equally *ch*eer and *ch*eck (and how effective the alliteration that proves the identity, from the perspective of nature's indifference, of blessing and curse). Further, they indifferently cheer and check men and plants, or rather, more extremely, "men *as* plants." In the face of his nature, what hope can there be for man to command his "brave state" (the state associated with day, we recall from Sonnet 12) but most inconstantly? The total leveling in the sonnet is impressive. It reminds us that the "when . . . when . . . then" poem, as we saw with Sonnet 12, moves in its seemingly random way from example to example in part to show the unrestricted universality—indeed the absolute oneness, whether in nature or in man—of the process.

Sonnet 73, though not a "when" sonnet, has the same quatrain organization as the "when" sonnets we have examined, and again the movement is from annual ruin in nature to permanent death in man.

That time of year thou mayst in me behold
When yellow leaves, or none, or few, do hang
Upon those boughs which shake against the cold,
Bare ruin'd choirs where late the sweet birds sang.
In me thou see'st the twilight of such day
As after sunset fadeth in the west,
Which by and by black night doth take away,
Death's second self, that seals up all in rest.
In me thou see'st the glowing of such fire
That on the ashes of his youth doth lie,
As the death-bed whereon it must expire,
Consum'd with that which it was nourish'd by.
    This thou perceiv'st, which makes thy love more strong,
    To love that well which thou must leave ere long.

Each of the metaphors is seen as if occurring *in* the poet, but how much less metaphorical (or rather, how much more than just metaphorical, how substantive) they become: from the bare boughs, the "sweet birds' " "ruin'd choirs," with their many subtly probing implications for the aging poet, to the twilight and its bleak promise of darkness. But in this second quatrain a metaphor within metaphor carries us closer to what most concerns the poet, even as we remain with nature; for "black night," which overcomes the last of twilight, is "death's second self, that seals up all in rest." It is for the third quatrain to bring us to death's *first* self, now seen in the expiring of another fire than the sun's, the modest flame of life in its last glow:

In me thou see'st the glowing of such fire
That on the ashes of his youth doth lie,
As the death-bed whereon it must expire,
Consum'd with that which it was nourish'd by.

We can use the three-quatrain arrangement of Sonnet 60 as a grand reprise to all these poems, as the total (and totally brilliant) confounding of nature and man: the endless fluidity of tides and the immeasurable flux of human time, the beauties of human features transformed to nature's plowed and blooming field awaiting the reaper.

Like as the waves make towards the pebbled shore,
So do our minutes hasten to their end,
Each changing place with that which goes before,
In sequent toil all forwards do contend.
Nativity, once in the main of light,
Crawls to maturity, wherewith being crown'd,
Crooked eclipses 'gainst his glory fight,
And Time that gave, doth now his gift confound.
Time doth transfix the flourish set on youth
And delves the parallels in beauty's brow,
Feeds on the rarities of nature's truth,
And nothing stands but for his scythe to mow;
    And yet to times in hope my verse shall stand
    Praising thy worth, despite his cruel hand.

Once more, and perhaps with the most impressive maestro flourishes yet, the several, seemingly parallel and coordinate images fuse into one. Still the synthesis, as it is won, is subtly won, is won in the process of winning it without seeming to.

There is yet another purpose which this unmethodical method, in the hands of Shakespeare, can serve: the solving of an insoluble problem at the end of a search for a metaphorical way out. There is a throwing up of metaphors that will not quite work on the path to one that will. But again the path is less random than the projected psychology of the speaker would suggest. Sonnet 34, the second in a sequence of sonnets on guilt and innocence in the poet and his beloved friend, is a helpful example. After a quatrain that summarizes the effect upon him of his awareness of the friend's guilty act dwelt upon in Sonnet 33, the rest of the poem seeks a way for the poet to excuse an irrevocable, seemingly inexcusable act. With the friend seen in Sonnet 33 and the first quatrain of Sonnet 34 as the heavily clouded sun, the poet must in the next two quatrains reject several metaphorical ways to dissolve the offense:

'Tis not enough that through the cloud thou break,
To dry the rain on my storm-beaten face,
For no man well of such a salve can speak
That heals the wound and cures not the disgrace.
Nor can thy shame give physic to my grief;
Though thou repent, yet I have still the loss:
Th' offender's sorrow lends but weak relief
To him that bears the strong offence's cross.

From the rain as "salve" to heal the "wound" to "shame" as "physic" for "grief" to repentance as relief for the poet's burden, none will work. But the last may open the way for the poet—or rather the friend—to find an escape: "Th' offender's sorrow lends but weak relief/To him that bears the strong offence's cross." The final word, "cross," promises more than we should have expected from the negative force of these lines which in this seem to resemble those that preceded it. With this word we have not only the prospect of the poet, as innocent, taking the sin upon himself, but also the introduction of hope, of the chance for ransom, for redemption. We are ready for the couplet which fulfills that hope, if with too much abandon and too little resistance: "Ah, but those tears are pearl which thy love sheds/And they are rich and ransom all ill deeds." Finally this metaphor works the trick, if only by fiat. The "ah" suggests the sudden, surprising discovery of the specious opening that the metaphor in the couplet offers him. The poet leaps to grasp the unearned transfer from "tears" to "pearl" to "ransom" which appears to solve his problem at an unsubstantive level of language only. Are we to see him as permitting himself to be deceived by his language in his desperation to exonerate his friend? May this not be the poet's sin whose consequences he willingly accepts in the following sonnets? And is this not the "ransom" which does fulfill the expectations of "cross"? The poet has ended by joining the friend in a search to evade the consequences of sin. The parade of rejected metaphors has not after all been pointless, has finally led to one which has worked at least verbally as the poet, in grasping at it as a miraculous transformation—"tears" into "pearl"—opens himself to the ransom that he, in taking on the sin, must pay. Thus the weaving dialectic and its further unpredictable consequences.

In Sonnet 65 a more desperate search for escape from a more inescapable trap leads to a less affirmative consequence, one that keeps us still in the box. The universal and indifferent reduction to "ruin" which we witnessed in Sonnet 64 ("When I have seen by Time's fell hand defaced") has been dramatically extended to the small helplessness of the poet's love in 65. If not the mightiest and most powerful, human or natural, can retain its "state," what chance for the poet's love? The poet searches for a metaphor:

O fearful meditation! Where, alack,
Shall Time's best jewel from Time's chest lie hid?
Or what strong hand can hold his swift foot back?
Or who his spoil of beauty can forbid?

But this time the poet seems to give up: "O, none!" He seems not to have come upon his discovery. Still, however it may appear, the dialectic is not really done with. For immediately after "O, none!" the poet takes it back with "unless": "O, none! *unless* this miracle have might/That in black ink my love may still shine bright." So the impossibilities have led to affirmation after all, through the bold appeal to miracle where less daring metaphors failed. But what is this miracle ("that in black ink my love may still shine bright") except a yet more daring metaphor, one which discards the material and worldly character of the rejected metaphors for the spiritual motive of the appeal to miracle, an appeal which is given to us in the absurd, even impossible, paradox of its material reflection—the brightness of love in the blackness of ink. Thus the rejection not only of the discarded metaphors but of the very strategy of making the desperate attempt in this futile direction, in accepting Time and his material world on his own terms. And again the dialectic has tightly controlled, even where it seems to have been ignored for less planned, more emotionally spontaneous methods.

In all poetic dialectic we are surprised. In the dialectic of wit we expect eventual surprise. We feel it has been well plotted in the very tissue of the seeming logic—very like the Aristotelian peripety in drama, distinguished by its combining of surprise with probability. But in the deceptive sort I am tracing here, the apparent dreamlike association suddenly become dialectic, we are surprised to be surprised; and so is the poet, we are convinced during our own double surprise, even if this conviction only attests to the greater perfection of the illusion of artlessness.

II

The second of the devices I shall mention of Shakespeare's deceptive dialectic, of the casual procedure turned inevitable, we have already ob-

Language in Shakespeare's Sonnets

served repeatedly in passing. We may term it pun as argument, using *pun* most broadly as coincidence of meaning and seeing it as the ground for the self-effacing, smuggled conceit. Not only does Shakespeare use his extra dimensions of meaning where he finds them ready-made in certain words; he also creates unique semantic dimensions for his language out of his construction of a unique syntax. And the critic working with this language must create—out of its internal relations—a special glossary for it.

We have repeatedly observed Shakespeare creating the added dimensions that make a word a nucleus of meanings from which his special dialectic can emerge. Remember what happened to "brave" in Sonnet 12 as it was used, first to characterize "day" in opposition to "hideous night," then in an alliterative relation to "breed" to borrow some of breed's strength in its heroic struggle with death's night. This combination of juxtapositions gives it a union of meanings which it can carry to its use in Sonnet 15 (man's "brave state") or even to Sonnet 33 (day's "bravery"). We have seen similar phonetic borrowings of meaning in Sonnet 12 in "bier" and "beard" and in "*ch*eer'd and *ch*eck'd even by the self-same sky" in Sonnet 15. And we may find these borrowings at the two ends of the climactic line of Sonnet 64, "Ruin hath taught me thus to ruminate": "ruin," echoed in "ruminate," is *in* the rumination, becomes its cause and its subject, its formative principle, even as its continuous process keeps the rumination from ever being complete. Or in Sonnet 6 the "self-kill'd" friend who refuses marriage becomes the "self-will'd" friend, as the rhyme allows identity to arise in the verbs despite the transfer of initial consonants—and of crucial meanings.

There are also many other juxtapositions that create new accretions of meaning as Shakespeare works up his unique glossary. We can look briefly and inadequately at the complex relations between "world" and "worms" in several sonnets, especially 71.

No longer mourn for me when I am dead
Than you shall hear the surly sullen bell
Give warning to the world that I am fled
From this vile world with vilest worms to dwell.
Nay, if you read this line, remember not
The hand that writ it, for I love you so
That I in your sweet thoughts would be forgot
If thinking on me then should make you woe.
O if, I say, you look upon this verse
When I perhaps compounded am with clay,
Do not so much as my poor name rehearse,
But let your love even with my life decay,

THE PLAY OF CRITICISM

*Lest the wise world should look into your moan
And mock you with me after I am gone.*

The poet, looking toward his death, asks his friend to be a wise enough worldling not to mourn him. But notice: he speaks, not of his death, but of his fleeing from this vile world to dwell with vilest worms, "vile world" and "vilest worms" occurring as echoes in one line. And in the couplet the friend is warned that if he insists on honoring dead love, he risks the scorn of the "*wise* world." Here once more is a remarkable collision of juxtapositions, of worms and world and their adjectives, "vile," "vilest," and "wise." The movement from the positive to the superlative degree of the adjective, "vile" to "vilest," in moving from "world" to "worms," is crucial: the worms are the furthest extension of the very tendency that makes the world "vile." The world as practical time-server that takes material truth as its total reality has the quality that is most purely represented in the activity of the worms. The vile world is a lesser worm. The friend's love, then, is to be permitted to "decay" even as the poet's "life" does; he is to feed on the body of love as the worms do on the body of life, since he is to see both bodies as suffering the identical limitation of the flesh. And the shift from the "vile world" of line 4 to the "wise world" of line 13 is the final evidence of Shakespeare's irony. For this world is wise—that is, shrewd, prudential—only as it is vile, only as it exercises those characteristics which ape the destructive perfection, the absolute cooperation with time, of the "vilest worms." The human impact Shakespeare packs into the earthy gluttony of the worms gives new force to their use elsewhere: in Sonnet 74 ("So then thou hast but lost the dregs of life,/The prey of worms, my body being dead"), in the anti-material address to the soul in 146 ("Shall worms, inheritors of this excess,/Eat up thy charge? Is this thy body's end?"), in Sonnet 6 (". . . thou art much too fair/To be death's conquest and make worms thine heir"), and, by implication, in the marriage plea to the narcissistic friend in Sonnet 1 ("Pity the world, or else this glutton be,/To eat the world's due, by the grave and thee") and in the "all-eating shame" that follows in Sonnet 2. The same charges and pleas fill Sonnet 9, although wormy self-consumption is related more insistently to the "world," a word that occurs with increasing force four times.

Sonnet 9 also marks the climactic joining of the several senses given the words "use" and "unuse" as a consequence of their earlier connection with "abuse" and "usury" in Sonnets 4 and 6. In Sonnet 4 ("Then, beauteous niggard, why dost thou *abuse*/The bounteous largess . . ./Profitless *usurer,* why dost thou *use*/So great a sum of sums . . ./Thy *unus'd* beauty must be tomb'd with thee,/Which, *us'd*, lives th' executor to be"), in Sonnet 6 ("That *use* is not forbidden *usury*"), and in the climactic Sonnet 9 (beauty "kept *unus'd,* the *user* so destroys it"). In these Shakespeare creates new possibilities for punning—creating the paradoxical possibility of a use that is a saving with interest and an unuse that is a using up—by forcing the relation of "use" to "usury," of finding "use" *in* "usury." Here we move toward his creation of a new semantic out of already existing coincidences of sound and meaning. There are innumerable examples of the use of double meaning to enclose narrow dimensions within broad, all-inclusive ones. We have observed in Sonnet 64 the effective manipulation of "state" that unites the narrowly political condition with the universal human condition, which proves in the end, alas, to be no more than political. Sonnet 124 ("If my true love were but the child of state") is an even more dramatic use of this maneuver, with its shockingly paradoxical turn, in which the great affirmation is that the poet's uncontingent, unpolitical love "all alone stands hugely politic," that is, as its own body politic. I could point also to the implicit reference to biblical typology under the more obvious uses of *figure* in Sonnet 6 ("Ten times thyself were happier than thou art,/If ten of thine ten times refigur'd thee") and 106, in which the praises of historical personages become "but prophecies/Of this our time, all you prefiguring" (and we can note the alliterative echoes as well among "praises," "prophecies," "prefiguring"). I could point to the forced union of three worlds in one by the pun on *husband* in Sonnet 3 ("For where is she so fair whose unear'd womb/Disdains the tillage of thy husbandry")—the pastoral, the domestic, and the world of proper management and conservation. Only by accepting the need to act as pastoral husband encouraging nature's yield and as sexual husband in the home can he husband—that is, conserve, keep from expending—the value that is himself. But, as I have said, the examples seem innumerable.

A more clustered use of the double meaning in a single poem leads to the kind of conceit that Shakespeare manages most effectively in the *Sonnets*, what I have called the smuggled conceit. It is not, of course, the self-conscious, witty sort that calls attention to itself as the organizing principle of the poem. Rather it arises, seemingly without pressure or even guidance, under our very eyes. It grows, in the background, out of the narrow range within which the secondary meanings are contained. Sonnet 30 is a splendid, if obvious, example.

The Play of Criticism

When to the sessions of sweet silent thought
I summon up remembrance of things past,
I sigh the lack of many a thing I sought,
And with old woes new wail my dear time's waste:
Then can I drown an eye, unus'd to flow,
For precious friends hid in death's dateless night,
And weep afresh love's long since cancell'd woe,
And moan the expense of many a vanish'd sight:
Than can I grieve at grievances foregone,
And heavily from woe to woe tell o'er
The sad account of fore-bemoaned moan,
Which I new pay as if not paid before.
 But if the while I think on thee, dear friend,
 All losses are restor'd and sorrows end.

As in many of the sonnets, the protestations of love come strangely trailing the language of crass finance. Such bits of soft sentiment as "sweet silent thought," sighs, wails, drowning eyes, grievings and moans, are held in the businesslike framework of "sessions," to which one is harshly summoned up, of woes that are "cancell'd," of "expense," accounts, and payments. We must be puzzled by "precious friends" or by "losses," which can be read into either world, or both; or by the telling over the "sad account," which can refer to the narrating of his sentimental tale or to the "telling" activity of the auditor. But it is just this language which has a foot in both worlds that seems to prove how thoroughly the poet has proved their union. Yet this union should be a shocking one, a yoking of elements that are surely most heterogeneous. And it is this union that aggravates the poet's losses since it emphasizes their immeasurability, their resistance to being balanced out, cancelled. It calls for nothing less than the total leap of love in the couplet.

  Sonnet 87 is a more spectacular example of the effective mingling of matters of money and affection.

Farewell! thou art too dear for my possessing,
And like enough thou know'st thy estimate.
The charter of thy worth gives thee releasing;
My bonds in thee are all determinate.
For how do I hold thee but by thy granting?
And for that riches where is my deserving?
The cause of this fair gift in me is wanting,
And so my patent back again is swerving.
Thyself thou gav'st, thy own worth then not knowing,
Or me, to whom thou gav'st it, else mistaking;
So thy great gift, upon misprision growing,
Comes home again, on better judgement making.

*Thus have I had thee, as a dream doth flatter,
In sleep a king, but waking no such matter.*

With the word "dear" in the first line, and the related "possessing" ("thou art too dear for my possessing"), the two poles of meaning that create the dialectic and the unity of the poem are sent forth. The unbroken multiplication of legal and financial terms shouts almost too loudly the poet's bitterness at having love's "dear" reduced to the merchant's "dear," to mere price. But the poem does so reduce it. Material reality will not permit love to be assigned where worths are so unequal. Only in the dream, from which the poet has been rudely awakened, can the beggar deserve a kingly love. This would appear to be an indictment of the shrewdness of the intellect, of the rational judgment of equivalence. But may we not see in this indictment a defense of the very strategy of language I have been tracing here? It is the controlled wit, under the service of the directing intelligence, that is being disdained for the seeming abandonment to an almost dreamlike associationism, with the bizarre equations and identities it produces. Why not, then, beggar and king in defiance of the world's rational denial?

III

There are, to be sure, sonnets in the sequence which do tumble in a more orderly manner out of an initially proposed and imposed conceit, whether it be the four elements in Sonnets 44–45 ("If the dull substance of my flesh were thought") or the careful comparison of love to food in 75 ("So are you to my thoughts as food to life"). How different this latter from the juxtapositions which we witnessed earlier, which, in discovering themselves, discovered the oneness of worminess and gluttony. The predetermined wit of the more obviously planned conceits is not the strategy Shakespeare handles well—or characteristically. It is rather out of the seeming abandonment to dream that, as in dream, unexpected, even unaccounted for, identities may arise—out of the accidents and miracles of a language that has been newly, and fully, empowered, even if by a masterful control that everywhere disguises itself as chance. The meanderings of dream, with the impossible reappearances, disappearances, and unions of contradictory identities, these meanderings at last discover themselves under the firm direction of art. The dream is yielded to as it is captured, flows even as it is frozen.[3] Caprice is transformed, while indulging its capriciousness,

---

[3] I call attention to the extensive development of this metaphor in "The Ekphrastic Principle and the Still Movement of Poetry," below.

into the inevitability of pattern. The *logos* affirms its hegemony by absorbing all that is wayward into the firm teleology of the word.

We have seen the double-reaching language of Sonnet 87 destroying the very judgment it seems intent on making, as the final lines establish the richness and beauty that, as dream, have been exploded ("Thus have I had thee as a dream doth flatter,/In sleep a king, but waking no such matter"), richness and beauty established only in the act of their vanishing, existing only in the discovery of their impossibility. We are reminded of the stubborn, if desperate, postulation of love's and poetry's miracle at the close of the universal ruin of Sonnets 64–65 (What chance? "O, none! unless this miracle have might,/That in black ink my love may still shine bright"), miracle in the teeth of rational impossibility. Without impossibility, no miracle; without reality, no awareness of the magic unreality of dream. The miracle, then, as dream, and poetry and love as the mutually enabling agents of both miracle and dream, in the teeth of the wise world's prose. We are beyond the limiting and limited world of wit—but not beyond the world of art and its breakthrough. We are rather following the words of Theseus, in the play appropriately for us called *A Midsummer Night's Dream,* who appreciates the "shaping fantasies" in which "the lunatic, the lover, and the poet/Are of imagination all compact." We follow his words to Prospero, that magician-poet-god of *The Tempest,* who transforms reality and knows of the dreamlike "stuff" of man. And we have a new sense of Prospero as Shakespeare's archetypal poet-as-maker—vision of his own best self; a new sense of Prospero's magical metaphysic as Shakespeare's magical poetic. In no one more than Shakespeare, and nowhere more than in his *Sonnets,* can we know and cherish the magic unpredictability of poetry's spell. The wisely sensitive critic can try only to pass it on as a noble contagion; he must treat it tentatively; he dare not try to capture it lest he loosen its hold on him.

3
The Dark Generations of *Richard III*

 Let me begin by remarking that I had half-jestingly thought of calling this essay "Richard III as Scourge and Purge." Not a highly serious way to begin a study of a work of the highest seriousness; but it should immediately indicate that I intend to break radically with the conventional treatments of the play as a Marlovian tragedy, even with those that allow the master Shakespeare a few extensions of the formula in his manipulation of it. For if we call Richard a scourge, then we are assuming that his victims somewhat deserve what he inflicts upon them, that they have been cruelly active themselves even if at the hands of Richard they are now rendered passive. And if we call him a purge, then we are assuming that he is in the service of the gods of a righteous future who must start afresh, that a guilt-ridden past, with all its weighty burdens, must be cast off by one of its own. If we think of Richard in these ways, then it is clear that the play is not uniquely his, nor the power and the evil uniquely his, as the Marlovian formula would have it.

Even looking only at Richard's motivations, however, we find more than is in the world of Marlovian psychology. One need hardly invoke the insights of Freud to see that the lust which impels him is not solely directed toward power. Admittedly, one can point to his opening soliloquy where—in a Marlovian manner which denies the possibility of self-deception and the psychological complexity that goes with it—he announces his villain's role and his prideful assumption of it. Indeed one can strike this note earlier, as early as his perhaps finer soliloquy in *III Henry VI* (III. ii. 124-95). Richard, then, does confront his villainy with a consciousness as candid as the actions which ensue from his villainy are consistent. But there is another and a less conscious motive being continually revealed in these speeches. He invariably couples the assertion of political power with the sexual assertion of manliness. And he admits that he embraces the former only because he is, as monster, denied the embrace of sexual love.

Early in the soliloquy from *III Henry VI* Richard despairs of ever attaining the crown as he lists those who would precede him in the line of succession. Well, then, he must turn to another source of masculine satisfaction: "I'll make my heaven in a lady's lap." But the dialectic proceeds:

O miserable thought! and more unlikely
Than to accomplish twenty golden crowns!
Why, love forswore me in my mother's womb;
And, for I should not deal in her soft laws,
She did corrupt frail nature with some bribe. . . .

There is no alternative, then. However impossible to attain, it must be power after all: "I'll make my heaven to dream upon the crown." In the opening soliloquy of *Richard III* he notes that the advent of peace demands that the warrior be transformed into the lover. Significantly, it is by a sexual image that he describes the warrior, so that the role as lover may follow naturally from the battle's end. The image tells us something also of Richard's deeper motives in the public life as well as in the private life.

Grim-visag'd War has smooth'd his wrinkled front;
And now, instead of mounting barbed steeds
To fright the souls of fearful adversaries,
He capers nimbly in a lady's chamber
To the lascivious pleasing of a lute.

It is clear from Richard's language that he dotes, perhaps perversely, on the sensual abandon in the battle of love—on the "sportive tricks" one plays with "a wanton ambling nymph." And again he decides there is nothing left for him but "to prove a villain" since he "cannot prove a lover."

His villainy seems to him to be chargeable to the heavens since it is but a moral reflection of his deformity.

The midwife wonder'd, and the women cried
"O, Jesus bless us! He is born with teeth!"
And so I was; which plainly signified
That I should snarl and bite and play the dog.
Then, since the heavens have shap'd my body so,
Let hell make crook'd my mind to answer it.
I have no brother, I am like no brother;
And this word "love," which greybeards call divine,
Be resident in men like one another,
And not in me! I am myself alone.

(*III Henry VI*, V. vi. 74–83)

The Dark Generations of Richard III

But if he is not a man among men, neither, of course, is he a beast. He may "play the dog," but he does so as a monstrous perversion of man. Thus he answers Anne, who insists that even the fiercest beast knows pity, "But I know none, and therefore am no beast" (*Richard III*, I. ii. 72). A unique monster, then, excluded from the order of men as from the order of beasts, he sees himself indeed as representing a gap in nature, a lump of chaos thrust into the midst of the natural order. And so he will do the business of chaos in the political and moral order. This dedication to chaos, physical and political, stirs him from his early soliloquy,

[Love] did corrupt frail nature with some bribe
To shrink mine arm up like a wither'd shrub;
To make an envious mountain on my back,
Where sits deformity to mock my body;
To shape my legs of an unequal size;
To disproportion me in every part,
Like to a chaos, or an unlick'd bear-whelp,
That carries no impression like the dam.

(*III Henry VI*, III. ii. 155–62)

to the speech before his final battle:

March on, join bravely, let us to 't pell-mell;
If not to heaven, then hand in hand to hell.

(*Richard III*, V. iii. 312–13)

And since force is the arm of chaos even as right is the sometimes feeble arm of order, so must he dedicate himself to force as well. It should be clear, however, that, far from being his essential motivation, force, like the power to which it leads, is a very derivative one. Shakespeare's probing instruments are too delicate to stop, with Marlowe, short of cutting away a little lower layer.

But there is even more psychological complexity than this to Richard. His will to political power is not merely a substitute for his frustrated will to sexual power, but, as his "mounting" warrior may have intimated, is a perversion of it so that sexual elements become curiously intermingled with political ones. His incapacities as a lover continue to torment him, but he welcomes and even relishes the torment. He parades his deformity before women even as he parades it before himself. And he takes an "underground" delight in both displays. His dialogue with Anne is a brilliant manifestation of this strange exhibitionism. Surely we cannot account for Richard's behavior in this scene solely on the grounds of his lust for power. Granted that

Richard feels this marriage to be a political necessity (as he tells us, I. ii. 157–59), that by their union the houses of York and Lancaster can be joined; nevertheless he hardly undertakes his wooing in a way that will ensure success. On the contrary he seems to enjoy this occasion since it presents every conceivable obstacle. It is the mostns inauspicious moment for him to woo her. Further, he makes it perfectly clear (I. ii. 160–62) that other foul deeds remain to be done before the marriage can serve its purpose; in other words, that there is no rush about wooing Anne, that he can await a more favorable opportunity.

Let us note the circumstances of the present occasion: Anne is the mourner in the funeral procession of her father-in-law, Henry VI, murdered by Richard, as Anne knows. And it is still but very little more time since the death of her husband, whom Richard co-murdered (*III Henry VI*, V. v). Of course, Richard's physical handicaps, in such marked contrast to Anne's murdered Edward—"fram'd in the prodigality of nature," as Richard disdainfully acknowledges—will always damage his chances; but they surely should prompt him to seek out a better time, if success is his primary objective. But both before and after the scene Richard indicates his special pleasure in wooing her at such a disadvantage. And he begins in the worst way possible, by forcibly interrupting the funeral procession, by allowing the conversation to enter those channels which must render him most hateful to Anne, by leading her to engage with him in a repartee that is on his side callously witty. His bantering appears calculated to inspire in her a loathing that must issue in her humiliating outcry, "thou lump of foul deformity." His love of self-torture having accomplished this much, he pursues her, still as her lover lest her revulsion abate. He speaks of the fitness of Henry VI for heaven and she, of Richard's for hell. Richard insists there is one other place for which he is fit:

Anne. *Some dungeon.*
Rich. *Your bed-chamber.*
Anne. *Ill rest betide the chamber where thou liest!*
Rich. *So will it, madam, till I lie with you.*

(I. ii. 111–13)

At this point fair Richard has turned Petrarchan lover. He blames Anne's beauty for his murderous actions, and when she threatens to destroy that beauty, like the sonneteer he answers,

These eyes could not endure that beauty's wreck;
You should not blemish it, if I stood by.

As all the world is cheered by the sun,
So I by that; it is my day, my life.

When she wishes that her eyes were basilisks to strike him dead, he again has the appropriate retort, even using the appropriate conceit:

I would they were, that I might die at once;
For now they kill me with a living death.

Once he has won her, Richard matches his contempt for her with his pride in himself.

Was ever woman in this humour woo'd?
Was ever woman in this humour won?
I'll have her; but I will not keep her long.
What! I, that kill'd her husband and his father,
To take her in her heart's extremest hate,
With curses in her mouth, tears in her eyes,
The bleeding witness of my hatred by;
Having God, her conscience, and these bars against me,
And I no friends to back my suit withal
But the plain devil and dissembling looks,
And yet to win her, all the world to nothing!

And his perverse self-mockery returns. If in spite of all these obstacles he has won the right to succeed his handsome predecessor, then, he ironically reasons, he must suppose himself to have underestimated his sexual attractiveness all along. He shall have to get mirrors and tailors to care for his fine figure and make a proper lover. In the opening soliloquy of the play he remarked that in this time of peace he, as a warrior who could not be a lover, had

. . . no delight to pass away the time,
Unless to see my shadow in the sun
And descant on mine own deformity.

Now he closes the soliloquy which follows his success with Anne by reverting to this idea, this time with the bitterness only renewed by his amatory conquest:

Shine out, fair sun, till I have bought a glass,
That I may see my shadow as I pass.

Toward the end of the play there is the similar scene with Queen Elizabeth when he woos her for her daughter's hand. Again he chooses the worst possible time since, his murder of her children having only recently occurred, she has come with his mother to join in cursing him. Again he seems to succeed, and again his success produces in him only contempt for her. Does it not appear possible, then, not merely that Richard pursues power as single-mindedly as he would a mistress, but also that he pursues power so that he may coerce a mistress—one who will have to play the game of treating him as lover and who, though it only aggravates her revulsion, will painfully sport with him as with one "fram'd in the prodigality of nature"? And in self-laceration Richard will enjoy it both ways: because his villainous intelligence has forced his mistress to receive him as lover and because his monstrous ugliness increases her horror and his pain in his unnatural role. Surely this is hardly a hero-villain of a single dimension.

I should like now to return briefly to the scene between Richard and Anne in order to ask an obvious question, one answer to which I find most illuminating. How is it, in view of Richard's handicaps of person and occasion and in view of his tactics, that Anne accepts him? We may ask a similar question about Elizabeth in the other scene I referred to—if we assume that she was sincere in her acceptance of him, an assumption that her later acceptance of Richmond makes doubtful for some readers. And we may ask similar questions about many other characters, some of them mostly openly at odds with Richard, who at times seem not to see through his transparent dissembling. Rivers, for example, whom Richard is shortly to dispose of, commends a sentiment of Richard's as "virtuous" and "Christian-like"; and Hastings, just before he learns that Richard has condemned him to death, says of Richard after observing his apparent good humor,

I think there's never a man in Christendom
Can lesser hide his love or hate than he;
For by his face straight shall you know his heart.

(III. iv. 53–55)

The usual answer to these questions seems unacceptable. If we take these characters at their face value, then Shakespeare is asking us to believe the unbelievable: that otherwise intelligent and sometimes brilliant characters (his women, for example, prove their brilliance in their repartee with Richard) are somehow fooled by an open hypocrite who has continually proved a villain even before the events of the play begin. Even if there were no other instance of this but the scene with Anne, does it not seem preposterous that Shakespeare would try to foist it upon his audience? Nor can the insistence upon Shakespeare's youth and inexperience in this early play and upon the improbabilities encouraged by Elizabethan dramatic convention explain away so irresponsible an attitude toward dramatic propriety.

The Dark Generations of Richard III

The alternative explanation is obvious. These characters know from first to last that Richard is a villain, so that they are never fooled by him. What they do they do in full knowledge of the truth. If they appear to be convinced by any poses he assumes, it is because they themselves are playing the hypocrite's role. Much of the difficulty in interpreting the play arises from an inability to recognize the villainy that pervades the entire stage. Perhaps once again it is because we have been too quick to see the play as if it were written by Marlowe, with a hero-villain gigantically alone in an inexorable surge which drowns all the innocents in his path. I shall eventually suggest that in *Richard III* there are no innocents; that rather than intruding himself as an alien force into the world of the play, Richard is a purified and thus extreme symbol, a distillation, of that world; that the evil stems not from Richard but from a history he shares with the others even if it finds its essential representative in him. Even the young princes, still children and thus still unsinning, must share with their forebears the burden of guilt.

The answer which common sense dictates—that the characters are not taken in by Richard but, consciously or unconsciously, must be engaging in deception themselves—finds support at several points in the play. It finds support, for example, in those minor and yet telling scenes in which Shakespeare lets us see what political facts are so obvious that even the common man is aware of them. Thus in a discussion of the affairs of the commonwealth by a group of citizens, one of them simply states, "O, full of danger is the Duke of Gloucester" (II. iii. 27). Even more precisely to the point, we find a scrivener commenting on the published report of Hastings' indictment issued after his execution in order to justify it:

Here's a good world the while! Who is so gross
That cannot see this palpable device?
Yet who so bold, but says he sees it not?
Bad is the world; and all will come to nought,
When such ill dealing must be seen in thought.
(III. vi. 10–14)

We are evidently being informed here of the deception, however enforced, which pervades the court. Surely we must acknowledge that what the scrivener and even the "gross" cannot help but see, the high characters of the play must see. Hastings himself, conscious that his pretended trust in Richard, quoted in part above, did not save his head, says in comment and in warning to the still remaining fawners as he is led off to execution,"They smile at me who shortly shall be dead" (III. iv. 109). He is recalling, no doubt, his own recent satisfaction in hearing of the execution of Rivers, Grey, and Vaughan, when he, still seemingly beguiled by Richard, could confidently mock (even as we know he himself has already been marked for execution):

But I shall laugh at this a twelve-month hence,
That they which brought me in my master's hate,
I live to look upon their tragedy.

(III. ii. 57–59)

Finally, it is quite likely that the confessed villainy and hypocrisy of Richard's first victim in the play, "false, fleeting, perjur'd Clarence," set the precedent for our moral evaluation of those who follow.

Richard, then, is a fox among foxes. He is wittier than the others and more successful. But his victories can be attributed not so much to the fact that he is more villainous than the rest, as to the fact that he is more consistently and self-admittedly villainous. Whatever reason Anne may give herself or him, she can accept him as successor to her sweet and lovely gentleman, his victim, for but one reason—her self-interest. A widow of the ousted House of Lancaster, she must sense that the ruthless Richard's star is rising. Thus she is serious in her toying acknowledgment to Richard, ". . . you teach me how to flatter you" (I. ii. 224). Disdaining the bitter role of her mother-in-law, Queen Margaret, she must instead take Richard, swallowing her curses and pretending to have been successfully wooed—which is of course precisely the game that Richard expects her to play and that his perverseness, as we have seen, demands that she play. It is one of the satisfactions he seeks in power. We must either believe this or believe not only in her apparent conviction that "the murderous Machiavel" has turned Petrarchan lover but also in her apparent desire for him, deformity and all.

Elizabeth is later equally politic in her reception of Richard's addresses to her daughter. One may argue that she *is* merely putting him off for the moment since she has intended her daughter for Richmond, as we learn in the next scene. But there is no evidence in her scene with Richard that she need fear him, nor does she fear him; for she is as outspoken as she pleases. Why, then, pretend to accept him? Why, having come to curse, does she remain to welcome his addresses? Is it not more likely that, with Richard still in power and Richmond's venture surely questionable at best, she will play it safe and mother a queen regardless of the victor? So she pretends to be won by Richard's oath (IV. iv. 397–417) and by his promised moral conversion.

And so it is with the others of his victims who play at being deceived by him. But like Anne and Elizabeth, these others have moral pretensions as well. We see these pretensions on display frequently: for example, in the solicitous mannerisms of the court (I. iii and II. i) and in the self-righteousness of the lamenting women (IV. iv). It may be that there is this difference between Richard's seeming hypocrisy and theirs: Richard's is only seeming; theirs is real. When Richard insists that he "cannot flatter and look fair," that as "a plain man" he wants only to "live and think no harm"; when he chides himself for being "too childish-foolish for this world," he knows he is in no danger of being believed. He is laughing at his pose and at their reception of it (often explicitly in an aside), knowing that as deceivers themselves they must play the game with a straight face. His wit enables him to delight in the farce as he forces them to appear to accept the most outrageous of his moralizing utterances. In short, while the others are pretending at being decent, Richard is rather pretending at being a hypocrite. No thoroughgoing and utterly unscrupulous villain need actually be one.

Richard would seem to be a self-conscious and consistent version of the other characters. They cannot bear to witness in Richard the logical consequence of their own tendencies—which is perhaps another reason that they often rush to accept his pretended pretensions. Nor can they endure to live with this purified reflection of their self-destructive instincts—which may metaphorically justify the fact that so many of them fall prey to him. Each falls prey to his own worst self. Anne is perhaps a perfect symbol here. Early in the action, as we learn more explicitly later, she is led by her personal and political ills to curse Richard and his future wife. It is of course herself she has damned: the torment she suffers while alive and the unnatural death which it is implied she suffers are inflicted by Richard only insofar as he is her agent carrying out her curse.

There are yet other indications of the unrelieved ugliness of the world of *Richard III*. Some of those who defend the Marlovian character of the play cite its humorlessness as evidence. No low-comedy vaudeville routines seem to be found here. But this is only a superficial view. For example, the scene between the two murderers as they confront first each other and then Clarence (I. iv) has all the earmarks of such a routine. We may miss the similarities because of the morbidity of the occasion: it is, after all, cold-blooded fratricide that is being committed. This stark reality may nag at us and mar our enjoyment of the quips leading to the brilliantly cynical discourse on conscience, which may well rival Falstaff's on honor in *I Henry IV*. But this is precisely Shakespeare's point, I take it. While much of the scene takes the form of so-called comic relief, it is a bitter perversion of this device. The scene indicates what has become of humor in the world Shakespeare creates here: it is a humor bitterly transformed to callous irony, a humor too chill to sustain even a suggestion of human warmth.

In the witty dialogue between the murderers all moral values are inverted. Conscience, "a dangerous thing," finally becomes "the devil," so that to obey it and spare Clarence is now a diabolical act. To resist it and murder Clarence is to be "a tall man that respects thy reputation." The lively and biting duels of wit between Richard and Anne and between Richard and Elizabeth are of course other examples of these fearful analogues to comic routines. They may even suggest to us, in an unguarded moment, the brilliance of Benedick and Beatrice in *Much Ado*. Even the terrifying moment of Queen Margaret's systematic and all-inclusive curse is not immune to Richard's ready and deadly wit (I. iii. 233-40). He toys with her at the height of her ritualistic fervor until, deflated, she weakly pleads with him, "O, let me make a period to my curse!" And even here his bantering does not stop.

There is bitter humor too in those moments when Richard turns his wit on himself in his public poses, although, of course, always in an aside or a soliloquy. When, responsible for it himself, he speaks forgivingly of those who have caused the imprisonment of his brother Clarence (I. iii), Rivers congratulates him:

A virtuous and a Christian-like conclusion,
To pray for them that have done scath to us.

Richard says aloud, "So do I ever, being well-advis'd." To himself he adds, "For had I curs'd now, I had curs'd myself." Always there is this final bitter twist. We can argue about whether all this ought to go by the name of humor or comedy, but the term is not important. It is important, however, to note that these passages are analogous to what in many other plays seems more properly comic and, therefore, that this brutal wit is as close to the comic as Shakespeare can come in the infernal world he is creating. It is true to this world and, in its differences from his wit elsewhere, it tells us much about the moral darkness through which his characters wander to their deaths—symbolically self-inflicted through Richard, one of their own.

The Dark Generations of Richard III

There is yet a rather evident argument for the general viciousness of the characters, but it is an argument which is conclusive. It asserts its force as early as Act I, Scene iii, when Queen Margaret appears and interrupts the self-righteous and yet haggling claims and counterclaims of the members of the royal court. And since to some extent she is Chorus as well as Nemesis, we must give credence to her characterization of them:

Hear me, you wrangling pirates that fall out
In sharing that which you have pill'd from me!
Which of you trembles not that looks on me?
If not that I am queen, you bow like subjects,
Yet that by you depos'd, you quake like rebels?

There is another reason why we should be especially moved by her words. She is, after all, the widow of the last king of the now deposed Lancastrian line, the line dear to the hearts of the Elizabethans, who associated the Tudors intimately with it; and she is addressing the far less favored Yorkists. They are, then, usurpers all, and all fall under her curse. Strangely, although it is Richard whom she most detests and most heatedly condemns, it is he who becomes the instrument of her vengeance. True, she cannot rest content until he is also fallen (IV. iv. 71–78). But before this final prayer for his death Margaret has recounted the murderous services which Richard, the Yorkist to end Yorkists, has performed for her; she has, in effect, thanked God for him.

O upright, just, and true-disposing God,
How do I thank thee, that this carnal cur
Preys on the issue of his mother's body,
And makes her pew-fellow with others' moan!

(IV. iv. 55–58)

So Richard does serve, in part, as an arm of Lancastrian justice.

But our problem is not so simple or so simply factional. For neither Margaret nor the Lancastrian cause is, after all, much less vicious than the Yorkist. We hear in the play about the previous curse laid on Margaret by Richard's father, the nobler Richard, Duke of York. It is the success of this curse which leads her to match it with her own. When we turn back to *III Henry VI* (I. iv), the circumstances which lead to York's curse frighten us with what they reveal of Margaret's unrestrained cruelty in her days of power. She is a termagant in the earlier play. Hers is a ruthlessness to match the later Richard's: she merits the curses she brings down upon herself as Richard merits his. We can, then, look to the Lancastrian—the injured party, the summoner of vengeance, in *Richard III*—for moral righteousness

47

no more than we can look to the Yorkists for it. If Margaret's curses settle our moral judgment of the Yorkists, immediate history as revealed in *III Henry VI* makes up our minds similarly about their predecessors.

History indeed holds the answer to all questions about the moral atmosphere of the play—or rather Shakespeare's dramatic version of history in the *Henry VI* plays which precede *Richard III* and in the plays from *Richard II* through *Henry V*, to which he turned shortly after *Richard III*. It seems reasonable to assume that Shakespeare, after *Richard III*, followed history back to Richard II in order to trace the origin and the course of the troubles that culminate in the War of the Roses and that—from the viewpoint of the confident Elizabethans—are removed with the death of the remover, Richard III, and with the advent of the Tudors. Shakespeare appears to have viewed English political history from the fall of Richard II until the rise of Henry VII as a single drama, and it is rewarding for us briefly to do so even though Shakespeare produced the first four sections after he had completed the final four. It is the usurpation theme which dominates the plays. The unruly, destructive forces unleashed by Bolingbroke roar uncontrolled through the land. What the eminently practical and calculating Bolingbroke meant to be a slight and limited blood-letting for the health of the state becomes a blood-bath which drowns generation after generation. Finally Richard III, the blood-bath personified in its purest form, cleanses the land of the last of the guilt-ridden generations, so that with his own bloody end England may begin anew with Henry Tudor, symbol of the conciliation of the past and its feuds. We see, then, why the world of this play must be so unqualifiedly ugly. It is worth noting too that England's salvation, Richmond, must come from outside, from France, like a breath of fresh air, since this world of England is so entirely foul.

As there is this spatial gap between bloody England and the forces of a new day, so in the beginning there was the temporal gap of a generation between the last of those who had a sound view of kingship and those, like Richard II and Bolingbroke, who courted national ill-health. In *Richard II*, only Gaunt and York, the last of the older generation, of the "seven vials" "of Edward's sacred blood," have a full and traditional sense both of the obligations owing to kingship and of the obligations owed by kingship. Richard II, with a decadent version of absolutism, is selfishly aware only of the former of these obligations. Bolingbroke, a modern who has broken with the absolutist principle, has no principle of governmental order to which to appeal except force and expedience, and these are hardly principles conducive to lasting order. Thus he usurps. And, unable to replace the dogma of divine right with another that would equally symbolize the maintenance of the state as an orderly and continuing establishment, he cannot reorder the chaos he has loosed.[1] Nor can those who follow, and blood begets blood.

It may hardly be original to state that Shakespeare relates analogically the traditional views of reason and emotion in the individual to those of order and chaos in the state. But it may be more original to use this analogy in order to establish the extent to which Richard III symbolizes his political and moral milieu. We need say little about the chaos which for Shakespeare must join with usurpation as ruler, upon the deposition of a rightful king—symbol of reason in the state—except to point to Ulysses' famous speech about cosmic, political, and psychological order in *Troilus and Cressida* (I. iii. 75–137). Toward the end of this speech is the intimation that when reason is perverted through enslavement to emotion, an overthrow of the proper hierarchy has occurred—a usurpation of mental authority and an introduction of chaos in the individual personality. It is the extremity mentioned in *Venus and Adonis* (792), "When reason is the bawd to lust's abuse." But to return to the words of Ulysses concerned with the loss of order:

Force should be right; or rather, right and wrong
(Between whose endless jar justice resides)
Should lose their names, and so should justice too.
Then everything includes itself in power,
Power into will, will into appetite;
And appetite, an universal wolf,
So doubly seconded with will and power,
Must make perforce an universal prey,
And last eat up himself.

But are these lines not a fine description of Richard as I delineated him earlier? Richard is surely the darling of almost a century of English history which has seized upon him and created in him a reflection of itself: he is an incarnation of the spirit of usurpation and thus of chaos. And we saw at the outset that he is, almost literally, a lump of chaos, physical and political, whose very existence defies the natural order. If chaos in the state reflects politically the perversion of the proper government of emotion, then we should expect this perversion in Richard. And we saw earlier too that in Richard the two most forceful emotions, the will to sexual power and the

[1] For evidence of a similarly corrupt moral atmosphere in the plays about reigns earlier than Richard III's, see Leonard Unger, "Deception and Self-Deception in Shakespeare's *Henry IV*," *The Man in the Name* (Minneapolis, 1956), pp. 3–17.

will to political power, are seriously perverted. Finally in Richard we have a brilliance of intellect, but criminally distorted in order to serve his perverse desires—again just what is required of usurpation incarnate.

But if history realizes itself in Richard as its representative, it also uses him—the embodied perfection of its horrors—to purge the world of itself, to end its reign. In a way English history is thus converted to eschatology with Richmond and the Tudors representing a Second Coming which gives birth to the golden world. I have already noted that Richmond returns from another country to be England's salvation. Only under his aegis, according to Elizabeth, can Dorset be safe "from the reach of hell" (IV.i.43). Richmond, who looms throughout the play as a source of help from afar, in effect plays the Saviour, even as the saintly if ineffectual Henry VI has served, like John the Baptist, to prophesy his dominion.

The spirit of usurpation and of chaos has been abroad in varying degrees among all of Shakespeare's characters after the deposition of Richard II. Thus Richard III, as we have seen, is its symbol too—a fearful projection of that worst self which they never dare confront. And for them to confront it reflected in Richard—as many of them have to—is usually fatal, since they are overcome by the unrelieved darkness of its aspect.

There is one final way in which the deadly weight of history enters the play: it asserts itself as ritual. The force of the dark generations past is felt especially through their curses. And the curse is a formalized affair, as we have seen from Margaret's insistence on giving it a proper ending. It must be formalized into ritual if, as a form of magic, it is to be efficacious. It invariably is efficacious. Margaret's extended curse contributes a structural framework to the play. In it she dispenses the fates of almost all the characters. The subsequent action is constructed largely in order to see her curse realized as, one after another, its objects succumb. Shakespeare induces us to keep count of them as her victims by the use of various devices: for example, by inserting brief pre-execution scenes in which the power of the curse is explicitly attested, and even once by having her reappear to calculate her bloody gains. And, in the realm of ritual and magic, the victims are hers rather than Richard's; for Richard is also her victim, one who is sufficiently destructive before turning self-destructive. I have already noted that Anne's earlier curse, of which we do not learn fully until considerably later, works only too well. Although it comes finally to be aimed at herself as well as at Richard, the curse once spoken cannot be unsaid nor its effects neutralized. Even the Duchess of York, the widow who matches in generation the

Lancastrian widow (even as Elizabeth matches Anne), must add her curse to the others her son must bear. And the night before Bosworth, the ghosts of Richard's victims deliver, again in proper form, the final curse, the same curse that Faustus had delivered upon himself: "Despair and die!" They also bless Richmond and, since they represent York as well as Lancaster, they put the seal of reconciliation on the House of Tudor. For example, the ghosts of the Yorkist princes say to the sleeping Richmond,

Live, and beget a happy race of kings!
Edward's unhappy sons do bid thee flourish.
(V. iii. 157–58)

But Margaret's is not the first curse in the play. We have seen that it is inspired by what has seemed to be the efficacy of York's earlier curse in *III Henry VI*. If his curse has bereft her of power and family, then why should she not answer it with one aimed at those who have been the executioners of his curse? With Margaret's curse reaching for its precedent back into the history that precedes the action of the play, it seems as if we could trace curse upon curse back through the bloody generations to Richard II. And when we turn to *Richard II* (written, of course, not long after *Richard III*), we find at the very start of civil strife speeches by Richard (III. iii. 85–100) and by Carlisle (IV. i. 136–49) which are half-prophecy of the bloodshed ahead and half curse calling for it.

There is another form of ritual in the play—the lamentation of the women and children. It is a competitive telling over of their woes, which, since they are of royal blood, are the woes of history. It takes the form of a stylized, chant-like rivalry of grief among those left by the dark generations to linger on the stage. A single passage will reveal how rigidly formalized it can be:

Elizabeth. *Give me no help in lamentation,*
I am not barren to bring forth complaints:
All springs reduce their currents to mine eyes,
That I, being govern'd by the watery moon,
May send forth plenteous tears to drown the world!
Ah for my husband, for my dear lord Edward!
 Children of Clarence. *Ah for our father, for our dear lord Clarence!*
 Duchess of York. *Alas for both, both mine, Edward and Clarence!*
 Eliz. *What stay had I but Edward? and he's gone.*
 Chil. *What stay had we but Clarence? and he's gone.*
 Duch. *What stays had I but they? and they are gone.*
 Eliz. *Was never widow had so dear a loss!*
 Chil. *Were never orphans had so dear a loss!*
 Duch. *Was never mother had so dear a loss!*

The Play of Criticism

Alas, I am the mother of these griefs!
Their woes are parcell'd, mine is general.
She for an Edward weeps, and so do I;
I for a Clarence weep, so doth not she;
These babes for Clarence weep, and so do I;
I for an Edward weep, so do not they.
Alas, you three, on me, threefold distress'd,
Pour all your tears! I am your sorrow's nurse,
And I will pamper it with lamentation.

(II. ii. 66–88)

There is no need to comment at length about the echoes and refrains in the passage, its symmetry, the effective closing of its first and last lines with the word "lamentation." Similar comparisons of sorrows occur among Margaret, the Duchess of York, and Elizabeth (IV. iv) and (though less clearly in the ritual pattern) between Elizabeth and Anne (IV. i). The very impersonality of the lamentation suggests its historic rather than individual authenticity. The characters are taking a recognized role, playing once for their generation a part that has been played many times, borrowing from history words and tears that have rarely gone unused.

In the ritual of lamentation and in the ritualistic curses which successive generations form in answer to one another, we are eventually carried back far beyond Richard II in history and tradition—back to those other dramas of lust and blood and Nemesis, to those extended cycles about family and domain with which Western tragedy began. Perhaps it is with Greek tragedy, rather than with Marlowe or even Seneca, that *Richard III* has its most essential and most intimate connections.

4
The "Frail China Jar" and the Rude Hand of Chaos

 Contrary to the usual impression, recent critical approaches to literature, at their most valuable, need not restrict themselves to the ivory tower of formalism, in which analytical ingenuity is paraded for its own sake. Elsewhere, arguing from aesthetic principles, I have tried to prove that, far from stifling extra-literary relations, the so-called new criticism can allow literature to be uniquely revelatory of life, to give us a new rendering of the stuff of experience. But here I should like to venture even further in an effort to correct the common misconception that sees modern criticism as no more than formalistic. For despite the fact that this criticism grew up largely in opposition to the historical disciplines, I shall here attempt to show how literature—if it is seen thoroughly and with new-critical care as literature—can illuminate in a rather special way even so un-new-critical an area as the history of ideas.[1]

To this end I should like to conduct a somewhat reckless allegorical excursion in order to assure myself the freedom I need to explore an extraordinary dramatic relation between perhaps the two greatest poems of the eighteenth century, "The Rape of the Lock" and *The Dunciad*. It may be that I shall have to construct a kind of mythology of idealized generaliza-

---

[1] Perhaps I shall be, in part, answering Roy Harvey Pearce's challenge to my book *The New Apologists for Poetry,* in his essay in the *Kenyon Review* of Autumn, 1958 ("Historicism Once More," pp. 554–91). There he asks me to extend my methodology into a new historicism, one that would move from my acknowledgment of the creative role of language in the making of the poem to an insistence on the historical dimension of this creatively endowed language. Consequently this language would be seen as expressing the inner stance of its author as a man in time and in culture: poetry would come to be treated as a kind of existential anthropology. While this essay was written before I saw Pearce's, it may very well have been his kind of objective that I have been looking toward.

tions which is to pass for the psychological history of the tensions of the eighteenth-century artist by allowing certain ideological commonplaces to bear more weight than the more careful historian may believe they can sustain. And I may end by doing violence to other more widely accepted commonplaces of the orthodox historian. But surely this is one of the chief functions of poetry, this violation of the commonplace. Finally, my claims may be seen to ignore the significance of the chronological relations among "The Rape of the Lock," *An Essay on Man,* and *The Dunciad* by assuming something like a simultaneity among poems spread over three decades. I hope that the facts of chronology will not be seen to disturb more essential dialectical relations among the works of this single poet. Let me add only this further apology: that I mean to suggest these dramatic and allegorical extensions of the poems no more than tentatively, even hypothetically—hoping only that by being suggestive they may be especially illuminating in a way that a more literal transcription would prefer to ignore, perhaps (let me admit the possibility) because the latter, in its scholarly caution, is more anxious to avoid being wrong. But the extensions that follow—at the worst—would have been nice if they were there to be justly read this way. They do make for an exciting drama of the eighteenth-century mind at work.

I

It is by this late date not at all original to claim that Pope's "The Rape of the Lock" is double-edged throughout, that in it he celebrates the artificial world of eighteenth-century social convention even as he satirizes it. Even Geoffrey Tillotson, the rather orthodox editor of the poem in the Twickenham Edition, acknowledges:

The social mockery of the *Rape of the Lock* is not simple, does not make a pat contribution to single-mindedness. The world of the poem is vast and complicated. It draws no line of cleavage between its "seriousness" and its mockery. Belinda is not closed up in a rigid coterie which Clarissa and the rest of the poem mock at. Pope, fierce and tender by turns, knows no more than Hazlitt, "whether to laugh or weep" over the poem. He is aware of values which transcend his satire:

Belinda smil'd, and all the World was gay

and

If to her share some Female Errors fall,
Look on her Face, and you'll forget 'em all.

The "Frail China Jar"

The poem provides a picture rather than a criticism; or, rather, the criticism is so elaborate, shifting, constellated, that the intellect is baffled and demoralized by the emotions. One is left looking at the face of the poem as at Belinda's.

But this is all he has to say. He follows his hunch no further. In a well-known essay, Cleanth Brooks argues in a more extensive and highly detailed fashion that our awareness, through Pope's double meanings, of the biological facts that lie just beneath the artful façade of the poem and of the social mannerisms of Belinda's world creates a two-way irony that admires even as it patronizes. Thus for Brooks also the poem does more than mock at a "tempest in a teapot." Many of my observations about the poem will be all too obviously related to his. But even he has not quite pursued his approach to this poem to a unified conclusion, resting content—as he all too often does in *The Well Wrought Urn*—with merely complicating the dimensions of the poem and of the irony it exploits and so leaving it, exposed but not regrouped, in all its multiplicity. Allen Tate, in an analysis he has never to my knowledge published, moves from Brooks' scattered insights to an over-all conception of the poem as metonymy and thus as what William Empson has defined as pastoral. It is this notion I should like to develop here.

Insofar as we view the poem as a mockery of the self-conscious seriousness displayed by trivial characters over a trivial occurrence, we see them, in their self-importance, indulging the logical fallacy of metonymy: they have mistaken the lock of hair, actually incapable of being violated, for the lady's body—vulnerable but unassaulted by the baron. Similarly, they have taken their rarefied and pomaded world of conventional play for the great world, that changeable heroic world of princes and states in which rape brings vengeance and catastrophe lurks. Hence the mock-epic. Granted that these are the delusions of the complacency fostered by an artificial society and that Pope forces us to see them as such. But surely, for all its absurdities, this self-contained and inconsequential "toyshop" world can manage an aesthetic perfection and (from the standpoint of an ugly, lurking reality) a disinvolvement that allow it a purity along with its thinness.

We may rightly smile—perhaps in envy as well as in disdain—at the metonymic wigs that are fighting in this world of decorum instead of the gory, if more glorious, lords of heroic mold; for, as Pope so brilliantly arranges things, the disembodied wigs fight, properly, with sword-knots instead of swords ("Where wigs with wigs, with sword-knots sword-knots strive"). The "toyshop" society that self-importantly mistakes itself for reality is defender, too, of "honor," that fashionable word out of Restoration comedy which so befits this world of fashion. Appearance is all. The lock of hair is to this world what the actual body is to the real world, except that the former is even more to be cherished since reputation is the only value in the world of fashion. So the rape of the lock is more to be avoided in honor's world than are the more sordid, but less openly proclaimed, assaults in classical legend and in London back alleys. Belinda, perhaps unconsciously, acknowledges as much in her lament to the baron:

Oh hadst thou, cruel! been content to seize
Hairs less in sight, or any hairs but these!

In honor's world the lock *is* the woman as the wig is the man and the sword-knot his weapon. There simply are no flesh and blood in these people—or rather in these artificially created shadows of people—so that, even without looking to John Milton, we should understand why it is fitting that

No common weapons in their hands are found,
Like Gods they fight, nor dread a mortal wound.

And of course not Belinda herself is flesh and blood—at least not the artful and perfected abstraction that Belinda creates of herself in administering "the sacred rites of pride." It is a brilliant stroke in this dressing-table passage that the real Belinda is only the priestess at the altar and that the goddess whom she decorates as she worships is her reflection in the mirror. She worships not fleshly or cosmic but "cosmetic pow'rs" whose kingdom is not of this world but of the elegant world of appearance. The Belinda who, fully created in artifice, is to enter honor's world on the Thames and in Hampton Court is not a woman but a goddess, a disembodied image: she is the insubstantial Belinda, composed of smiles that have been repaired and of the "purer blush." Deprived of the imperfections that mar—even as they humanize—flesh-and-blood reality, the painted blush is indeed aesthetically purer than a natural blush, an improvement upon it. And it is morally purer too, for it is caused not by blood—by any natural, unmaidenly immodesty—but by the cool calculations of art. It is far less spontaneous, or suggestive, than the blush earlier induced in her dreams by the disguised Ariel:

A Youth more glitt'ring than a Birth-night Beau
(That ev'n in slumber caus'd her cheek to glow).

The "Frail China Jar"

This world of images, from which—as in Yeats' Byzantium—the fury and the mire of human veins are excluded, is also the world of play and, thus, of innocence. And it is the sense of play that justifies Pope's frequent and brilliant use of zeugma in the poem. When Ariel suggests to his "sylphs and sylphids" what catastrophes may threaten Belinda, he couples[2] "real" dangers with merely fashionable ones:

Whether the nymph shall break Diana's law,
Or some frail China jar receive a flaw;
Or stain her honour, or her new brocade;
Forget her pray'rs, or miss a masquerade.

Elsewhere "the virgin's cheek" pales in a fear that yokes maidenly dishonor to the loss of the card game:

She sees, and trembles at th'approaching ill,
Just in the jaws of ruin, and Codille.

Or kings captured in battle are yoked to aging virgins, fierce and unrepentant tyrants to an imperfectly dressed young lady. To be sure, these and similar instances emphasize the triviality of the action and thus the poem's mock-heroic aspect. But given this world where images and wigs and sword-knots replace real men and women, where fashion replaces emotion, where "honor" replaces moral earnestness, this very triviality should alone be taken seriously. Utterly inconsequential in contrast to both the heroic world and the sordid everyday world, the insubstantial quality of the world in which woman is recognized as woman only by the clothes she wears and the way her hair is dressed makes it actually unworldly. As a world of play and of art, it is utterly self-contained, self-justified. Absurd as it may be from the standpoint of the heroic and of the everyday world, it is yet an idyllic world whose very purity gives it a unique value—thus Tate's characterization of it as pastoral. Even as Pope condescends to its creatures, may he not envy them? May he not be suggesting his admiration of a world in which dress is more significant than tyranny, maidenly attitudes more significant than

---

[2] I am using the term *zeugma* in a broader sense than its strict grammatical meaning would permit. For example, in the two couplets I quote in what follows, only the line "Or stain her honour, or her new brocade" is an actual instance of it. Obviously it is only a triangular affair, so that the two objects must be yoked by the single, double-visioned verb. In this sense, the other lines are merely antitheses of four distinct parts, with each object controlled by its own verb. My point is, however, that in a rhetorical if not a grammatical sense, there is a similar yoking of two disparate worlds in all these instances. In rare cases this yoking is reflected in the short-circuited perfection of the grammatical device; the other cases are effective but less complete and thus less brilliant examples yielding the same rhetorical effect.

victories and defeats of princes—and more to the point, the flawing of a china jar more significant than the violation of a virgin? How precious and delicate a world, if utterly thin, irresponsible, and unreal! Or should I not say precious and delicate *because* utterly thin, irresponsible, and unreal? The price of substance, responsibility, and reality—of conscientious social significance—Pope knew only too well, as we do. He computed it for us in the bitterness of his satire elsewhere, and especially in *The Dunciad*. It is as if, seeing as Henry James later did that "life persistently blunders and deviates, loses herself in the sand," the artist Pope, like James, wanted to preserve "his grain of gold." And part of him wanted, as a devotee of art for art's sake, or of the world for art's sake, to salvage the world of fashion as that grain of gold.

II

We must ask, then, whether the epic tone and machinery are so easily and so uniformly seen as incongruous as our normal understanding of the mockheroic would have us believe. Belinda, seen repeatedly as rival to the sun, is treated throughout as a goddess. Now of course this is absurd, as it is meant to be. But is it only absurd? Is it not really, as we have seen, that it is the image of Belinda that appears as the goddess, a kind of sun-goddess? And to the extent that we see her as the world of fashion does—as disembodied and thus not of the dull world of substance and consequence—is she perhaps not in some sense a goddess after all even while she remains the shallow fool of social convention? We have seen already that in a strange sense the terms in which Milton's airy beings do battle are not totally inapplicable here. When early in the poem our humorist asks, "In tasks so bold, can little men engage?" he may be playing a more complex game than that of mere mockery.

Belinda, of course, is warrior-goddess, too. From the time her "awful beauty puts on all its arms," we know that the war between the sexes— limited by the rules of the drawing room rather than of any Geneva convention—is on. All is directed to the final superhuman battle at the end. We learn that her locks of hair are "nourish'd" and nourished "to the destruction of mankind"; and we are warned by the general claim

Fair tresses man's imperial race ensnare
And beauty draws us with a single hair.

We begin to suspect that Belinda, Amazon as well as nymph, may be the aggressor as well as the assaulted in the war of love. For after all, the realistic, common-sense view that Pope forces before us, too (and that Clarissa later so painfully represents), makes us recognize that behind the masque of the drawing room lurk the biological and domestic facts of life. The war is finally but a game that disguises the uninspiring realities of the social and sexual mating urge. Since the war is only symbolic and as innocent as mere war-games, no wonder no one is harmed. In Canto V, when the issue is joined, we see death being scattered around by the eyes of various nymphs with wits dying in metaphor and in song and reviving as the lady's frowns change to smiles. Allusions to the sexual act abound in secondary meanings even as on the surface, in the living deaths and the burnings in the flames of love, the stale love-song clichés—dull remnants of a long-outworn Petrarchan convention—continue the melodramatic pretense on a heroic scale. The players must take the game seriously, play it as war—though happily a war without war's consequences—in order to preserve that artful and idyllic purity of their innocent make-believe. Yet, of course, this final battle is not the only one in the poem. To pile absurdity upon absurdity, Pope prepares us for the war-game at the close with the "combat on the velvet plain"—the game of Ombre, that earlier military maneuver disguising sexual reality, in which Belinda barely escaped "the jaws of ruin, and Codille." The card game is a symbolic prophecy of the final battle which, ironically, is itself only symbolic. The earlier battle, symbol behind the symbol, proves the game-like quality of the later: it establishes the later one as pure nonsense, as pure as itself, as pure as games alone are. If all this reminds us of the play-theory of art, it reminds us also of my earlier claim that Pope loves Belinda's world as a true aesthete.

Of course, the unaesthetic world of biological and domestic fact lurks always beneath. Pope is not afraid for us to see it beneath his language, since he wants us to know that he can cherish Belinda's world only in continual awareness of its evasions and delusions: it evades the real world by deluding itself about its own reality. Indeed, Pope is so anxious for us to be aware of his awareness of the real world that he forces an explicit representative of it upon us by inserting Clarissa's speech into a later edition of the poem. But he has shown this awareness to us all along in the sexual secondary meanings of phrase after phrase and in the "serious" half of zeugma after zeugma. We must remember also the suggestion that Belinda after all is the aggressor, and that at the crucial moment, before the baron acts, Ariel is rendered powerless by viewing

> . . . *in spite of all her art,*
> *An earthly Lover lurking at her heart.*

Surely this is the baron, so that Pope is suggesting that on one level—that of flesh-and-blood reality—Belinda is, to say the least, a willing victim, shrewd enough to know the truth of the pronouncement later made by "grave Clarissa": ". . . she who scorns a man, must die a maid." But Belinda also—or at least her painted image—is dedicated to the game and will play it through at all costs. So the show of resistance must be maintained, with the mock-battle of love and its sexually suggestive overtones as its proper consequence.

Once Pope feels secure that he has established Belinda's world as one we can cherish, but always with a chuckle, he dares introduce materials from other and realer worlds more openly as if to prove the power of his delicate creation. Thus the biological realities are paraded in the Cave of Spleen whose queen, be it noted, rules "the sex to fifty from fifteen." Or earlier Pope introduces figures of the great world—"Britain's statesmen" and "great Anna"—only to reduce them through zeugma to the pastoral level of his central action, the statesmen foredooming the fall "Of Foreign Tyrants and of Nymphs at home" and Anne, in the famous line, taking tea as well as counsel. Is the great world being transformed to the petty or the petty to the great? A question appropriate to the double-edged nature of the mock-heroic. Surely it can increase the stature of normally trivial subject matter by playing up that within it that surprises us with its hidden grandeur. There is also Pope's daring glance at the sordid everyday world in which

The hungry Judges soon the sentence sign,
And wretches hang that jurymen may dine.

But this break into Belinda's world is no defect. It rather reinforces the wonderfully inconsequential pastoralism of that world. This brief, terrorizing glance at the alternative should send us clutching at the innocuous grace of the "toyshop," where we need fear neither hunger nor execution though we may have the make-believe equivalent of each. And, as if to prove the point, Pope turns almost at once to Belinda, who like the statesman wants victory in war and more important, like the judge, wants to assign her own arbitrary sentence of execution: she will "foredoom" in her own way:

Belinda now, whom thirst of fame invites,
Burns to encounter two advent'rous Knights,
At Ombre singly to decide their doom.

Of course, it is Clarissa who furnishes the most serious intrusion upon Belinda's world by the alien world of undeluded common-sense reality. It is she, Pope tells us in his note, who is "to open more clearly the moral of the poem." How inspired a touch that earlier it was Clarissa who perversely furnished the baron with the scissors he used to commit his assault.[3] By all means let her be the earlier Clarissa who even then, in her anti-pastoralism, plotted the downfall of the make-believe world of artifice. In her speech she breaks all the rules, says all that is unmentionable, shatters the mirror in order to replace the painted image with the flesh-and-blood creature of fleeting charms who marries, breeds, ages, wears, and has all sorts of dire consequences—eventually dust and the grave. Of course, she alone speaks only the truth. And so she does open the moral, but only to make us recognize its price. No wonder that "no applause ensu'd." She is intolerable even if she is right. In Belinda's world the fancy cheats too well to be abandoned for its grim alternative.

Even the sylphs, Pope's magnificent addition to his heroic machinery, are implicated, at least by negation, in the quarrel Belinda's world has with Clarissa. We have seen that Ariel first appears to Belinda in her dream as so attractive a youth as to cause in her a blush of desire. And we may see him throughout the poem as an unearthly rival to the baron, the "earthly Lover." It is Ariel who speaks the magnificent couplet

Know further yet; whoever fair and chaste
Rejects mankind, is by some Sylph embrac'd.

What a stroke to rhyme "chaste" with "embrac'd"! Surely the latter word is to retain its fully sexual flavor here as Ariel is in effect telling Belinda to save herself for him. And as we turn to Pope's words in his dedicatory epistle to Arabella Fermor, his Belinda, we note the different, the more-than-mortal sort of embrace that sylphs are capable of. How uproariously he toyed with the poor girl:

For they say, any Mortals may enjoy the most intimate Familiarities with these gentle Spirits, upon a Condition very easie to all true *Adepts,* an inviolate Preservation of Chastity.

This embrace, then, is the empty equivalent of the sexual act in that rarefied world of fashion guarded by the decorous sylphs. Ariel is warning Belinda away from flesh and blood, from yielding to the realistic truths of life and marriage and death attested to by Clarissa. As an image, eternalized in art, dehumanized in perfection, she must remain Ariel's alone. It is he, anxious

---

[3] Although Pope in this note speaks of her as a new character, he must mean, as Tillotson supposes, that she is new as a speaking character.

to protect his own, who keeps her safe from assault and seduction. And so, as he tells Belinda, he comes to represent "honor," the word used by us "men below" to characterize the maidenly purity the sylph has ensured. No wonder, then, that he is so solicitous and that, once he spies

An earthly Lover lurking at her heart.
Amaz'd, confus'd, he found his pow'r expir'd,
Resign'd to fate, and with a sigh retir'd.

He must, with Belinda, yield the field to the baron. But she yields only the metonymic symbol rather than the thing itself; and she yields only momentarily, since she returns to Ariel's world of honor by calling for war. The sylphs, then, "wondrous fond of place," with their innumerable ranks reflecting all the levels of cosmic and human order, are the ideal superhuman attendants of the empty and yet perfect world of fashionable decorum. And they are as ineffectual, their airiness being an extension of the airiness of that disembodied world whose integrity they claim to protect.

As his translation of Homer shows Pope to have viewed it, in the old and revered heroic tradition the world of serious significance and consequence and the world of high play and the grand manner were one. Actuality was somehow hospitable to decorum. But in the dwarfed mock-heroic world Pope sees about him, actuality, in becoming sordid, rejects all style: its insolent insistence allows decorum to make only a comic appearance as its pale reflection. Instead of the all-accomplishing Homeric heroes, Pope must accept either the jurymen and wretches or the wigs and sword-knots, either Clarissa's breeder or Ariel's nymph of the "purer blush."

All this must return us to my earlier insistence that insofar as Pope values Belinda's world, which from the standpoint of reality he must satirize, he values it for an aesthetic purity that frees it from ugliness even as it leaves it utterly insignificant. It is, as I have said, a world created for art's sake, one in which the zeugma can finally create a miraculous inversion, so that the "frail China jar" becomes more precious than virginity—in effect comes to be not merely a symbol for virginity, but even an artificial substitute for it in this world of artifice.

III

But is there not, in Pope's day, a larger and more important, if equally unreal world, created for art's sake: the world of Epistle I of *An Essay on Man?* (I call a halt after Epistle I, since Pope opens Epistle II with those brilliant and tragic lines on man's middle nature.) Here, the aesthetic perfection of the universe is set forth and adored. In the conclusion to the epistle, we are warned in our blindness not to claim any imperfection in the infallible order that enfolds all. And in these famous lines occur the parallel oppositions that are to fade as we recognize the full and true cosmos:

All Nature is but Art, unknown to thee;
All Chance, Direction which thou canst not see;
All Discord, Harmony not understood;
All partial Evil, universal Good.

Is not such a universe decorum itself, decorum erected into a cosmic principle, all the spheres and the links in the chain of being taking and keeping their places with a propriety resembling that of the sylphs, and of the drawing room? And the seeming disturbances within it are seeming only: the discord that is a false front for harmony reminds us of the battles in "The Rape of the Lock" that are only decorous and conventional mock-battles, war-games that secure rather than threaten the world of fashion. The dangerous casualty of flesh and blood gives way to the controlled inevitability of art.

In *An Essay on Man* we are given a kind of *ersatz* and decapitated replica of the unified, catholic, psychologically and aesthetically soothing thirteenth-century universe. It is a replica that represents a last, desperate, brilliant postulation in the face of the devastations of the Renaissance and of modern science that left the medieval world (or dream world) a shambles. It even rationalizes the static generalizations of early modern science by analogizing them and coming up with the "Newtonian world-machine." It thus represents also a supreme act of human will, the will to order—and to sanity. It is, finally then, an aesthetic construct only—hence Pope's insistence in these final lines of Epistle I that we leave this delicately created china jar unflawed. (One can, of course, see the same forces, the same insistence on order at all costs, reflected in Pope's indiscriminate reduction of the troublesome dimensions of his world to the uniformity of his perfected version of the heroic couplet.) As the Humes and Kants convincingly reveal in shattering the false, dogmatic security of this world, the price of the construct is a metaphysical flimsiness—a naiveté, the reverse side of its symmetrical delicacy—that made it easy prey to the rigors of critical philosophy and the ravages of social-economic revolution.

Is it not, however, rather smug of us to assume that minds as sensitive and probing as Pope's could believe in their dream world so utterly and simply, that they could rest so secure in an unquestioning acceptance of this architecturally perfect model universe? Perhaps at some level of their consciousness they were alive to the ultimate futility of their desperate postulation. Nevertheless, postulate they had to in Western man's final attempt to resist universal disintegration. But in this last assertion of cosmic solidarity there may have been the insecurity that was aware of its vulnerability and of the surrounding hordes of modernism already closing in. I am here suggesting, of course, that "The Rape of the Lock" is Pope's testament of the aesthetic universe, one that reveals a nostalgic yearning for it along with a critical acknowledgment of its impracticability, and that *The Dunciad* is his bleak acceptance of the chaotic forces he most feared.

One can account in a general way for the enlightenment's ethic and metaphysic as well as for its aesthetic by treating as synonyms for what is to be avoided all the first terms in the two couplets I have quoted from *An Essay on Man,* and as synonyms for what is to be sought all the second terms: thus nature, chance, discord, yielding partial evil; and art, direction, harmony, yielding universal good. And it is clear why the unchanging permanence of art must be preferred to the dynamic casualty of history, the china jar to unpredictable flesh and blood. But the spirit of Clarissa has been abroad and it leads away from art to the realities of history. It is ultimately to the last book of *The Dunciad* that she points, to Pope's prophecy of the chaos that modern historical reality brings. Perhaps we can reinterpret a couplet from this last book for our own purposes:

But sober History restrain'd her rage,
And promis'd Vengeance on a barb'rous age.

Here in the victory of Dullness is her vengeance, what she has saved for us in the world of jurymen and wretches.

It is clear that *The Dunciad* extends in its satirical range far beyond the literary world to the ethical and metaphysical. It is clear also that to the mock-epic quality of the poem is joined a more serious, a not much less than epic—almost Dantesque—quality. There is nothing slight about the Empire of Dullness. The significance of its action is hardly beneath heroic treatment. For these creatures literally absorb all the world. Unlike the action of "The Rape of the Lock," their action has consequences indeed, woeful ones. Their action is heroic in scope; it is repulsive and base on the very grandest scale. While it reverses all heroic values, it does so in heroic terms:

Then rose the Seed of Chaos, and of Night,
To blot out Order, and extinguish Light.

The "Frail China Jar"

The delicate world for art's sake is overcome by ponderous dullness, by what James termed "clumsy Life again at her stupid work." Throughout the last book of *The Dunciad* it is the discord of partiality that acts the role of destroyer: "Joy to great Chaos! let Division reign." We find the dunces, like their Laputan cousins in Swift, divorcing words from things and thought, cherishing minute parts for their own sakes, refusing to relate them to any whole. Division indeed, and subdivision. And what is chaos for Pope but the multiplication of parts run wild? Discord is no longer resolvable into harmony, or partial evil into universal good. Pope is looking forward to the destruction of totality, to the destruction of the long vogue of naive philosophical Realism, by critical philosophy—and ever more critical philosophy even down to our contemporary Oxford school. The increasing attractions of partiality to man's microscopic tendencies and the dogged dedication to immediate truth replace the dream world with a piecemeal chaos.

In *The Dunciad* Pope sees this infinitely divided world, the modern world, as the one finally suited to man, imperfect and partial as he prefers to be. Pope sees the wholeness and sameness and sanity of the art-world as beyond man, now with the placid classic vision no longer his. Man will prefer to be Clarissa, who would destroy an aesthetically satisfying world for the dull truths of homely reality and utilitarian candor. Perhaps Pope comes to feel that he has hoped for too much from man: the capacity for a willful naiveté that will leave undisturbed the golden world, well wrought like the china jar. Perhaps this is part of what Pope had in mind in dedicating *The Dunciad* to Swift who, in a famous letter in 1725, had chided Pope and Bolingbroke for a rationalistic optimism that rated man too high and that could result only in an unreasoning hatred of man for falling short. Swift was ready from the start to settle for less, to acknowledge the sordid, to avoid fabricating a purified, pastoral, anti-Clarissa world, as a comparison of the dressing rooms of his poetic heroines with that of Belinda will readily testify. Perhaps Pope's dedication was his way of acknowledging that Swift was right and that the poem which was to follow is a testament of hatred to those who have proved him wrong, even as he had always feared himself to be. For the usual picture of Pope as pure rationalist must be balanced by that of the subterranean Pope who is the pure and frightened skeptic. By the time of *The Dunciad*, Book the Fourth, Pope may know the dream is shortly to be smashed forever. But his was not a dogmatic slumber, or a slumber at all. It was an artful delusion—of himself and of us—by a mind too aesthetically fine to accept the universe as less than a work of art. He would have the china jar, no matter how frail, although the prophet within forced from him at last the poem that acknowledged its destruction by the rude hands swinging out from the motley mob that clutters *The Dunciad*.

IV

My fullest measure of Pope's utterance, then, would find a voice given to the felt subterranean pressures that moved his age despite his and its overt assurances—pressures generated by the tensions between rationalism and empiricism, between classicism and modernism, between confidence in a mechanism that roots the hospitable universe and anxiety about the unknown alien something or nothing that may finally lurk underneath everything out there. As a poet, through the plasticity of his brilliantly controlled and maneuvered language, Pope reached into the unvoiced capacities for praise and wonder and laughter and lament in his world and surmounted the ideological commonplaces of his time to voice all at once; even, of course, while never yielding his finally classical hold on the things of life, those precious if dainty things that in their arbitrary and nonsensical way order life and preserve sanity—and civilization. For these are the things that shape a culture even as they create its vulnerability, the transience that is built into it as one of its most charming features.

In doing all this, Pope was also proving the role and the power of poetry. He was demonstrating the special privilege of poetry to move beyond those facile propositions—drawn from a few "spokesmen" in prose and from the most obvious voice extorted from its poets—that supposedly characterize the inner "spirit of an age"; the privilege of poetry to reveal the more-than-propositional (and less-than-propositional) existential shape, the true inwardness, of that inner spirit, that which makes it of man's spirit rather than of a textbook's logic. Thus to the extent that Pope, through his maneuvers of language, becomes involved, at whatever level of consciousness, in any of the complexities of attitude and value, of hopes and frightening realizations, that I have been claiming to find—and I might call also upon the testimony of his friend Swift to support me—I would want to claim that it is in such as these that the full history of ideas in Pope and in the eighteenth century must be found; that any intellectual history which ignores these dimensions in the interest of lesser men's "documents" (and Pope himself was frequently a lesser man, as is any poet in his less than most creative moments) has sacrificed adequacy to discursive convenience. It is

The "Frail China Jar"

incomplete, dehumanized, forcing the true "spirit of the age" into an historian's *a priori* (or at least unexistential, pre-poetic) categories. For the ideas of an age may stem out of the more-than-ideological fullness of the poet rather than make their way into his work as a commonplace element that reduces it to themselves. And, so long as this remains a conceivable hypothesis, the historian of ideas had better worry about whether ideas—the ideas that finally come to found intellectual institutions—may not prior to their formulation as ideas be born, in an existential non-ideological form, in the fullness and the tensions of a poet's work rather than come to die there after a long, dull, existentially unchallenged institutional life of their own.

"Tott'ring . . . without a wind" by virtue of its very delicacy, Pope's aesthetic construct of a universe is unable to withstand the merest touch of the hand of reality. It now lies in the "glitt'ring dust and painted fragments" of "rich China vessels fall'n from high." But it did not *only* crash, though *The Dunciad* chronicles that it did. Thanks to Pope, we can cherish with him the very fragility that assured its perfection even as it guaranteed its destruction. For, like Belinda's lock, even as it ceased being a force down here, the muse "saw it upward rise." We have perhaps been too taken with the brilliance of Pope's satire and mock-heroics to sense fully the almost single-minded tribute to the lock and thus to Belinda's world contained in the moving final lines in which Pope enshrines the lock eternally in his heavens. It is, after all, one of the stars the Empire of Dullness threatens with extinction at the apocalyptic close of *The Dunciad*. So Pope's universe, seemingly destroyed, does with Belinda's lock "upward rise,"

Though mark'd by none but quick, poetic eyes:
(So Rome's great founder to the heav'ns withdrew,
To Proculus alone confess'd in view)
A sudden Star, it shot through liquid air,
And drew behind a radiant trail of hair.
Not Berenice's locks first rose so bright,
The heav'ns bespangling with dishevel'd light.
The Sylphs behold it kindling as it flies,
And pleas'd pursue its progress through the skies.
  This the Beau monde shall from the Mall survey,
And hail with music its propitious ray. . . .
  Then cease, bright Nymph! to mourn thy ravish'd hair,
Which adds new glory to the shining sphere!
Not all the tresses that fair head can boast,
Shall draw such envy as the Lock you lost.
For, after all the murders of your eye,

When, after millions slain, yourself shall die;
When those fair suns shall set, as set they must,
And all those tresses shall be laid in dust,
This Lock, the Muse shall consecrate to fame,
And midst the stars inscribe Belinda's name.

As in *The Dunciad* Pope acknowledges the death of the art-world he has already immortalized in "The Rape of the Lock," so here he finally can afford to acknowledge Clarissa's truth about the death of the physical Belinda, but only because he is granting a resurrection to that metonymic lock which has been appropriately hailed by the "Beau monde" that it symbolizes.

For, after all the murders of your eye,
When, after millions slain, yourself shall die;
When those fair suns shall set, as set they must,
And all those tresses shall be laid in dust,
This Lock, the Muse shall consecrate to fame,
And midst the stars inscribe Belinda's name.

The poem, too, is inscribed there! And with it that illusory universe, like the "Beau monde" constructed as a work of art, whose very artificiality testifies to the persistence, the indomitable humanity of its creator's classic vision—and to his awareness that the insubstantial nature of this universe could allow it to transcend all that chaos ground into "glitt'ring dust." Powerless against chaos—that disintegrating force of historical reality whose "uncreating word" extinguished "Art after Art"—the frail universe could win immortality with the very evanescent quality that doomed it: for "quick, poetic eyes" it glows, gem-like, a sphere beyond the reach of the "universal Darkness" that buried all.

5
"Dover Beach" and the Tragic Sense of Eternal Recurrence

 What are the characteristics of Matthew Arnold's "Dover Beach" that have earned a place for the poem so far above that of those maligned Victorian works which critics commonly consign to our willful neglect? To what extent has it earned its exemption from the common charges they bring against many of its contemporaries?

It would seem clear enough that in "Dover Beach" Arnold brings along his usual equipment, or, I might better term it, his *impedimenta*. The usual techniques and the usual patterns of thought which infect much of his verse and render it unsuccessful are apparent at once. The surprise is that the joining of them in this poem proves as happy as it does. There is, first, the well-known Arnold melancholy: the man of little faith in a world of no faith, who still hopes to maintain the spiritual dignity which the world of no faith now seems to deny him. There is also the typical nineteenth-century didactic formula which Arnold rarely failed to use by allowing his "poetic" observer to extort symbolic instruction from a natural scene. Finally there is here as elsewhere the mixture, perhaps the strange confusion, between a poetic diction and a diction that is modern, almost prosaic.

Arnold's easy but uneven rhetoric of melancholy often leads these characteristics to fail as he compounds them, but here they succeed, and in a way that reaches beyond the limitations of Arnold's period and of his own poetic sensibility. "Dover Beach" bears and rewards contemplation from the vantage point of the modern, and yet ancient, concept of time which has stirred our consciousness through writers like Mann, Proust, Virginia Woolf, T. S. Eliot—a concept of time as existential rather than as chronologically historical, as the flow of Bergson's dynamics, as the eternal and yet never-existing present. This awareness which we associate with our sophisticated contemporary can be seen somehow to emerge from Arnold's highly Victorian "Dover Beach." We must determine how it manages to do so, how the very weaknesses that generally characterize Arnold's poetic imagination serve here to create this tragic and extremely modern vision. It is a vision which Arnold achieves neither as a nineteenth-century optimist nor as a vague and confused rebel of his period who turns to an equally nineteenth-century pessimism and simple melancholy; it is a vision which he achieves by transcending his period and foreseeing the intellectual crisis which we too often think of as peculiar to our own century.[1]

A cursory reading of the poem discloses that all the stanzas but the second are built on a similar two-part structure and that each recalls the ones which have gone before. The first section in each of these stanzas deals with that which is promising, hopeful; the second undercuts the cheer allowed by the first section and replaces the illusory optimism with a reality which is indeed barren, hopeless. In these subdivisions of stanzas there is also a sharp contrast in tone between the pleasant connotations of the first section of these stanzas and the less happy ones of the second. In each of them, too, there is a contrast between the appeal to the sense of sight in the first section and the appeal to the sense of hearing in the second.

And yet, these three stanzas are not, of course, mere repetitions of each other. Each marks a subsequent development of the image—the conflict between the sea and the land. With each succeeding stanza the sea takes on a further meaning. I said earlier that this, like most of Arnold's poems, deals with a natural scene and the moral application of the meaning perceived within it: the vehicle of the metaphor and then the tenor carefully stated for us. In this poem, however, the development from the natural scene to the human levels into which it opens is much more successfully handled than elsewhere in his work. Each level grows into the succeeding one without losing the basic natural ingredients which initiated the image.

We can see that the natural scene described in the first stanza is value-laden from the beginning. It is clear that nature itself—or at least nature as sensuously perceived—does have immediate significance, and moral significance, so that when the development and application are made later, we do not feel them as unnatural. By the third stanza the sea has of course

---

[1] This paragraph may seem to imply that Nietzsche, whose phrase I have borrowed for my title and my theme, is a twentieth-century mind. In the sense in which Arnold is predominantly a nineteenth-century mind, Nietzsche may very well appear rather to belong in our own century.

become the "Sea of Faith,"[2] but the human relevance of the sea-land imagery is justified by the transitional second stanza. In addition, the image is handled completely in the terms which characterize its natural use in the first stanza. The sea-land conflict is still with us, still the motivating force of the insight the poem offers. And in the last stanza the sea-land conflict exists in the present, but, for Arnold and for these lovers, representative here of humanity at large, the historical present. The aphoristic impressiveness of the final lines of the poem is again justified in terms of the initial image of the first stanza, which they here recall and bring to its final fruition. The archetypal image of the sea, of the tides, and of the action of these as the sea meets the land—all these have been merged with the destiny of that humanity to which they have meant so much throughout its mythopoetic history.

As nature has thus—if I may use the word—*naturally* merged with man, so, through the use of the middle part of the poem, has history merged with the present, has the recurrence, of which the sea, the tides, the meeting of land and sea have always stood as symbols, merged with the ever-historical present. This is why the second stanza of the poem is excluded from the parallel development of the others. It is the stanza which makes the poem possible, which brings us to "the ebb and flow of *human* misery," and brings us to the past even as we remain in the present. The image and its archetypal quality are indispensable to the poem. For the tidal ebb and flow, retreat and advance, and the endless nature of these are precisely what is needed to give Arnold the sense of the eternal recurrence which characterizes the full meaning of the poem.

But now to examine some of these general comments in greater detail by looking at the poem more closely. The first eight lines give us the scene as it appeals immediately to the sight of the poet viewing it. It is a good scene, one which finds favor with the poet. The value of the scene is indicated by adjectives like "calm," "full," "fair," "tranquil," "sweet," "moon-blanched." There is a sense of satisfaction, of utter completeness

---

[2] The surface triteness of this phrase is typical of Arnold's frequent and stereotyped use of a metaphorical sea, as in the many variations on "the Sea of Life" which dot his poems. (See, for example, "To Marguerite," "Despondency," "Human Life," "Self-Dependence," "A Summer Night," and "The Buried Life.") His failure to exploit this image freshly or even to show an awareness of the need for doing so accounts in large part for his poetic weaknesses elsewhere. We shall see later that "Dover Beach" is distinguished by Arnold's ability here to make his usual conception come alive through his manipulation of the central image of the poem.

about the scene. But of course it is the sea which gives the feeling of ultimate pleasure. In the two places in which the land is mentioned there is something a bit less steady in the impression. The light on the French coast is not, after all, a steady light, and as it gleams and is gone so the cliffs of England, which seem to stand so steadily, yet are glimmering even as they are vast. The land, then, provides the only inconstancy, indeed the only qualification of the perfection of the scene.

The word "only" in line 7 introduces the contrasting mood which will characterize the later portion of the stanza. But before this later portion is given to us, there is the remainder of line 7 and all of line 8, which serve as a reminder of the satisfying first portion of the stanza, although "only" has already been introduced as a transition—one which serves to awaken us to the more unhappy attitude that is to follow. And with the word "listen" at the beginning of line 9, we are to be shocked out of our happy lethargy even as the poet is shocked out of his. The sharp trochaic foot and the long caesura which follows re-enforce this emphasis. And with this word we are transferred from the visual world to the auditory world.

One might almost say that the poet, until this point remarking about the perfection of the scene, has been remarking rather casually—that is, after an almost random glance at it. But here he meets the scene more intimately. He does not merely glance but comes into closer rapport with the scene by lending the more contiguous sense, that of his hearing. He now pays close attention to the scene, and what he hears replaces what he has merely seen as a casual onlooker. What he discovers is far less satisfying, and yet it is more profound than his earlier reaction because he now begins to catch the undertones and overtones of the scene before him, which he before was content to witness superficially. And here the sea is used much as, for example, Conrad and Melville use it. Its superficial placidity, which beguiles its viewer, belies the perturbed nature, the "underground" quality, of its hidden depths. As the more intimate, more aware, and more concerned faculty of hearing is introduced, the turmoil of sea meeting land becomes sensible. The shift in tone from the earlier portion of the stanza is made obvious by Arnold's use of "grating roar" immediately after the appeal to the ear has been made.

One may see in the shift from the eye to the ear also another purpose. It is Arnold's way of moving us from the here and the now to the everywhere and always, from the specific immediacy of the present scene to the more universal application his image must have to serve the rest of the poem.

What we *see* must be a particular scene which is unique and irreplaceable, while our hearing may be lulled by similarities to identify the sounds of other places and other times with those before us now.[3] No sight is completely like any other; sounds may be far more reminiscent and may thus allow us to fancy that we are in another time, in another country. Identity of sound may lead the imagination to an identity of occasion.[4] Then not only is the sense of sight inadequate to grasp the profound perplexities of the situation so that the more subtle sense of hearing must be invoked, but, unlike the sense of hearing, the sense of sight is also incapable of permitting us to break free of the relentless clutch of the present occasion to wander relaxedly up and down the immensities of time.

The "eternal note of sadness," then, caused by the endless battle without victory and without truce between sea and land; this note representing the give-and-take of the tide which symbolically echoes the basic rhythmic pattern of human physio-psychology—this eternal note of sadness, heard also by Sophocles, connects the past at once with the presentness of the past and connects also this rhythmic pattern with the humanity who has taught it to serve them and yet ironically, as the Greeks among others have shown us, has instead served it. Even in the first stanza we saw nature as animated by the human mind, as immediately meaningful in human terms. In the second stanza its human relevance is made explicit. The word "turbid" (line 17) effectively joins the natural sense of the image to its human application as it combines the meaning of "muddied" with that of "confused." As Sophocles serves to read man into the natural image of the first stanza, thus making him one with the natural world, so with the final word ("we") of line 18 the present is read into the past;[5] and the circle of

---

[3] I am indebted to Michael W. Dunn, who first suggested to me that Arnold is here using the greater dependence of the sense of sight on a single time-and-place occurrence.

[4] One can see a similar conceit operating in Wordsworth's "To the Cuckoo" and Keats' "Ode to a Nightingale." In each of these works, too, the poet (who here cannot use his sense of sight since he is unable to see the bird) allows himself to fancy, because only the sound of the bird's song reaches his senses, that the bird itself is somehow immortal even while it has temporal existence, that it has sung in other times and in other places. The illusion fostered by this romantic operation of synecdoche could become a valuable poetic instrument in the hands of such writers as these. See pp. 120–21, below, for an extension of this discussion as it applies to these poems.

[5] The effecting of this union may be aided by what may seem to be something like an unusual internal rhyme between two neighboring vowels, between the last syllable of *misery* and *we*. (It would of course be difficult to maintain this as an internal rhyme if one admits that the last syllable of *misery* is probably unstressed.)

the natural order, now including within its circumference the wheel of human destiny and man-made time, is closed.

The third stanza, in a manner parallel to the first, breaks into two contrasting parts. The first three lines present the promise of the visual image, the last five the despair of the auditory. In the first portion, to the sense of fullness and perfection which was ours in the first lines of the poem is now added the illusion of protectiveness—hence the "girdle" image. Not only is the sea characterized by its complete and self-sufficient perfection, but, like the divine "One" of Plotinus, it must overflow its bounds to salve, indeed to anoint, the imperfect land. Thanks to the passage on Sophocles, the extension of the sea to the human problem and hence to the "Sea of Faith" is now literally as well as metaphorically justified, although the image must remain true to its earlier formulation. And it does. After the "but" (line 24), which here has the same qualifying function as the disappointed "only" in the first stanza, we are returned to the sense of hearing and to the struggle between land and sea which it first introduced. The inevitable cycle must continue and every resurgence be followed by the equally necessary retreat. The advance we have made from the sea to the sea of faith and the added quality of protectiveness given by the "girdle" image bestow a new dimension to the hopelessness of the "naked shingles of the world," the words which close the stanza.

While the first line and a half of the last stanza, in which the poet addresses his beloved, may seem digressive, although they are prepared for in line 6 of the first stanza, they are involved in the development of the poem by the crucial adjective "true," which here means "faithful": the poet is posing the only and the hardly satisfying alternative—the personal alternative of mutual fidelity—for our abandonment by the sea of faith. And again there follows the antithesis between the vision which yields the Apollonian attitude and the cacophony of Dionysian turmoil. Here, however, the balance is swung more heavily than before in the direction of despair. For, we are told explicitly, the world of perfection now merely "seems" (line 30); the world of chaos exists "really" (line 33). The final image of battle, though far-grown from the land-sea conflict of the latter lines of the first stanza, is thoroughly consistent with it and can take its meaning only in terms of it. We are returned in effect to the pre-human natural world of the first stanza and to its primitivism as the clashing armies are finally characterized by the poet as "ignorant." The clash is endless, as endless as time and tide, and, viewed without faith, in terms of nothingness, is as purposeless.

Man himself has now drawn his circle closed or rather has acknowledged the closeness of nature's circle—perhaps the same thing—and has joined with an ungrounded nature to assert his ignorance, his irresponsibility, his doom. But the doom man carries with him he carries only to assert with it his eternal recurrence, even if that which recurs does so but to be doomed again. For paradoxically, doom too is eternally recurrent.

We are, then, worse than returned to what I called a moment ago the pre-human natural world of the first stanza and its primitivism. For the "nature" of the first stanza, being, as we have seen, value-laden, existing only in terms of human perception, was indeed a nature that was humanized. It was seen as meaningful, indeed as purposive. The telic quality of the human was read into nature and, by animating it, made it also telic. But in the primitivism of the "*ignorant* armies" humanity is seen as atelic. The relationship has been reversed as the non-purposive quality of the nature of modern science has been read into man. As nature was humanized at the start, so here man is naturalized and, thus, deprived of his purposiveness, deadened. He has indeed become part of nature and hence, in the words of Keats, "become a sod." The poet, of course, rises above this death-in-life by his dedication to the personal, the I-and-Thou, relationship to his beloved, now that any more inclusive relationships have been shut off from him. But, more important, the poet's assertion of his still-lingering humanity consists primarily in his insistence on realizing fully the sense of its loss, in his refusal to be "ignorant" of it.

The poem may seem at first, despite some sideroads, to have a unilinear chronological development. After the natural scene of the present is given us in the first stanza, the word "eternal" in the last line of this stanza permits the poet to move back to Sophocles. Then, after briefly returning to the present in the latter part of the second stanza, the poet moves us back again in time, but now to the Christian Middle Ages.[6] With the introduction of the modern world and its skepticism in the latter part of the third stanza, the poet has prepared us to return to the present dramatic scene of the last stanza. But whatever sense of chronology this arrangement allows us is seen to be purely illusory because of the return in the final image of the poem to the primitivism and everlastingness of the image of tidal conflict with which we began. Similarly, in the very close parallelism of structure of the first,

[6] Here we see Arnold managing to return to one of the favorite laments of so much of his prose as well as his verse: the irreplaceable psychological efficacy of the Christian medieval unity which, unfortunately, had to turn out to be so scientifically erroneous, and thus to him unacceptable, in its theological foundations.

third, and concluding stanzas we feel the unprogressiveness of man's ever-repetitive circular history.

The handling of the metrics and rhyme scheme reflect the other elements we have observed in the poem. The inexorable quality of the unending struggle as it is felt in such passages as

> . . . *the grating roar*
> *Of pebbles which the waves draw back, and fling,*
> *At their return, up the high strand,*
> *Begin, and cease, and then again begin* . . .

is obvious enough. But perhaps more significant is the development of the patterns of line-length and rhyme, which begin as relatively undefined and conclude as firm and under full control. Through the first three stanzas the intermixture of pentameter lines with shorter ones is unpredictable, and, similarly, there is no determinate rhyme scheme. While the poem clearly is written in rhyme, the echoes of the final syllables of the lines surprise us since there is no pattern which enables us to foresee when the sounds will recur. And yet they continually do recur in this seemingly undetermined way. Only the final word of line 9 ("roar") seems not to have any rhyme in its stanza; and even this may be claimed to be an off-rhyme with "fair" (line 2) and "air" (line 6), functioning to set up a tension between this line and the earlier pleasant portion of the stanza—precisely what we should expect of the noun which is characterized as "grating."

Thus until the last stanza is reached, the patternless rhymes suggest a continual recurrence, but one on which human meaning and form have not yet been bestowed. The echoes multiply, but they have not yet been cast into a significant mold. In the final stanza a clear rhyme scheme at last emerges (*abbacddcc*), and, further, for the first time the line-lengths even out. Between the initial trimeter and the concluding tetrameter are seven consistently pentameter lines. The problem of the poem, while certainly not resolved (poems rarely resolve problems, or ought to), has at last emerged as fully comprehensible, in terms of the poem at least. The meaning of the recurrence has become tragically and profoundly clear.

It may—and perhaps with some justice—be claimed that, if my prosodic analysis is valid, this manipulation of line-length and rhyme is, after all, a not very cunning trick, indeed is a highly mechanical contrivance. Or the poet's attempt to make the technical elements so obviously expressive may be charged and booked under Yvor Winters' "fallacy of imitative form." I shall skirt these issues since my purpose here is primarily explicative. In terms of this purpose it is enough to say that the versification, like the structure, the diction, and the archetypal imagery, marks out the repetitive inclusiveness of the human condition and its purposeless gyrations. The poem's form thus comes to be a commentary on the problem that is being poetically explored, a mirror which allows the poem to come to terms with itself.

But if the form helps indicate the price of eternal recurrence for a world robbed of its faith—the fate of being pitilessly bound by the inescapable circle—in the regularity it finally achieves, it indicates, too, the sole possibility for victory over the circle and freedom from it: the more than natural, the felt human awareness of its existence and its meaning. The tragic is at least an attainment, an attainment through the painful process of utter realization, realization of self, of nature, and of history. And the contemporaneity of the Western tradition in the poem is Arnold's way of proving that he has realized *it* and himself as its child.

6
The Marble Faun and the International Theme

*The Marble Faun,* of all Nathaniel Hawthorne's fiction, may be the clearest acknowledgment of the uncertainty with which its author maintained his famed Puritanical morality. If the novel has been seriously underestimated, as I believe it has, it is because critics have commonly drained off its life by applying to it an *a priori* notion of Hawthorne's moral austerity which the novel itself does not justify. It is unfortunate that commentators have failed to accord to Hawthorne the benefits of the critical generosity usually reserved for Henry James in his later versions of "the international theme" that makes its earlier and influential appearance in *The Marble Faun*. Even writers who concede that James was indebted to this novel in his formulating this theme and who normally allow to James the controlled transcendence of his moral opposition between American and European values continue to see Hawthorne as the priggish provincial who condescends to his Italian experience and idolatrously creates cold New England saints to protect himself from it and purge it from his pages. However, it is not only that in Hawthorne, as later in James, the novel is grounded in a profound conflict between the limited claims of American moralism and of European aestheticism, but also that in Hawthorne, as later in James, the totality of the novel in its multi-dimensionality sees round any single restrictive moral vantage point. The earlier as well as the later writer is aware, in the moral-aesthetic polarity, of an irresolvable *either/or* and displays an ambivalence toward either pole that forces any total choice to be made only with a tragic sense of loss. It is as much a mistake to deny Hawthorne a finally cosmopolitan awareness of the mutual attractions and disadvantages of his alternatives as it is to deny him the awareness of the conflict itself.

None of this is to deny that his heroine Hilda is, for the most part, an intolerably pallid New England version of a human being; but it is to deny that, to the total neglect of Miriam's claims, we can blandly identify Hilda with Hawthorne's conception of the human ideal and thus can rub off her insufficiencies on him. After all, some of James' ambassadors from Woollett, Massachusetts, are no more humanly satisfying, and yet we see the total structure of the novel revealing an awareness that towers over their dwarfed sensibilities. It is risky to assume that Hawthorne was so much less an artist, that he projected his limitations so single-mindedly that we can turn our reactions to Hilda upon her creator, when he has really protected himself against them by seeing her inadequacies, intending them to be seen as such, and containing them within a structure that defines and judges them in the full dramatic density of their human relevance.

But are Hilda's limitations in fact Hawthorne's? Even before we reach *The Marble Faun* itself, our expectations concerning his New Englander's insularity may lead us to underestimate the depth of the experience described in his *Italian Notebooks,* to dismiss his Italian experience by assuming that he self-righteously dismissed it. It is this experience, and the problems revealed in it, that are projected onto the novel. The complexity of one is clue to the complexity of the other. Thus it is worth stopping to observe the tensions revealed in the journal since they make their way, equally unresolved, into the novel.

The journal continually shows Hawthorne profoundly perplexed by the art and the sense of the past which engulf him in the seat of Catholicism. This is not to say, as some have, that his experience was refracted through a narrowly provincial Puritan mind which would allow no value to anything it encountered. At the same time it is certainly true that there was much in Italy of which he was contemptuous, even much that he hated. This is truer in his earlier pages, written in days and nights of physical discomfort; but throughout the journal we see him bored by the endless and wearying exhibition of art, shocked by the pagan nudity of the sculpture, and morally outraged by the general corruption and filth of Rome and its people. But as he comes more and more to be captivated by certain works of painting and sculpture and forced into admiration for certain aspects of Catholicism, we become increasingly aware of another side to this sensitive New Englander. Finally, he could not quite make up his mind about Italy, but unquestionably he saw that he could not reject it uncritically, that he could not bring himself to spit it out even if he never dared swallow it.

Thus it is with a sense of unavoidable loss that, at the end, he takes up

The Marble Faun—*International Theme*

his Americanism and tries to forget the enigma that Rome became for him:

> . . . nor do I wish ever to see any of these objects again, though no place ever took so strong a hold of my being as Rome, nor ever seemed so close to me and so strangely familiar. I seem to know it better than my birthplace, and to have known it longer; and though I have been very miserable there, and languid with the effects of the atmosphere, and disgusted with a thousand things in its daily life, still I cannot say I hate it, perhaps might fairly own a love for it. But life being too short for such questionable and troublesome enjoyments, I desire never to set eyes on it again.

Yet he has earlier lamented his need to return from Rome and to be plagued by the seductions of his memory of it. He worries, "What shall we do in America?" He has worried earlier, in an unresolved way, about the future effect of his daughter's attachment to Rome:

> We shall have done the child no good office in bringing her here, if the rest of her life is to be a dream of this "city of the soul," and an unsatisfied yearning to come back to it. On the other hand, nothing elevating and refining can be really injurious, and so I hope she will always be the better for Rome, even if her life should be spent where there are no pictures, no statues, nothing but the dryness and meagreness of a New England village.

There are many similar passages in which America comes off as poorly and Italy as favorably, although none is as sharp or as shocking as that indictment of Americans—prompted by his admiration of Florence—as "the meanest and shabbiest people known in history." I shall cite but one more:

> I had a quiet, gentle, comfortable pleasure, as if, after many wanderings, I was drawing near Rome, for, now that I have known it once, Rome certainly does draw into itself my heart, as I think even London, or even little Concord itself, or old sleepy Salem, never did and never will.

In these passages we find in Hawthorne a sense of nostalgia at the loss of Europe's historic depth and aesthetic richness not much less than that of Lambert Strether, Henry James' richly confused ambassador. It is the judgment of a sensibility that, against its wishes, has been made somewhat cosmopolitan. He can even go so far as to "recognize the truth," in defense of an American expatriate, that "an individual country is by no means essential to one's comfort."

Most of these passages occur when we are well along in the *Notebooks*. Since his devotion to Italy increases with the length of his visit, we may assume that here is a man who is challenged and who is changing. After his early apathy and disdain in Rome, we find him increasingly drawn by the Uffizzi Gallery in Florence. Upon his return to Rome, everything appears more beautiful than before, so that he wonders at his previous insensitivity. At his first carnival he held himself aloof, scornful of what seemed to him to be artificial, scheduled merriment. At his second he joyfully joins in the throwing of confetti.

But of course Hawthorne is not quite so simple, and I do not mean to err in the other extreme. We must remember, for example, that not long after his new joy at returning to Rome as to home, he is able to lament:

I hate the Roman atmosphere; indeed, all my pleasure in getting back—all my home-feeling—has already evaporated, and what now impresses me, as before, is the languor of Rome, its weary pavements, its little life, pressed down by a weight of death.

His moral consciousness, his scrupulosity, never leave him utterly, so that at best his attitude is ambivalent. The tradition and age of Rome sometimes impress him favorably, even arousing his admiration as an inheritor of Western culture and his envy as a patriotic and apologetic American; but at the same time he sees this enormous burden of the past oppressing the present with the massive legacy of centuries that have multiplied sin with brutality. The very aesthetic heritage which draws him to the Church binds it irrevocably to the paganism which Catholicism superseded (or, Hawthorne might prefer to say, adapted) in Rome. He is profoundly struck by what in the novel he calls (and not always condescendingly) the "convenience" of Catholicism, by the unfailing understanding through which the Church has adapted itself to all human weakness and all human needs, by the easy and pleasant and beautiful comfort it has made of religion. What better evidence of how moved he is than that he allows the inviolable Hilda, Puritanism itself, to avail herself of this "convenience," the Confessional, at a most crucial moment—and to be saved by it! Still never quite absent from his awareness is the feeling that this very paternal solicitude, however humanly soothing, contains an impurity and a corruption which can be avoided only by a hard and severe, individual and immediate religion, without worldly priestly intruders, illuminated by the light of heaven unfiltered by the deceptive man-made splendor of the stained-glass window.

Hawthorne's unresolved double vision in the *Notebooks* should warn us to expect no simple thematic resolution in *The Marble Faun*. The writer of the journal could hardly produce a partisan victory. And the closeness of

The Marble Faun—*International Theme*

the novel to the journal is striking in detail as well as in the larger thematic concerns that we have been observing. Since Hawthorne thought of himself as a romancer rather than a realistic reporter and since he indeed was a most inventive storyteller, a maker of fables, it is surprising to find so much material carried over from the *Notebooks* into the novel without being significantly reshaped to fulfill a uniquely fictional purpose. And when we recognize the thematic and even symbolic use to which borrowings from the *Notebooks* are put, our surprise at the similarity of fact and fiction, of personal reaction and aesthetic creation, increases. These occurrences suggest that Hawthorne in his original autobiographical involvement was already thinking in the thematic and symbolic terms out of which the novel later emerged. And our observations have tended to confirm this suggestion. Italian works of art offer especially persuasive further evidence. Hawthorne makes special use of painting and sculpture which he had observed in Italy. Having made extensive moral-literary interpretations of them in the journal, he creates much of his thematic structure in the novel from them. Yet many of these interpretations in the novel seem reproduced almost bodily from the journal. For example, a comparison of his journal comments on the *Faun* of Praxiteles, Story's *Cleopatra*, Guido's *Beatrice Cenci*, and Guido's *Archangel* with his dramatic use of them shows how little artistic transformation has taken place. Even the chronological structure of the novel is significantly related to that of the Italian visit recorded in the *Notebooks*. While his stay extends from late winter, 1858, until late spring, 1859, it is the two carnivals which seem essentially to frame his journal. The novel similarly runs from one early Italian spring to the next, ending in the carnival. And in both the *Notebooks* and the novel the background of Rome yields to a less uncomfortable location in the summer, although in both, too, the travelers are to return, and to return transformed.

I have said that it is surprising to find in a novelist of Hawthorne's kind so great a dependence on relatively unaltered materials from life. Even if we view the *Notebooks* as a sort of apprenticeship to the central issues of the novel, still we must wonder why the materials were not forced to respond more plastically to the demands of Hawthorne's "romance," which, according to his own prescriptions, must create a reality of its own distinct from that of ordinary existence. And the major difficulty in *The Marble Faun*, the weakness probably responsible for its unfortunate neglect, stems from his inability to create a unique realm of being for the characters and incidents in the romance; that is, his inability to decide whether the novel's reality was to stem from the Italian actualities borrowed from the *Notebooks* or from a special, fabulous world created in terms of its own symbolic necessities.

In his famous metaphorical definition of a romance in the lengthy introductory chapter to *The Scarlet Letter,* Hawthorne has told us of the romancer's power to "dream strange things and make them look like truth." He can manage this power because his romance is an independent, specially illuminated world, "a neutral territory, somewhere between the real world and fairyland, where the Actual and the Imaginary may meet, and each imbue itself with the nature of the other." In Hawthorne's metaphor familiar, even commonplace objects are acted on first by the cold lucidity of moonlight and secondly by the genial domesticity of a dim coal fire. The first transforms the objects into intellectual abstractions; the second informs those abstractions with the warmth of life, turning them "from snow-images into men and women." It is perhaps this metaphor Henry James refers to in his book on Hawthorne when he objects to unjustifiably abstract or allegorical elements in his predecessor by complaining of them as "moonshine" or as the products of a "lunar" mist.

The failings of *The Marble Faun* are mainly of this kind, but they occur because Hawthorne tries to ground his "lunar" elements in the precise and detailed realities provided by his *Notebooks.* Despite his intentions, his work, alas, is only half romance, and it cannot satisfy two realms of probabilities at once. An author is quite justified in establishing his own world, with its special laws, if he will not remind us too much of ours. But fantasy is difficult to follow or allow when it takes place before so vividly reported a backdrop as Hawthorne's Rome. He needs Rome and its many masterpieces which give meaning to the action and allow conversations which importantly reflect the speakers. But he must pay the price in realism for his use of this scenery. It is here that he becomes half-hearted, unable to make his fantasy literally sensible and not quite unwilling to try. He multiplies coincidences that often, with his encouragement, seem mystically induced and then belatedly and without conviction tries to account for them. He cannot manage to make Miriam's persecutor either man or Satan, although on differing occasions he tries to make him both, even as these several occasions and their presuppositions about the persecutor are mutually contradictory. He has a similar problem with Donatello as man and/or faun.

Finally, the very source of the action depends on an ever-deepening

The Marble Faun—*International Theme*

mystery about Miriam's family and personal history and her relations with her persecutor. The intrusion of vague Gothic elements which remind us of unspeakable and unholy terror—a metaphysical horror which makes *any* action possible—cannot satisfy us. We simply do not believe that Hawthorne can satisfy us, that any literal reality can satisfy the supernatural requirements he has placed on his situation, and we can believe that the terror remains unspeakable only because the author dare not speak lest it evaporate before the breath of a reality that he cannot make impressive enough. So we never do find out the details. Late in the novel we are told that Kenyon has been the author's narrator and his sole source of information, even though only an omniscient author could have told us much of the story that has preceded. But Hawthorne introduces this narrator in this *ad hoc* way in order to impose this limit upon his omniscience so that we shall excuse him for not knowing what we must never find out. When he feels pressed by exasperated readers to add his chapter of "Conclusion," he apologizes for his Gothic vagueness by reinvoking his definition of romance and then, with regrettable coyness, at once provides inadequate explanations and introduces further mystifications to cover up for them. And again we feel the futility of this attempt at a romance in which, perhaps thanks to the borrowings from the realities of the *Notebooks,* he cannot totally believe. He cannot root his allegory in bedrock reality, even though it is biographical and geographical reality which permits it to take shape.

It is in the Preface to the novel that Hawthorne relates his notions about romance to his opposition between Italy and America, feeling that especially in Italy history can provide mystification (or mythification):

> No author, without a trial, can conceive of the difficulty of writing a romance about a country where there is no shadow, no antiquity, no mystery, no picturesque and gloomy wrong, nor anything but a commonplace prosperity in broad and simple daylight, as is happily the case with my dear native land. It will be very long, I trust, before romance-writers may find congenial and easily handled themes within the annals of our stalwart republic, or in any characteristic and probable events of our individual lives. Romance and poetry, ivy, lichens, and wall-flowers need ruin to make them grow.

This passage, dedicated to the distinction between realism and romance, fact and fancy, the literal and the symbolic, also returns us to Hawthorne's duality of attitude toward the old world and the new. And as we recall my earlier discussion of the aesthetic-moral conflict between these worlds and my observation that his original definition of romance in *The Scarlet Letter* at once opposed the real to the allegorical and human warmth to cold intellectual abstraction, we may be permitted to wonder whether the aesthetic difficulties we have seen him fall prey to in the novel are not the reverse side of the moral perplexities and indecisiveness we have seen him fall prey to in Italy. Could it not be that his inability to choose consistently between actuality and symbolic overlay or to synthesize them into his "neutral" realm of romance is a reflection of his inability to choose consistently between the inhuman austerity of New England moralism and the all-too-human license of aged Italian aestheticism or to synthesize these? Thus the relation of the *Notebooks* to the novel, of both of these to his notion of romance in contrast with reality, and of all these to the conflict between corrupt warmth and intellectual frigidity reveals how unified the aesthetic and thematic dimensions—and difficulties—of *The Marble Faun* come to be.

Hawthorne's own aesthetic, as we can derive it from what he says about the romance, indicates how much he concedes to the need for human warmth and how clearly he relates this need to the need for historical depth, even as the latter brings sin in its wake. The warmth of the hearth is the romancer's only protection against sheer moonshine, the only way to bring men and women out of snow-images. Hawthorne gives to Kenyon, his American sculptor in *The Marble Faun*, a similar artistic problem. Working in marble, he must imbue his objects with the warmth of humanity. And in moments of despondence he fears that after all the cold severity of his medium has proved too much for him. When his American moral overscrupulosity leads him to turn aside from Miriam in her need to confess to him, she cries, "You are as cold and pitiless as your own marble." Again Hawthorne's equation of the unfeeling virtue of moral severity with coldness and the yielding grace of faulty humanity with warmth. And again his aesthetic problem and his thematic problem are seen to join, his aesthetic sense conditioning his moral sense in broadening his awareness as a romancer even as it did in broadening his reactions to his Italian experience.

The structure of the novel is primarily controlled by the dramatic terms given the oppositions which have been concerning us, and with about the same ultimate indecisiveness, which explains why I quarrel with the common relegation of the novel and with the facile disposition of Hilda's place in it. Hilda must rather be seen as a person who is in one sense admirable, if not saintly, but in another sense seriously incomplete. Again it is the grim confrontation of cold and warmth, together with the grimmer insistence that there is no acceptable bridge between them. Each has the derivative qualities we have noticed: warmth has Catholicism, aestheticism, and tradition; cold

The Marble Faun—*International Theme*

has Protestantism, moral simplicity, and immediacy. Each set of qualities has its desirable and undesirable consequences: Catholicism is "convenient" but corrupt, aestheticism is enriching but pagan, and tradition is profound but carries along its burden of sin. The alternative qualities invert these attributes, correcting the moral deficiencies but losing their relevance to the needs of the human heart. Thus Protestantism is seen as a religion for angels and Catholicism as a religion for men. If the former will not bend to man to help him in his need, the latter cannot raise him so as to obliterate that need.

It is of course in Miriam and Hilda that this opposition realizes itself. Miriam not only is the essence of Rome but is made its literal incarnation. If Rome, home of the universal and traditional religion and of the pagan world's universal state is an exquisite choice as the symbol of warmth, Miriam is an exquisite choice as the symbol of Rome. She is beautiful, brilliant, charming—attractive in every way. Yet there is a fatality about her which is inevitably associated with her sin-ridden heritage. In the not quite idyllic early scene in the Villa Borghese, Rome's bloody inheritance from the ages and its own fatality, together with its beauty, are juxtaposed to hers. Rome is likened to Eden, but it is like Eden in its fatality—here represented by malaria—as in its loveliness. Immediately after this description Miriam warns Donatello to protect his innocence by avoiding her. He answers, "I would as soon think of fearing the air we breathe." Her reply completes the metaphor: "And well you may, for it is full of malaria. . . . Those who come too near me are in danger of great mischiefs, I do assure you." The murder she commits through Donatello is consistent with this metaphor. He hurls the persecutor-model from the Tarpeian Rock in what amounts to a pagan execution ceremony. Not only has Miriam given the assent of her eyes, but just before the act she has defended the principle behind the ancient Roman use of the Rock. Thus her crime, initially precipitated by an evil to which she was born but of which she was innocent, is committed in a manner similarly dictated by history.

If Miriam is the Roman ideal, certainly Hilda is the Puritan. She is as spotless and as unearthly as the doves who at once symbolize and accompany her. But despite her transcendent moral perfection, she is humanly insufficient. At the start she has no knowledge of sin, and when its existence is forced upon her, her sole reaction is fear of contamination. She fears that, once mixed, evil will appropriate good rather than good evil. In her severity she fails Miriam irrevocably and crucially as a friend. Miriam forcefully and repeatedly charges her willful blindness to the evil principle and her austere refusal to acknowledge and combat it with being serious human, if not moral, shortcomings. Her moralistic lover Kenyon joins in making these accusations, on occasion with surprising intensity; and even Hilda herself acknowledges their justness. All insist, however, that her action is right for her, that her nature makes it inevitable. Still there remains the unmistakable implication that this nature of hers is woefully inadequate.

The opposition between Miriam and Hilda is also developed in response to several paintings. Guido's *Beatrice Cenci* is an especially eloquent vehicle. The essence of this picture, as Hawthorne describes it, consists of a girl's intimate but guiltless awareness of evil. At the start of the novel she is the mirror of Miriam, who desperately tries to flee the sins of the ages which have descended upon her in her innocence. When Miriam sins, she enmeshes in this ancient and awesome network which has also claimed Donatello the innocent Hilda who, as witness to the deed, now takes up the place that Miriam held. And from this point it is Hilda who is reflected in Beatrice. Confession is made centrally relevant in this sequence. When Miriam was our Beatrice Cenci, she felt urgently the need to unburden herself; but Hilda was of course out of reach, Kenyon put her off, and Donatello perpetrated her crime the night before she was to tell him all. We are allowed to suppose that confession might have saved her. Hilda's knowledge later oppresses her similarly, but the Church's "convenience," the confessional, gives her the relief she needs. At the same time we may be sure that Hilda could not have fallen in any case, since she also has the faith for which Miriam envies her. This faith allows her to use the "convenience" safely, Kenyon's foolish fears of her conversion notwithstanding, since she can live only in "the pure, white light of heaven." Her direct relationship to God can never be finally threatened.

But the contrast between our alternative heroines is perhaps seen most clearly in their reactions to Guido's *Archangel*. Miriam has never cared for the picture which moves Hilda to ecstasy. Only Hilda can appreciate the placid disdain of Michael in his triumph over Satan (or is it Miriam's persecutor-model?). Miriam, on the other hand, herself involved, sees this conflict between good and evil as bloody and cruelly fought with a complete commitment on both sides, even if she is heretically uncertain about who will finally win. Guido's painting seems totally inadequate to her. Her magnificently frightening description of what the picture should have been

The Marble Faun—*International Theme*

so moves Kenyon that even this conservative commentator begs Miriam to paint it. And Kenyon's word ought to be rather good authority to persuade us that Miriam has some share of truth in her view and that Hilda, after all, can be as optimistic as she is only because, out of fear of the Manichaean alternative, she can never give due credit to the existence of evil.

The Donatello story, obviously enough, is a parable of the fall of man. Through him the problem is clearly put to us at the end: was the Fall fortunate? If it was, then the existence of evil is theologically justified since good will come of it. And Puritan insufficiency, as represented by Hilda's refusal to compromise with the human state, is indeed proved to be insufficient. As we might expect, Miriam believes the Fall was fortunate, Hilda is shocked at the very notion, and Kenyon vacillates. Here again, as in the other opposed alternatives Hawthorne has treated, the answer is not definitive and any gain carries its consequent loss along with it. The loss of Donatello's perfect but amoral and unintellectual innocence must be mourned; but the moral consciousness and intellectual awareness which replaced it have brought him a new richness of person. Only his crime could have effected this transformation. And before he gives himself up to punishment, we find him for a moment both a Faun and a sensitive human being. Even his final imprisonment cannot shake our belief in what is after all a spiritual development. But at what a price! Perhaps Kenyon gives us a compromise, if compromising, answer in his statement that in the present world the innocence of Eden is an impossible incongruity. Thus Donatello's fall could be inevitable, and even fortunate, in view of the demands of reality, without forcing us to view the original Fall in this way. Of course, "the hopeful and happy-natured Hilda" cannot accept this modest formulation either.

Obviously this quarrel still concerns the problem of mixing good and evil. Are we to have Hilda's Michael, Miriam's Michael, or Satan? Will good remain aloof, will it struggle with evil and win, or will it struggle and be overcome? Indeed, can it struggle without being overcome in the process, win or lose? This is to ask whether we can have Miriam's Michael without having him inevitably transformed to Satan. The development of Donatello would seem to be clear evidence that for Hawthorne some good can come from evil. It would then be evidence, too, that for Hawthorne Hilda again fails as an all-encompassing ideal. She is, in the end, as she has always been, only half the story and half its meaning, even if the two halves continually overlap and cross over. Forced into a choice, we may have to choose her in the end, however great our losses, but only with the great sorrow of having been shown that our novel has made a choice necessary.

All that we have seen in *The Marble Faun* may partially confirm Henry James' insistence that Hawthorne used his Puritan heritage only as an objectively transformed element in his work, that this heritage represented his data rather than his commitment. But Hawthorne is not quite James, and we must also avoid the other extreme which would totally divorce Hawthorne from any subjective concern with Puritanism. It would seem fair to insist, at the very least, that on his European trip Hawthorne became increasingly open and aware—and thus increasingly troubled, if increasingly perceptive—and that *The Marble Faun,* considered in its fullness, achieved a cosmopolitanism that foreshadowed one of the most important themes in our literature. Of course all the awarenesses that are loosed in the novel have not yet achieved their total fusion in it and often seem rather to be mutual blockages. But for all its faults, this novel was impressive evidence that the American sensibility, without sacrificing its own unique vision, was, together with its forms of literary expression, coming to full maturity.

7
From *Youth* to *Lord Jim*: The Formal-Thematic Use of Marlow

 I find in Joseph Conrad a combination rare in modern fiction generally and in the recent history of the English novel especially. To those disposed to categorize them neatly—perhaps too neatly—most novelists of the last hundred years may be seen primarily either as defenders of prose fiction as a sophisticated and highly disciplined art form or as artless assailants of the dark crises of moral existence. The first group may often seem deliberately modest, unadventurous, even narrow in the scope of their material, and the second defiant of all the refinements needed if the novel is to deserve a place as an equal among its fellow literary genres with their much longer histories of traditional disciplines. The first, defenders of order, find this order reflected in their aesthetic form, while the second, plunged in chaos and dedicated to it, refuse to succumb to form as if to celebrate their underground home. Thus, if the first emphasizes a form that often is so self-conscious as to restrict content, the second yields to a despairing, a desperate theme, a soul-shattering substance that overruns all restraining bounds. One might oversimplify further by terming this an opposition between the French idea of the novel and the Russian, especially as the later nineteenth century viewed this conflict. In Conrad, I believe, the oppositions disappear.

Perhaps what makes Conrad unique is his Slavic sensibility that immigrated (by way of France) to England, carrying with it the Pole's hatred of Russia, which turned him westward in his aesthetic as well as his political preferences. Yet this sensibility remained lurking within his work. Thus, Slavic despite his scorn for what he saw as the formless Russian novel, he could combine the underground awareness of a Dostoevsky with the technical improvisations of a James, the licentious stirring of the romantic agonist with the order and finesse of aesthetic sanity—and ethical sanity too, for always Conrad reveals the English moral earnestness he adopted so well, an uprightness that allowed him to skirt the abyss in the very act of charting it to its immeasurable depths.

Probably it was Marlow, the wise, the mature, the adventurous and yet sound, the warmly sympathetic and yet morally unyielding man of the world and of the sea, who was Conrad's most brilliant invention, allowing him to be at once in the abyss and on solid English ground. Thanks to his narrator, Marlow, Conrad could let loose the reckless agent who summons him to vicarious daring and could learn from him, even as he maintained his own access to a healthier and more reassuring vision. Conrad could allow the socially dangerous representative of outlaw sensibility a freedom of action while purging the outlaw tendency within himself by having his alter ego, Marlow, furnish a moral alternative to it in the very act of projecting it narratively with a warmth that suggests the danger of identification. Just as Marlow, then, is Conrad's alter ego, so the errant romantic may threaten to become Marlow's alter ego as Marlow tries to transcend him through the act of becoming his narrative creator.

Conrad created Marlow for *Youth,* where the narrator, soberly changed from his romantic earlier days with their fond illusions and expectations not unlike Lord Jim's, dotes condescendingly and yet sympathetically on his own reminiscences. Thus *Youth* is a most helpful entry into the study of Conrad. An initiation for Conrad even as it concerns the rites of initiation for his Marlow, it initiates us as readers of his later Marlovian works. It is, of course, not one of his most searching fictions, but it reveals in modest and undeveloped form many of his characteristic devices and themes. If these devices and themes are undeveloped here, they are also simple; as such they are useful to the student seeking to find a way to cope with Conrad's grander and graver works. For enough difficulty and complexity abound in his work generally for the student to profit from this initiation. He can use whatever assistance he can get.

The most obvious and thus the most frequently cited of Conrad's devices is the narrator point of view and its most eloquent instrument, Marlow, who makes his first appearance in *Youth*. In addition to the balanced double vision which Marlow allowed to Conrad's themes, he was a device who was invented for his technical significance. And perhaps, after James, Conrad contributed as much as any other writer to the development of the discipline we have of late come to associate with fiction, the manipulation of point of view. I think it worth recapitulating what Conrad, through his narrator, brought to fictional point of view. By this phrase we refer to the manner in which the events of the tale are relayed to the reader—whether indirectly, through the intervening presence of an omniscient, unidentified author who leads us by the hand and has all the information when he wants it, or through the intervening presence of a first-person, the "I" of the tale; or directly, by allowing the reader to witness the events and conversations without an intervening presence making its commentaries. The last, the purely dramatic point of view, would probably have been seen by a Conrad or a James as properly confined to the drama, since it did not exploit the special resources for narration that fiction made available to its author. Further, Conrad was apparently anxious to avoid the limitations both of an "I" and omniscience. The latter was for him too diffuse, lacking in focus, covering its story like a blanket. And if one was dealing, as he was, with delicate examinations of delicate moral beings, in which refined subjective responses were all-important, omniscience would be especially clumsy. Now it is true that through the first-person the story comes to the reader subjectively, refracted through a single consciousness. Unfortunately, however, there is no way of getting outside the "I," of permitting either a more objective view or other competing subjective views filtered through other sensibilities. Limited by the single set of perceptions available to an "I," Conrad would not be able to multiply dimensions and perspectives.

In his invention of Marlow, and with him the narrator point of view, Conrad combined the advantages of the two opposed points of view, the omniscient and the first-person. There is also the advantage of the narrative frame, the distance and the sobriety lent by the dramatic situation in which Marlow unfolds his tale. And there is Marlow's easy acceptance of fixed and unquestioned values, of his membership in a moral fraternity that gives meaning to his crucial phrase "one of us." Conrad's simultaneous pursuit of the two occasions, the one we are being told about and the one of the telling itself, allows us to be at once outside and inside our narrator, his story, and his view of it. Unlike an omniscient author, the narrator gives us a particular perspective upon the series of events. Further, unlike an "I," he has a specific identity, an objective reality, for us. We must not lose sight of the obvious fact that everything he says is in quotation marks, that we view him from the outside as a character. This makes all the difference when there is a need for us to have several contrasting perspectives upon a situation. After all, if we are restricted to a first-person narrator and cannot get outside him, we cannot get an outside view of our lens so as to judge his judgment of the events he relates to us, to understand the refraction, the limitations produced by his single angle of vision. We see through the window but are not made sufficiently aware of the existence of the glass and its distorting properties. In contrast, Conrad can also, as in *Lord Jim,* introduce characters and incidents that we see at times through Marlow, at times directly; or, again as in *Lord Jim,* he can use other lenses besides Marlow—quotation marks within quotation marks. Finally, to the extent that he uses Marlow to tell his story, he can accentuate certain aspects and suppress others, can go round and round still others by performing involutions of the time sequence and proceeding in a way that is anything but chronological.

In *Youth,* however, matters are managed more simply, for the narrative device is not exploited to yield its more complex effects. In *Youth,* indeed, the reader may think that, in effect, Marlow is nothing more than the usual first person telling his story. Aside from a couple of paragraphs at the start and a short one at the end to frame his narration, it is all Marlow, speaking in his own person. But is this narrative frame needed? Why not simply start and finish with Marlow, have him simply transcribing his own youthful reminiscence? For one thing, we would lose the dramatic situation in which Marlow unfolds his tale: several successful, sedate, middle-aged men—all of them once long ago young and adventurous and at sea and thus now feeling this tight bond of kinship—are having an evening together over a bottle of wine. Marlow shares much with them: his career from romance to solid propriety; his attitudes both past and present, of youth and middle-age; his sense of what is lost and how necessary—if painful—it was to lose it. The rhetorical tone of the tale, and of the general philosophical commentaries that accompany it, arises in large part from Marlow's easy confidence of group understanding, from an exclusive, fraternal sense of belonging. This tone, permitted only by the dramatic situation that frames the monologue, helps Conrad establish the contrast between the then and the now, the freshness and idiocy of romance and the wrinkled weariness of solid, circumspect reality. So does the sense that this narration is being spoken aloud help him attain this effect. In addition, there are those significant returns to the present dramatic situation in Marlow's repeated requests for his hearers to "pass the bottle." At times these occur when the narration threatens to become too sentimental or dramatic, too lost, in its recollections. Marlow breaks the mood, indeed destroys it utterly—as Conrad means him to—with his most unsentimental and undramatic requests. He is jarring the

From Youth *to* Lord Jim

reader—as he is jarring Marlow's listeners and even Marlow himself—out of the beckoning, tempting grasp of romance. What is being told us, we are forcibly reminded, is past, irrevocably behind us, faded and done with, despite the teasing and deceptive vividness of narration. For always the vividness is accompanied by Marlow's conversational rhetoric that establishes the perspective of time and of a sad, aging wisdom.

There are in *Youth* ironies and incongruities which the distanced narrator's role can emphasize. Although there is a wide gap of time and of temperament between narrator and protagonist so that with gentle irony Marlow can condescend to his former, youthful self, at the same time the older Marlow sees in the younger one a certain value and validity that in his honesty he dare not evade. The fact that Marlow is spinning the tale and that it concerns his own earlier self—not that of someone else—enables him to be inside the young man's sensitive psyche even as Marlow's present age, with the skepticism it has brought, allows him to view the youthful dedication rather critically. And even as, through Marlow, we are allowed to look through the young man's eyes as well as to observe him looking through them, so we are allowed to look through the older Marlow's eyes and—since he is an objective character in the story—to observe him observing his own past, to judge the distortions produced by our lens, to understand his reactions in terms of his own limitations of age, sedateness, his mild and moderate disillusionment. And finally we cannot be certain which Marlow is our protagonist—the youthful or the middle-aged—which it is whose psyche is most worth observing. For indeed it is both, in their interrelations. This multiplication of perspectives gives the story its value, and it is the narrator point of view that allows them so to multiply and to vie with each other for supremacy, and for our sympathy.

Yet, as I have suggested, Conrad's use of his narrative device in *Youth* is but a weak shadow of what this method becomes as he comes to live more familiarly with his talkative creature, Marlow. There is in this initial use of his narrator some stylistic difficulty in reconciling the flowery rhetoric the early Conrad so enjoyed using with the sense of colloquialism demanded by the oral narrative situation. How to be both lofty, even romantic, in diction and yet casually conversational in tone? There are inflated phrases like "rectitude of soul," "terrestrial globe," or "a pestiferous cloud defiling the splendour of sea and sky." How is language as pompous as this—and there is much of it—to be reconciled with the breezy carelessness of those passages in which Conrad is trying to emphasize the spontaneity of Marlow's extemporaneous narration? Perhaps the most objectionable of the latter is the refrain "Pass the bottle." Its function, as I have observed, is evident enough—and of course crucial to Conrad's theme. But Conrad puts too heavy a strain on what is after all a rather crude mechanical contrivance all too obviously meant to shatter the reader's illusions even as time has shattered Marlow's. For the most part Conrad is in other writings more subtle in gaining his effects. While of course some of the contrast in the narrative itself between the pompous and the colloquial is consistent with Conrad's ironic intention, unfortunately the incongruities of style also occur, sometimes closely juxtaposed, in passages when Marlow's attitude seems constant. As he grew, Conrad was usually able more successfully to weld the tone of Marlow, the descriptive polysyllabic raconteur; Marlow, the pompous philosopher; and Marlow, the breezy drinking companion.

Further, while I have tried at some length to justify Conrad's use of his peculiar narrator technique in *Youth*, I must admit that he gets far more out of it elsewhere, especially in *Lord Jim*. There the number of perspectives upon a single action or single problem comes to be endlessly multiplied so that one's view of it is endlessly complex, as it should be in Conrad's world, where relativity rules supreme and objects have reality not in themselves so much as in their effect upon the consciousness of the character concerned with them. Only in *Youth* does one find the narrator-Marlow's role so circumscribed as to be related only to a single other character, himself, and his technique of storytelling so inhibited as to restrict him to a simple chronological recital of a sequence of events. Yet even here, less exploited as he is, Marlow manages, as I have shown, to function for his master most effectively.

The theme of *Youth* is similarly related to themes in Conrad's other work. And Conrad had a most serious interest in his themes—themes of a special nature—as one might by now expect, of an especially complex nature. As we shall see, all that Conrad had to say in his own voice on the subject of art and truth reveals—as does his circuitous method—that he is primarily concerned with how much his work can mean but that the meaning which concerns him is anything but simple, is at least ambiguous, if not utterly ineffable. In *Youth* there is a resistance to choice between the romantic striving that may from a more sober view seem essentially aimless and the sensible compromise with reality that speaks of an inglorious weariness even as it boasts of wisdom. We cannot choose any more than Marlow himself can. He would not return to the folly that alone permitted

From Youth to Lord Jim

the blind courage he still admires, nor can he give up his calm knowledge even though it has stripped from him the possibility of a heroism he knows he misses even if he has made his peace without it.

But again *Youth* is but a frail shadow of Conrad's other work. The symbolism by which he expresses his theme here is surprisingly transparent, indeed explicit. It neither demands nor deserves more than a superficial notice in passing. For the symbolism does not enrich the story, which is only an illustration of it, any more than it is enriched by the story, which in no essential way adds to or deepens its meaning. Marlow introduces the symbolic note early and openly:

> You fellows know there are those voyages that seem ordered for the illustration of life, that might stand for a symbol of existence. You fight, work, sweat, nearly kill yourself, sometimes do kill yourself, trying to accomplish something—and you can't. Not from any fault of yours. You simply can do nothing, neither great nor little—not a thing in the world—not even marry an old maid, or get a wretched 600-ton cargo of coal to its port of destination.

All this, at the outset of the story, is terribly grandiose. It puts a tremendous burden on any story that is to live up to this advance notice. And it supplies us with too calculated a commitment. Marlow reinforces this statement, and about as explicitly, a bit later: "To me she was not an old rattle-trap carting about the world a lot of coal for a freight—to me she was the endeavor, the test, the trial of life." And speaking of the old ship, whose worn body cannot support the glorious dream of youthful enthusiasm, he clearly demonstrates her symbolic place in the theme: "Her youth was where mine is—where yours is—you fellows who listen to this yarn. . . ." There is also, of course, the obvious significance of the ship's motto, "Do or Die," and the finally conclusive characterization of "the sea that gives nothing except hard knocks—and sometimes a chance to feel your strength. . . ." There is one passage in which the theme achieves a more brilliant and metaphorical expression, but after a moment's study it should not be much less obvious than the others:

> Oh, the glamour of youth! Oh, the fire of it, more dazzling than the flames of the burning ship, throwing a magic light on the wide earth, leaping audaciously to the sky, presently to be quenched by time, more cruel, more pitiless, more bitter than the sea—and like the flames of the burning ship surrounded by an impenetrable night.

This is effective, but one can make the evident equations readily enough to pass quickly on. Not that obviousness or clarity in literature is necessarily bad. Far from it. But the special virtue of Conrad's work generally is its complex treatment of our moral life; thus work as thin and as thematically limited as *Youth* seems to be, in comparison with his other fictions, has its special value in its capacity to initiate the reader into that absorbing world Conrad everywhere creates. For it is a world unique and revelatory enough to demand such initiation.

Most of the thematic elements that are, for Conrad, all too neatly contained in *Youth* appear more monumentally elsewhere, again nowhere more crucially than in *Lord Jim*. There, too, we have the story of an education, the fitting out for life of a dedicated young man. There too we have a trial, and it is also a self-imposed trial. That is, our hero's romantic mind, having projected itself outward upon common-sense reality so as to convert this reality into illusion, now sees this imagined outside world as imposing exaggerated romantic demands upon him. But unfortunately the cruelly indifferent, unromantic world refuses to cooperate with the sensitive dreamer, thus frustrating his unswerving and uncompromising quest for honor and for the highest and noblest fulfillment of moral duty.

Once again the problems are severely simplified in *Youth* and, unusual as it is in Conrad, simplified in a comic direction. The romanticism of the young Marlow is undercut by more than the ironic skepticism of the older Marlow who reconstructs him. It is undercut most immediately by the objective facts of the situation, by what is undeniably the triviality—indeed the farcicality, the sense of the ridiculous—that characterizes the ship, its captain, its cargo, the difficulties in getting under way: in short, the entire adventure. The whole affair is hardly respectable. There is not objective ground sufficient to sustain young Marlow's fervor, so that there is difficulty in our taking him seriously throughout the tale any more than we can take seriously his "first command," his captaincy of the lifeboat at the end. To be sure, this may be as the older Marlow meant it to be and why he is patronizing and ironic toward the memory of his younger self. Still, in his tribute to the glories of youth implied throughout the story and stated explicitly at the end, our narrator *is* being serious, perhaps more serious than the earlier situation has allowed for. For the challenge young Marlow sees thrust upon him is seen—by the older Marlow and by us—to be too illusory for us to admire his answer sufficiently. Granted that for awhile there is a real element of danger for the ship and its crew. But there is enough that is comic in the way this is presented to keep us from sympathizing fully with their devotion in the face of it.

But let Conrad stack the cards differently: let him have much the same sort of young hero, but since this hero may not succeed, let him be someone other than Marlow himself. After all, if we need to see inside the hero, Conrad can complicate his point of view so as to allow him also to function as a lens. Now let Conrad create a situation that inherently deserves, indeed demands, courage and devotion. And it thus becomes more than a matter of *pure* illusion. Our romantic youth, who makes such unrealistic demands upon his resources for heroism, is now confronted by a situation that has its own heartless demands. Must not some human failures reveal themselves—here in the real world with knighthood no longer in flower? And must not these failures be fearfully exaggerated by our hero's sensitive, uncompromising mind? All this is, in effect, what happens when we move from the relatively shallow world of *Youth* to the profound world of *Lord Jim,* from illusions deriving from a farcical reality to illusions deriving from a terrifying reality. Reality, we are told in *Lord Jim,* is "the destructive element." And the romantic hero, having failed his dream like most of us but, unlike most of us, unwilling to give it up, can learn to live with himself and in the world only by "immersing" himself in "the destructive element," reality, while cherishing still his youthful illusions of honor and courage. Of course at the hands of this reality, which lives up to Conrad's phrase, this hero can expect only his destruction, but a destruction through which his faithfulness shines and his truest self is realized. But here, in *Lord Jim,* in this profound modulation of the themes we find so modestly displayed in *Youth,* we are brought to the very edge of the tragic, that fearsome and lonely realm through which Joseph Conrad became one of our most moving and most instructive guides.

Let us turn fully, then, to *Lord Jim,* observing its more complex ways from the more complex manipulation of Marlow, at once Conrad's formal device and his thematic ground. After *Youth,* Marlow appeared as narrator immediately again in *Heart of Darkness,* where he shared the protagonist's role with the famous Mr. Kurtz.[1] *Lord Jim,* in which Marlow's role recedes

---

[1] I have a detailed treatment of Marlow's formal-thematic function in *Heart of Darkness*—his relation, as semi-protagonist, to Kurtz—in *The Tragic Vision* (New York, 1960), pp. 155–65. I excerpt the following from my conclusion there:

As at once the sensitive and the normal man who has both been shown by Kurtz and been horrified by him, Marlow is our ideal lens and narrator even as he becomes the protagonist of a kind of *Bildungsroman*. And he willingly pays for his education. Normal enough to see the need to reject Kurtz but sensitive enough to qualify his rejection and to see the even greater need to be captivated by Kurtz, Marlow can sensitize us to the phenomenon of Kurtz as he appreciates it, because we can trust him ethically as "one of us." . . . Our own need enables us to understand his—and to

considerably before the protagonist so that he is converted almost totally into narrator, followed quickly, having been started earlier, although Conrad apparently put the tale aside before reaching the point at which Marlow entered it. Indeed, since he started *Lord Jim* as a short story, it may be that he did not originally intend using Marlow and decided to borrow him only as the magnitude of the tale asserted itself along with the value of his narrator in the tales he had so recently finished. In any case, in *Lord Jim* Conrad has come to live more familiarly with his talkative creature, and so have we. As soon as we have his name and learn he is once more spinning a yarn at an evening gathering of friends—those bound by common fealty within the "us" of whom Jim is repeatedly asserted to be "one"—we know all about him. We know the values and attitudes he represents and know that these will figure importantly in the tale, as they collide with the values and attitudes of the romantic hero, so that Conrad need no longer present him to us with the biographical detail we found in his first appearance. Nor does Marlow disappoint us, either in his standards or in the tentativeness with which he urges them.

Marlow does not disappoint us as a function of Conrad's form any more than he does as a function of Conrad's theme. Entering the story of an omniscient author, he takes it over and makes it his own even as he liberally—but discriminately—shares perspectives with others. Through Marlow also, Conrad manipulates time, as he manipulates point of view, again in order to emphasize subjective reality over objective and classifiable fact. One can see Conrad's contempt for fact in the thoughtless ease with which he uses his chronological waywardness again and again to dispose of

---

accept his willingness to pay for having it satisfied, to acquit himself of his debt to Kurtz by something surely less than identification with him but uneasily approaching it in the totality of its moral involvement. But Marlow has cracked our moral austerity enough for us to countenance all this, even if—through the example of Kurtz—he has made us distrustful of that other, that self-appointed immoral austerity as well. . . .

. . . Marlow is all awareness, perhaps too much awareness to allow any final commitment—except to the compromising unidealistic world that scorns commitment. The limitations on even this commitment explain why he is open to the extremity of Kurtz, while his refusal to abandon the commitment (to non-commitment) explains why he remains in need of Kurtz.

Since Marlow is incomplete even while he is comprehensive, he cannot furnish the answer to Kurtz. Marlow has no answers: he cannot even quite dare to ask Kurtz's questions. He shows us that we cannot afford the vision of Kurtz if we are to manage, as social beings, to struggle along in our daily drudgeries. But neither can we do without it unless we are to become enslaved to these drudgeries and thus take them as our reality.

any incipient suspense we may feel about how things will turn out. What counts about Jim's story, as Marlow at once sees at his hearing, is that which is not reducible to fact: "They demanded facts from him, as if facts could explain anything!" Jim recognizes this understanding in Marlow, the "white man who sat apart from the others," who "seemed to be aware of his hopeless difficulty" in communicating the reality underlying that moment of his irrevocable faithlessness. Indeed, Marlow continually echoes Conrad's distrust of facts, his interest in the ineffable qualities of our profoundest and our most personal experiences. Thus, in *Heart of Darkness*, Marlow, in the same spirit, tells his listeners

... it is impossible to convey the life-sensation of any given epoch of one's existence,—that which makes its truth, its meaning—its subtle and penetrating essence. It is impossible. We live, as we dream—alone. ...

It is no wonder that in *Heart of Darkness* a special quality is attributed to Marlow's stories, as subsequent critics have attributed it to Conrad's stories in general:

... to him the meaning of an episode was not inside like a kernel but outside, enveloping the tale which brought it out only as a glow brings out a haze, in the likeness of one of these misty halos that sometimes are made visible by the spectral illumination of moonshine.

And in his own voice, in his famous Preface to *The Nigger of the "Narcissus,"* Conrad defines art as

... a single-minded attempt to render the highest kind of justice to the visible universe, by bringing to the light the truth, manifold and one, underlying its every aspect. It is an attempt to find in its forms, in its colours, in its light, in its shadows, in the aspects of matter and the facts of life, what of each is fundamental, what is enduring and essential—their one illuminating and convincing quality—the very truth of their existence.

But, as we must suspect even from what we have learned from *Youth*, this "truth" that goes beyond the "facts" is no simple matter. Thus Conrad must tell us also in this Preface that "it is not in the clear logic of a triumphant conclusion; it is not in the unveiling of one of these heartless secrets which are called the Laws of Nature." For Conrad means us to feel that the density, the indefiniteness, the merest intimation of a frightfully complex moral reality, escape the neat formulations of any ethical code. This becomes a major intention in his tales: their need to demonstrate through extreme examples the many-sidedness of our moral experience, a many-sidedness which makes the stories more indispensable to our understanding and our living than the inadequate oversimplifications of moral philosophy. Thus in Conrad, as in Marlow, there is to be found no single dimension of meaning. Always there is the qualification, the sense of balance, of irresolution, so that every gain has its loss and every loss its gain. All is dilemma; there is no best way; indeed, at times we may doubt that there is an indisputably better way. For Conrad's art is not designed to give us final answers, and he would have us distrust any art that pretended to do so. His art can teach us to tread our moral way only with a light foot and a heavy heart.

Consequently, in *Lord Jim* the incompatible demands of fidelity—fidelity to self, fidelity to one's society, fidelity to what Marlow, with more assurance than he has a right to feel, calls a "fixed standard of conduct"—and the awesome downward pull of human weakness and self-distrust produce an unhappy array of alternative possibilities for action which can only persuade us of the vast chasm between our deepest vision and our most necessary decision. How, in the final choice, to reckon the relative claims of what must be at all costs saved, and what sacrificed—even betrayed—in the cross-purposes that send vision and action against each other, when faithfulness and treachery refuse to assert themselves independently, each seeming to become the mask for the other? Satisfactory mediation is seen as a fond illusion; what we are left with are mutually exclusive and thus unsatisfactory choices based on costs beyond our ability to pay and hopes for glory too lofty for our wisdom to ascertain.

All these multiple and simultaneous awarenesses and counterawarenesses argue persuasively for Conrad's need to afford us the complexity of vision yielded by his use of Marlow and his disruption of chronology. Add to these the parade of further commentators and of characters in positions analogous to Jim's, all made available to us by Marlow, and we have a brilliant series of variations upon a theme. And, most crucially of all, add also Marlow's special characteristics as a person, and we discover why this theme is one we have to take with considerable "high seriousness." We have seen his distrust of facts, which is an echo of Conrad's. But what about Marlow's distrust of himself; indeed, of us all? It is a distrust of which his distrust of facts is symptomatic. Were he finally confident of that "fixed standard of conduct" of which the English traditions of seamanship were for him a symbol, Jim, though "one of us," could not worry him as he did. But the kinds of ineffable truth he looks for in the endlessly suggestive stories he tells, his denial of facts—like Conrad's denial of "the clear logic of a

From Youth to Lord Jim

triumphant conclusion"—reveal Marlow's awareness of the mysterious and underground depths which tug at our actions and unfix our standards. Jim's case plays on this awareness and turns it into a gnawing self-doubt. He cannot push his doubts into a conviction of his own depravity—as does the ill-fated Captain Brierly, that romantically brilliant success, the happy counterpart of Jim—for this would also be a single-minded conclusion, however *un*triumphant. But he must pursue Jim's case in all its meandering uncertainties through the miles and years to the last outpost and the last moment, grabbing onto every person who can furnish new information or a different opinion. Nor is Marlow unaware of the causes of his special interest in the case:

> Why I longed to go grubbing into the deplorable details of an occurrence which, after all, concerned me no more than as a member of an obscure body of men held together by a community of inglorious toil and by fidelity to a certain standard of conduct, I can't explain. You may call it an unhealthy curiosity if you like; but I have a distinct notion I wished to find something. Perhaps, unconsciously, I hoped I would find that something, some profound and redeeming cause, some merciful explanation, some convincing shadow of an excuse. I see well enough now that I hoped for the impossible—for the laying of what is the most obstinate ghost of man's creation, of the uneasy doubt uprising like a mist, secret and gnawing like a worm, and more chilling than the certitude of death—the doubt of the sovereign power enthroned in a fixed standard of conduct. It is the hardest thing to stumble against; it is the thing that breeds yelling panics and good little quiet villainies; it's the true shadow of calamity. Did I believe in a miracle? and why did I desire it so ardently? Was it for my own sake that I wished to find some shadow of an excuse for that young fellow whom I had never seen before, but whose appearance alone added a touch of personal concern to the thoughts suggested by the knowledge of his weakness—made it a thing of mystery and terror—like a hint of a destructive fate ready for us all whose youth—in its day—had resembled his youth? I fear that such was the secret motive of my prying. I was, and no mistake, looking for a miracle. The only thing that at this distance of time strikes me as miraculous is the extent of my imbecility. I positively hoped to obtain from that battered and shady invalid some exorcism against the ghost of doubt.

Marlow later comments even more forcefully on the evasive wisdom of getting Jim out of his consciousness:

> To bury him would have been such an easy kindness! It would have been so much in accordance with the wisdom of life, which consists in putting out of sight all the reminders of our folly, of our weaknesses, of our mortality; all that makes against our efficiency—the memory of our failures, the hints of our undying fears, the bodies of our dead friends.

This fear of common human guilt cannot attack someone as unromantically mature as Marlow, as trustworthy in his unfailing espousal of the reliable virtues, without its attacking us. And, with all the objectivity of his performance, with his capacity to examine and re-examine the underpinnings of action from every side, he persuades us of his disinvolvement, appropriate to his status as officer and as our narrator. But we have seen that Marlow has persuaded us also that a part of him not only is involved with but is wholly committed to Jim out of his fear that the two of them are identified in the "us." And Marlow's two motives seem to work against each other, one lending itself to Jim as the other judges him. But in another sense, a sense relevant to fictional technique, the two are complementary; for Marlow's role as narrator demands both the disinterest that solicits our trust and the obsession that forces him to pursue the case in the tireless way he does. As new informants and new commentators are turned up by Marlow, as the course of events is traced over again and again, in all varieties of chronological order and from all varieties of points of view, revelation—the relief of final revelation—seems always beyond the next turning for the prying Marlow and for the reader whose desperate sympathies he has enlisted with his own. And the ineffability, so vital to the theme, not only becomes the justification for the technical employment of Marlow and for his freely playing with the succession of events, but also proves to be a product of his search as well as a motive for it, thus becoming a justification also for his desperation and ours. But this returns us once again from technique to theme, from aesthetic control to the restlessly and resistantly existential. Still we can return to theme only by way of technique; and to make this claim is to assert their essential identity for Conrad, especially in *Lord Jim*, where the maturity in handling the one assures the maturity of the other.

So we end as we began, with the observation of Conrad's unique capacity to bring his innovations in fictional technique to the service of his profound existential probings. Instead of thinning his surface reality to the enclosed drawing rooms of James, instead of yielding to the unrestrained urge to indiscriminate revelation as Dostoevsky often did, Conrad—and nowhere more than in *Lord Jim*—finds an aesthetic control, a virtuoso manipulation, that, even while revealing fully and fearfully, is able to affirm the moral and the aesthetic order that can stand only in spite of the revelation.

8

The Ekphrastic Principle and the Still Movement of Poetry; or *Laokoön* Revisited

Let me interpret the proposed subject for these papers, "The Poet as Critic,"[1] as referring to the poet as critic in his poem, the poet as critic in the act of being poet; which is, in effect, to rephrase the title to read, the poetic in the poem. It would seem extravagant to suggest that the poem, in the very act of becoming successfully poetic—that is, in constituting itself poetry—implicitly constitutes its own poetic. But I would like here to entertain such an extravagant proposal.

Central to a poem's becoming successfully poetic, as I have tautologically put it, is the poem's achieving a formal and linguistic self-sufficiency. I could go on to claim, as I have elsewhere, that this formal and linguistic self-sufficiency involves the poem's coming to terms with itself, its creating the sense of roundedness. That is, through all sorts of repetitions, echoes, complexes of internal relations, it converts its chronological progression into simultaneity, its temporally unrepeatable flow into eternal recurrence; through a metaphorical bending under the pressure of aesthetic tension, it converts its linear movement into circle. But in making these claims, I am being pressed to metaphors of space to account for miracles performed in time, even if—thanks to the powers of poetic discourse—in a specially frozen sort of aesthetic time. The spatial metaphor inevitably becomes the critic's language for form. Many a self-conscious literary critic has been aware of the debt he owes to the language of the plastic arts—perhaps sculpture most of all—in his need to find a language to account for poetry's formal movements, its plasticity, if I may use the very word that most gives the temporal game away to space.

---

[1] The subject of the first conference of the Iowa Center for Modern Letters, held at the University of Iowa, October 28–30, 1965. This essay was the opening paper of that conference.

THE PLAY OF CRITICISM

Very likely it was just this self-conscious necessity that created the tradition of *ut pictura poesis* from Simonides to Winckelmann, the tradition that drove Lessing to the classical good sense of his *Laokoön* and its insistence on keeping distinct among the arts what belonged to Peter and what to Paul, what to space and what to time. It is surely too easy to try to make poetry and sculpture meet and even fuse (as John Dewey, for example, tried to do anew in *Art as Experience*) by seeing the poem's transcending of mere movement through circular form as being one with the statue's transcending of mere stasis through its unending movement. But still the language of space persists as our inevitable metaphor to account for the poem's special temporality, its circularizing of its linear movement.[2]

I would take as my model statement Eliot's words in "Burnt Norton" about words and their relation to "the still point of the turning world":

Words move, music moves
Only in time; but that which is only living
Can only die. Words, after speech, reach
Into the silence. Only by the form, the pattern,
Can words or music reach
The stillness, as a Chinese jar still
Moves perpetually in its stillness.[3]

These words, in turn, are an echo of the words of the Fourth Tempter in *Murder in the Cathedral*, themselves echoes of Thomas' earlier words about the Women of Canterbury:

You know and do not know, what it is to act or suffer.
You know and do not know, that acting is suffering,
And suffering action. Neither does the actor suffer
Nor the patient act. But both are fixed
In an eternal action, an eternal patience
To which all must consent that it may be willed
And which all must suffer that they may will it,

---

[2] The beginnings of the sort of study I am undertaking here were made by Joseph Frank in his essays on "Spatial Form in Modern Literature" in *The Sewanee Review*, LIII (Spring, Summer, Autumn, 1945), which appear in revised form as the first chapter of his book *The Widening Gyre: Crisis and Mastery in Modern Literature* (New Brunswick, 1963), pp. 3–62. But Frank is interested more in the use of these spatial metaphors by recent authors than in the generic spatiality of literary form and—even more to *my* point—in the inevitability of spatial language by the critic or by the poem as its own aesthetician. French literary critics of time-consciousness and space-consciousness, like Gaston Bachelard and Georges Poulet, also touch matters relevant to my interests here—though with a crucial difference of emphasis, as should become clear toward the end of this essay.

[3] This quotation and the one which follows are from T. S. Eliot, *The Complete Poems and Plays 1909–1950* (New York: Harcourt, Brace & World, Inc., 1952), pp. 121 and 193 respectively.

The Ekphrastic Principle

That the pattern may subsist, that the wheel may turn and still
Be forever still.

I mean to take from Eliot's words about the still movement—like the Chinese jar—of verbal form the suggestion that the poet himself, in seeking to find an eloquence to account for the forms his words seek to turn themselves into, has done well to turn to metaphors from the spatial arts. Thus the poem that in the very act of becoming successfully poetic implicitly constitutes its own poetic may do so, as Eliot suggests, by turning itself into the Chinese jar. It violates Lessing's injunction most strenuously by claiming for itself another order than its own, by substituting the Platonic claim to oneness for the Aristotelian theory of well-policed classes of Peter's and Paul's, with mutual appropriation prohibited.

I use, then, as the most obvious sort of poetic within the poem this anti-Lessing claim: the claim to form, to circular repetitiveness within the discretely linear, and this by the use of an object of spatial and plastic art to symbolize the spatiality and plasticity of literature's temporality. Actually, of course, a classic genre was formulated that, in effect, institutionalized this tactic: the *ekphrasis,* or the imitation in literature of a work of plastic art. The object of imitation, as spatial work, becomes the metaphor for the temporal work which seeks to capture it in that temporality. The spatial work freezes the temporal work even as the latter seeks to free it from space. *Ekphrasis* concerns me here, then, to the extent that I see it introduced in order to use a plastic object as a symbol of the frozen, stilled world of plastic relationships which must be superimposed upon literature's turning world to "still" it.

There are, of course, many less explicit ways for the poem to proclaim as its poetic what I might term its ekphrastic principle, if I may broaden the ekphrastic dimension beyond its narrowest and most literal employment—as I must confess I intend eventually to do. For I would like finally to claim that the ekphrastic dimension of literature reveals itself wherever the poem takes on the "still" elements of plastic form which we normally attribute to the spatial arts. In so doing, the poem proclaims as its own poetic its formal necessity, thus making more than just loosely metaphorical the use of spatial language to describe—and thus to arrest—its movements.

A critic like Sigurd Burckhardt goes so far, in attributing plasticity to poetry, as to insist—and persuasively—that the poem must convert the transparency of its verbal medium into the physical solidity of the medium of the spatial arts:

> . . . whether [a painter] paints trees or triangles, they are corporeally there for us to respond to. . . . The painter's tree *is* an image; but if the poet writes "tree," he does not create an image. He *uses* one; the poetic "image" is one only in a metaphorical sense. Actually it is something that evokes an image, a sign pointing to a certain pre-established configuration in our visual memory. . . . The so-called poetic image achieves its effect only by denying its essence; it *is* a word, but it functions by making us aware of something other than it is. If many key terms of literary analysis—"color," "texture" and "image," for example—are in fact metaphors borrowed from the other arts, this is the reason: poetry has no material cause. Words already have what the artist first wants to give them—body.
>
> I propose that the nature and primary function of the most important poetic devices—especially rhyme, meter and metaphor—is to release words in some measure from their bondage to meaning, their purely referential role, and to give or restore to them the corporeality which a true medium needs.[4]

Thus, by calling attention to the poetic function of words as substantive entities, one might extend the ekphrastic impulse to every poet in search of the sculptor's fully plastic medium.

But, as I have said, it is most useful to begin with the literally and narrowly ekphrastic, the poems which, in imitating a plastic object in language and time, make that object in its spatial simultaneity a true emblem of itself—and of poetry's ekphrastic principle. Jean H. Hagstrum, in his pioneering work *The Sister Arts,* finds his prime example of this mastery of space in time in Homer's description, in Book XVIII of the *Iliad,* of the shield of Achilles wrought by Hephaestus. Hagstrum acknowledges Homer to be a painter, but only as a poet could be:

> The passage remains faithful to the demands of verbal art and is by no means only an enumerative description. The shield becomes an emblem of the life of man: of nature and society, of the seasons of the year, and of cities at war and in peace; of agricultural scenes and the diversions of the rural day. There is obviously much that is non-pictorial: sound, motion, and sociological detail all "appear" on the surface of Hephaestus' masterpiece.[5]

---

[4] "The Poet as Fool and Priest," *ELH,* XXIII (December, 1956), 280.

[5] *The Sister Arts: The Tradition of Literary Pictorialism and English Poetry from Dryden to Gray* (Chicago, 1948), p. 20. Hagstrum, trying to be etymologically faithful to the word *ekphrasis,* uses this word more narrowly than I do as I follow its other users. To be true to the sense of "speaking out," he restricts it "to that special quality of giving voice and language to the otherwise mute art object." The other descriptions of spatial works of art, those that are not made to "speak out," he merely calls "iconic," even as he admits this is a narrower use of *ekphrasis* than that of his predecessors (*The Sister Arts,* p. 18n.). Since I confess from the start that I intend to broaden poetry's ekphrastic propensities, it would be expected that I also am using *ekphrasis* here to include what Hagstrum calls "iconic" as well as what he calls "ekphrastic."

In this total mastery of moving life, the capturing of it in a "still" pattern, do we not seem to have the whole of Homer's world? In this emblem all is at an instant, though it is only in time and language that its simultaneity is created. The emblem is the constitutive symbol, the part that seems to contain the dynamic whole.

From the start, as in my title, following the example of Eliot in the quotations I have cited, I have been openly dependent upon the pun on the word *still* and the fusion in it of the opposed meanings, never and always, as applied to motion.[6] Having, like Eliot, borrowed it from Keats, I have freely used it as adjective, adverb, and verb; as still movement, still moving, and more forcefully, the stilling of movement: so "still" movement as quiet, unmoving movement; "still" moving as a forever-now movement, always in process, unending; and the union of these meanings at once twin and opposed in the "stilling" of movement, an action that is at once the quieting of movement and the perpetuation of it, the making of it, like Eliot's wheel and Chinese jar, a movement that is still and that is still with us, that is—in his words—"forever still." Thus my rendering and free borrowing of the "still" of Keats' "still unravish'd bride of quietness" in the poem which Leo Spitzer taught us profitably to view as a most splendid example of *ekphrasis*.[7] Further, Spitzer taught us to view the ekphrastic and imitative element in the poem not merely as its object but also as its formal cause. In keeping with the circular, "leaf-fring'd" frieze of the urn it describes, Spitzer tells us, ". . . the poem is circular or 'perfectly symmetrical' . . . thereby reproduc-

---

[6] There is a very different and common use of *still* in the aesthetic realm to which I must call attention since it is so single-minded in its rejection of Keats' secondary and more subtle meaning. The "still" of the genre called still-life painting unhappily means only "stilled," inanimate, even in a sense dead—as we are told in the equivalent French phrase, *nature morte*. This sense of the timeless, of the motionless, may recall, for example, Pope's use of *still* to deny change in *An Essay on Criticism*:

First follow Nature, and your judgment frame
By her just standard, which is *still* the same:
Unerring Nature, *still* divinely bright,
One clear, unchanged, and universal light. . . .

(I, 68–71 [my italics])

How much less aware is this "still" than the pun which restores vitality, and an eternal vitality, to a word that means primarily to deny motion and sound. For a more profound vision of *nature morte*, one that is more just to the dynamics of the still-life genre in painting, see Rosalie L. Colie, "Still Life: Paradoxes of Being," *Paradoxia Epidemica: The Renaissance Tradition of Paradox* (Princeton, 1966), pp. 273–99.

[7] "The 'Ode on a Grecian Urn,' or Content vs. Metagrammar," in Leo Spitzer, *Essays on English and American Literature*, ed. Anna Hatcher (Princeton, 1962), pp. 72–73.

ing symbolically the form of the *objet d'art* which is its model."[8] In a footnote to this passage Spitzer generalizes on this practice:

> Since already in antiquity the poetic *ekphrasis* was often devoted to circular objects (shields, cups, etc.), it was tempting for poets to imitate verbally this constructive principle in their *ekphraseis*. Mörike's poem on an ancient lamp shows the same formal circularity motivated by the form of the model as does Keats's ode on the urn. . . .

So the spatial metaphor about the "shape" of the poem is not quite metaphorical, is in a sense literal. Only a little less immediately iconic than George Herbert's poems of imitative graphic form, the poem seeks to attain the "shape" of the urn. In this iconic attempt to shape itself in the form of its content, the poem seeks to perform in a way similar to the way the urns themselves, as sepulchral receptacles, sometimes sought to perform, if we can sense them as Sir Thomas Browne momentarily does in his *Urne Buriall*. For the urn, container of ashes of the dead, seems to take on the form taken by its contents in life, thus becoming a still remaining form of a form that is no more. Browne's description is magnificently far-reaching:

> While many have handles, ears, and long necks, but most imitate a circular figure, in a spherical and round composure; whether from any mystery, best duration or capacity, were but a conjecture. But the common form with necks was a proper figure, making our last bed like our first; nor much unlike the Urnes of our Nativity, while we lay in the nether part of the earth, and inward vault of our Microcosme.[9]

In "the Urnes of our Nativity" we see a further circularity, a further reaching toward stillness (in both major senses): we see at once the end and the beginning, the receptacle of death simultaneously as the receptacle and womb of life, even while, as tomb, it takes on a spatial permanence in its circular imitation of the living form. This added circularity introduces new possibilities for temporal complexity in the use of the urn as the object of *ekphrasis,* a raising of it beyond the linear chronology of life's transience. These are possibilities that Cleanth Brooks seems to have foreseen in *The Well Wrought Urn,*[10] in which he assembles several complex uses of *urn* in

---

[8] *Ibid.,* p. 73.

[9] *Hydriotaphia, Urne-Buriall, or A Brief Discourse of the Sepulchrall Urnes Lately Found in Norfolk,* in *The Works of Sir Thomas Browne,* ed. Geoffrey Keynes (London, 1929), IV, 23.

[10] *The Well Wrought Urn: Studies in the Structure of Poetry* (New York, 1947). He discusses "urn" in "The Canonization," "The Phoenix and the Turtle," "Elegy Written in a Country Churchyard," and "Ode on a Grecian Urn." See pp. 16-20, 101, 112-13, 139-52.

The Ekphrastic Principle

poems, some of which I shall be referring to; although, interested primarily in single interpretations, he does not press their ekphrastic implications.

There is a climactic couplet in Alexander Pope's "Eloisa to Abelard" that serves at once to summarize and to symbolize this poem's studied futility. Eloisa, now denied sexual satisfaction with her lover not only by edict and by physical separation but even more irrevocably by the fact of his emasculation, becomes increasingly and more bitterly conscious of the tragic irony in the underlying sexual meaning of her repeated imperative to him: "Come!" She reaches the bitterness of the lines

Come, Abelard! for what hast thou to dread?
The Torch of Venus burns not for the dead.

(lines 257–58)

He is the walking dead, deprived of all flame. If he defies Church and even the laws of space, his coldness yet prevents all or anything. And as his beloved, Eloisa is doubly cursed since *her* heat has not been subdued: ". . . yet Eloisa loves." And then the masterful couplet to which I want to call attention:

Ah hopeless, lasting flames! like those that burn
To light the dead, and warm th' unfruitful urn.

(lines 261–62)

Here "urn," in its simultaneous relations to flame and death and fruit, becomes in an instant the constitutive symbol for the multiple agonies of the speaker of this monologue. As both tomb and womb, the urn is the receptacle at once of death and of love, of the remnants of the flame and of its height, of the congealing of life and the flowing of life. And a few lines later, in as daring an image, Pope adds the needed liquid element, derived of course from her tears:

In seas of flame my plunging soul is drown'd,
While altars blaze, and angels tremble round.

(lines 275–76)

What is left but for her to direct her flames toward God, as Abelard's rival, in the questionable frenzy of religious ecstasy?

My point is that it is the urn of line 262 that, if I may pun myself, *receives* these meanings, at once preserves and gives life to them, as it gives life to the poem. Receiver of death as it is not permitted to be the vessel of life, it is warmed by the "hopeless, lasting flames" of a desire that dare not—indeed cannot—feed it. And the flames are at once of heat and of cold: at once agent of sexuality, of the life that is its consequence, and agent of the ashes, cold residue of life's flames and death's. The enforced, permanent chastity, this death in the midst of life, is of course reminiscent of the double-edged "stillness," the always-in-motion but never-to-be-completed action that, as with Keats' urn, accompanies the introduction, in accordance with the ekphrastic principle, of spatial forms within literature's temporality.

How different at all is Shakespeare's introduction of the urn, at the close of "The Phoenix and the Turtle," to be at once the repository of the separate ashes of the ideal lovers and the guarantor of their resurrection in the "mutual flame" of their new-born union, in accordance with the Phoenix riddle? Or Donne's introduction of the "well wrought urn" in "The Canonization" as the equivalent of his poem, an ever self-renewed memorial to his true lovers? Both these uses have been properly exploited by Cleanth Brooks in his appropriately titled book.[11] Or we may move forward in time, across the centuries to William Faulkner's *Light in August*, to see the urn crucially, and similarly, functioning. It has been pointed out[12] that each of the three major strands of the novel derives its symbolic characterization in metaphorical and ekphrastic descriptions that by now should sound familiar to us. Let me cite the three passages.

The indomitable Lena Grove, in her endless and endlessly routine—even automatic—movements is, properly enough, given an ekphrastic symbol:

. . . backrolling now behind her a long monotonous succession of peaceful and undeviating changes from day to dark and dark to day again, through which she advanced in identical and anonymous and deliberate wagons as though through a succession of creakwheeled and limpeared avatars, like something moving forever and without progress across an urn.[13]

Continual, deliberate advance, a "succession," yet a forever movement, "without progress." The rolling wheels of all the interchangeable wagons are not finally very different from the wheel spoken of by Becket and the Fourth Tempter in Eliot's *Murder in the Cathedral;* for, like that wheel, these are

[11] *Ibid.*, pp. 17–20.
[12] C. Hugh Holman, "The Unity of Faulkner's *Light in August*," *PMLA*, LXXIII March, (1958), 155–66, especially pp. 159, 161, 164. There is reference here also to Norman H. Pearson's treatment of Lena in terms of Keats' "Grecian Urn" in his "Lena Grove," *Shenandoah*, III (Spring, 1952), 3–7. Faulkner's awareness of Keats' urn as a source for allusion is more explicitly shown us in *The Bear*.
[13] *Light in August* (Modern Library ed.; New York: Random House, Inc., 1950), p. 6; Copyright © 1950 by Random House, Inc. Other references are to this edition.

The Ekphrastic Principle

fixed in an eternal motion, at once action and patience, action and the suffering of action (with the appropriate puns on *patience* and *suffering*). The eternal circularity of Lena's urn and the wagon wheels that bear her round it is further enhanced by the transcendent notion of the "avatars": the god in an ever reappearing, ever indestructible, ever freshly embodied movement, continually in touch with the world and yet remaining intact.

There are similarly definitive passages for Joe Christmas and the Reverend Hightower. First, the young Joe Christmas' vision after his discovery of the uglier facts about female physiology:

In the notseeing and the hardknowing as though in a cave he seemed to see a diminishing row of suavely shaped urns in moonlight, blanched. And not one was perfect. Each one was cracked and from each crack there issued something liquid, deathcolored, and foul. He touched a tree, leaning his propped arms against it, seeing the ranked and moonlit urns. He vomited. (page 165)

Then Hightower's vision of the "seminary," that etymologically shrewd word, as the protected retreat from living, as the tomb of the seed killed within him:

When he believed that he had heard the call it seemed to him that he could see his future, his life, intact and on all sides complete and inviolable, like a classic and serene vase, where the spirit could be born anew sheltered from the harsh gale of living and die so, peacefully, with only the far sound of the circumvented wind, with scarce even a handful of rotting dust to be disposed of. That was what the word seminary meant: quiet and safe walls within which the hampered and garmentworried spirit could learn anew serenity to contemplate without horror or alarm its own nakedness. (page 419)

We should note, first, that while Joe Christmas' urn and Hightower's classic vase exist as metaphorical definitions of their visions, Lena is an actual figure on an urn of our narrator's envisioning. Christmas' vision, distorted by the ugliness of human perversity, sees the foulness of death flowing from what should be the vessel of life and love. Hightower's vision, rendered bloodless by his withdrawal from the living, sees the vacancy of purity in the aesthetic containment and non-commitment of the "classic and serene vase." (And how appropriate that what Hightower sees is a vase— devoid of contents—rather than an urn, a vase as the aesthetic equivalent of the urn while resisting that latter's involvement with either life or death.) But Lena, the creature of the endlessly repetitive, generative fertility principle, is seen as an actual figure partaking of the still movement of the life on the urn. And how different an urn from those of Christmas' vision, one that holds death as part of the ongoing life process, one that—as Sir Thomas

Browne saw it—holds the body of death as the womb holds the body of life, and in the symbol that recalls the womb. So there is Christmas' death-dealing vision; there is Hightower's vision that, in desperate retreat from that of Christmas, denies life as well; and there is Lena's, the vision of wholeness under the aegis of a primal sanctity. Lena's naiveté of course does not permit *her* to have this vision, as Christmas and Hightower have theirs. Instead, all-existing rather than envisioning, she must live it unselfconsciously, herself crawl round the urn's surface, and be made part of the narrator's vision—and ours.

I have already suggested that the shift from urn to vase, as we get to Hightower's life metaphor, is a significant one, confirming in this sterile symbol the shift from the pulsing, dark and deathly existential concern of Joe Christmas and the Apollonian living grace of Lena's procreative innocence to the pulseless aesthetic distance of Hightower's non-living purity. If we view the vase symbol generally as the aesthetic equivalent of the urn, the resistance to the urn's involvement with death and life—whether death-as-life (Lena) or life-as-death (Christmas)—then we can move easily to Eliot's Chinese jar and think of the latter as an echo of the "frail China jar" of Pope's "The Rape of the Lock," itself an echo of the china vases Pope speaks of elsewhere in this poem.

In "The Rape of the Lock" there would surely seem to be no place for the urns, if we take seriously their ritual involvement with the actualities and consequences of flesh-and-blood existence. Better, in this supercilious celebration of the airiness of the world of play that resists flesh and blood, to replace them with vases and jars, *objets d'art* in the toyshop unreality of Belinda's art-world. We have just seen Hightower's more serious and less successful attempt to withdraw from the consequential world-winds lead to a similar conversion from the urn to its life-free aesthetic equivalent, the vase, whose cognate term, vessel, perhaps better reminds us that it is but an extension of the urn. For, as I have elsewhere argued at length,[14] Pope's poem is created out of a wistful idolatry of the disengaged and—in terms of flesh-and-blood reality—the inconsequential, pure if fragile world of social play. Finally, I claim, the mock-heroic world of the lock, where empty symbols rather than bodies are the objects of rape and battle, becomes a metaphor for the poem itself, even as the "frail China jar," *objet d'art*, becomes the toyshop substitute for our blood-filled vessels of breathing life. The recurrent use of china as symbol of honor's empty equivalent for

[14] In "The 'Frail China Jar' and the Rude Hand of Chaos," above.

chastity was commented upon earlier by Cleanth Brooks.[15] This use is indicative enough of the transformation of the world of bodies to the wrought world of empty objects:

Whether the Nymph shall break Diana's Law,
Or some frail China Jar receive a Flaw . . .
(Canto II, lines 105–6)

Or when rich China vessels, fall'n from high,
In glitt'ring dust and painted fragments lie!
(III, 159–60)

'Twas this, the morning omens seem'd to tell,
Thrice from my trembling hand the Patch-box fell;
The tott'ring China shook without a Wind . . .
(IV, 161–63)

We may note that this very use of china as a generic term for ceramic objects is a metonym made in the spirit of Pope. Pope himself extends the significance of this metonymy in yet another passage in the poem, one whose brilliance sustains the others. It occurs in his description of the pouring of coffee:

From silver spouts the grateful liquors glide,
While China's earth receives the smoking tide . . .
(III, 109–10)

Here in this wrought ceramic world we have the transformation of earth into art; indeed, in these earthen objects is the only earth that is admitted in this poem. China is, after all, the aesthetic form of China's earth, the aesthetic reduction of China for this social company. Again we are reminded of Sir Thomas Browne, this time his relating the purgative crematory fire to man's "earth":

But all flies and sinks before fire almost in all bodies. . . . Where fire taketh leave, corruption slowly enters; In bones well burnt, fire makes a wall against it self. . . . What the Sun compoundeth, fire analyseth, not transmuteth. That devouring agent leaves almost alwayes a morsel for the Earth, whereof all things are but a colony; and which, if time permits, the mother Element will have in their primitive mass again. (*Urne Buriall*, pages 30–31)

The jars and vases and cups of Pope's airy world, vessels subject only to the smoking tides of coffee poured from silver spouts, are the real China of that world, from which all other earth has—by the transmuting ceramic fire—been purged. Browne helps remind us of that more destructive purgation of earth in the fire of cremation. And the remnants of this cremation, we

[15] *The Well Wrought Urn*, p. 87.

remember, have as their container that which also is fired out of earth. But the urn, as a created form, is one created—as Browne has already told us—in imitation of the living form as an echo of the womb which forms life. As a fired, earthen icon of what its contents had been—the earthly form consumed by fire—as holder of life and death, the urn transcends both. For it has attained the pure and permanent circularity of form and, in its frieze, has the forms of life eternally captured as, like Keats' figures or Lena Grove, they trace a still movement around it.

The sepulchral urn's aesthetic equivalent of breathing life, an equivalent that at once captures life's movement and perpetuates it, accounts for the suspended purity we have seen in the figures of Pope and Keats and Faulkner. To appropriate the term from Eloisa, we might say the "unfruitful urn" in one sense leads to a fruitful urn—the fruitful poem—in another. There is an enforced chastity binding Eloisa and Abelard, not altogether unlike the aesthetically enforced chastity binding Keats' figures on the urn. We can see this enforced chastity in Eloisa's description of Abelard, which precedes her hopeless and bitter invocation to him ("Come, Abelard!") which we witnessed earlier:

For thee the Fates, severely kind, ordain
A cool suspense from pleasure and from pain;
Thy life a long dead calm of fix'd repose;
No pulse that riots, and no blood that glows.

(lines 249–52)

It is just this being "fix'd" in a "cool suspense" from the rioting pulse and glowing blood that lends the creatures of Pope's world of artifice in the "Rape" and the creatures trapped on Keats' urn their precious transcendence—and their unworldly incompleteness, their dance that denies the very notion of consequence. Belinda's "purer blush," Keats' "maidens loth," the mock love-battle at the end of the "Rape," the unanswered factual questions in Keats' "Ode"—these testify to the inconsequential, unbound, free nature of the chaste aesthetic transmutation of breathing existence.

There are, then, three kinds of earth and three ways of its being fired—all finally expressive of the circular tradition that moves from earth to earth. There is, first, man's living earth—his flesh—that, fired by sexual desire, fills the earthly vessel with the flowing fruit of life, of more earth; there is, secondly, as timely consequence of the first, man's dying earth that, fired by the funeral rite, is reduced to the ashes that, in urn burial, fill the third kind: the earthen vessel, an artifact that, transmuted by the ceramic fire of human craft, becomes a permanent form. The latter is at once unfruitful and still-moving, the transcendence of earth in the earthen, the transcendence of flesh in the artifice of eternity; and—where it is urn, too—it is also the receptacle of the remnants of that other earth, the flesh, that is conceived in fire and consumed by fire. Further, the urn may, as Browne describes, imitate the shape of the human conceiving urn; still further, it may have the figures of life as a frieze forever running round it, either in pursuit of desire (the first kind of firing of man's earth which I have spoken of) or in celebration of death (the second kind of the firing of earth)—the two very actions captured on Keats' urn. And, as in the case of Keats' urn, these are captured on the object that, as the third sort of the firing of earth, is in its shape the icon of the others and their container, holding them at once within it and on its circular surface. Thus it celebrates both time past (the ashes within) and time forever now (the circular pattern of scenes that is the frieze), even as, in its shape, the container of death mimics the container of life, tomb as womb. No wonder an amazing multiple pattern is projected by the purified metonymy of sexual meanings ceramically purged and yet insisted upon in "The Rape of the Lock," where "China's earth receives the smoking tide" pouring from the "silver spouts," well heated since "the fiery spirits blaze." Here is a ceramic masque, an earthen playing out of that most earthly action. Can we resist expanding these meanings to include those which range about the china vases and jars of this poem as they relate to frail sexual purity? Or, if we can consider also the "unfruitful urn" in the abortive firing of Eloisa's desires, can we resist seeing vase as the vessel that is related, without sexual consequences, to the urn, with the jar as the semantic generalizing of the ceramic impulse? And we must marvel at the resuscitation of the urn, so unpromising an object of death, into a symbol of life in death: of art. We must marvel at the choice of the urn as the ekphrastic object *par excellence* to unite the stilled and the still-now movement by concentrating within and upon itself the several sorts of earth and the several manners and consequences of their being fired.

But all, even the most aesthetically transcendent, still remain literally movements from earth to earth, from living-dying time to time both affirmed and arrested. This is reason enough to deny that one other kind of the firing of earth as a possible fourth kind: the religious firing that is to transform man's earth to pure spirit. Eloisa, her earth now fired so unfruitfully by Abelard, claims this different kind of firing by God: "But let Heav'n seize it [the soul], all at once 'tis fir'd:/Not touch'd, but rapt; not waken'd, but inspir'd!" (lines 201-2). Nevertheless, this is a figurative firing only: it can move her toward the "flames refin'd" that "in breasts seraphic glow" (line 320) only by denying her literal earth, her earthly status as creature. Which is why Eloisa remains so ambivalent, why in seeing God as Abelard's rival and successor (". . . for he/Alone can rival, can succeed to thee" [line 206]), she must involve her sexuality in her religious impulse. She must confound the firing of her earth with the smothering of earthly fires which constitutes the religious metaphorical firing that she seeks. This denial of all kinds of earth and of earthly fires, sexual and aesthetic, replaces the movement from earth to earth with the Platonic movement from earth to heaven as the last movement, the permanent stilling of movement. It is destructive of the aesthetic, of the earthen, of the ekphrastic principle; is a fraudulent alternative and, for her, a false resolution. Time is merely stilled in the simple sense, the sense of "still life"; it is killed in the sense of the French translation of still life, *nature morte*. And the brilliant multiplicity of time's possibilities for running free and yet running around, repeating circularly, the brilliant revelations of the *ekphrasis*, of the urn at once fruitful and unfruitful—these are forever sacrificed. To alter Horace and defy Lessing, as with the urn, so with poetry.

Keats' urn, a pure *ekphrasis*, is an object especially created to celebrate the teasing doctrine of circularity. If this doctrine is aesthetically complete in creating, through enforced chastity, a fruitful urn of the aesthetic sort out of the unfruitful urn of the empirically human sort, in its chaste circularity it touches the empirically human only fitfully. In its freedom from what Yeats called "the fury and the mire of human veins," in its purging—at once Yeatsian and Aristotelian—of "complexities of fury," it asserts the transformation of the empirical into the archetypal ("the artifice of eternity"), in this way obeying the Hegelian injunction to move from the concrete to the concrete-universal. In the drama of poetry we recognize the creatures as creatures like us, like us most of all in their intense individuality, their here-and-now unique concreteness. But the motions they make—rituals of love and death—through aesthetic pattern and thus through the principle of echo, of repetition, become forever-now motions. This principle frees these motions from the singleness of chronology's linearity and of the empirical sort of finitude. Thus though concrete, the characters in this sense attain universality. They are converted from the merely individual to the casuistic; their motions achieve formal finality even if they never merely finish. Theirs is the finality-without-end, if I may so adapt Kant's definition of aesthetic experience. As creatures fixed on Eliot's wheel or Keats' urn, they show us the movements we all are and have been eternally fixed upon making, though we each make them but once, in singleness, and without awareness of our fixed turning.

To the usual notion of poetry's archetypal nature that moves too quickly from the particular to the universal, indeed that merely universalizes the particular, I would prefer this sense of the archetypal dimension of each poem as it struggles to capture the empirical in all its movement.[16] It must be at once as movement and as movement overcome, as movement joined and mastered, that the individual poem can make its movement eternal and still significant to us in our empirical singleness.

Yeats' Byzantium poems, as I have shown in my quoting from them, at once enunciate this aesthetic and create the ekphrastic symbol, the golden bird, that embodies it. The bird has been placed—indeed "hammered"—into these poems to continue with them their manufactured, artificial perfection forever. Purged, as the "images of day" with their "complexities of mire and blood" are "unpurged," the well-wrought object is both bird and golden handiwork even as, through miracle, it can be both at once, so that it is indeed "More miracle than bird or handiwork." Like the earthen urn or Pope's china, it is the product of the transmuting and purifying fires, alchemical medium of eternal creation, so different from the destructive fire that reduces the aged man's earth to ash. As "God's holy fire," it partakes—like "the gold mosaic of a wall"—of "the artifice of eternity" and can so transubstantiate the "aged man," the "dying animal," into the golden creature—both in and out of nature—of wise and eternal song.

Without this express insertion of the ekphrastic object, there are other birds that turn legendary under the pressure of their poetic contexts; indeed there is a chain of them leading to Yeats' golden bird that may be seen as their appropriate embodiment. And always it is this Platonic opposition between empirical singleness and archetypal inclusiveness that stirs the movement toward the golden incarnation.

In Wordsworth's treatment of his cuckoo, the poet must make a judgment about this very duality in the bird: it is a "wandering voice" even as it remains "bird," it is "far off" even as it is "near," it brings the poet "a tale/Of visionary hours" even as his sense of reality recognizes that it is only "babbling." This duality has the experiential basis we find in many of

[16] I clearly mean here to propose an alternative view of poetry as archetype to that of Northrop Frye.

The Play of Criticism

Wordsworth's poems: the moment celebrated is a conjunction of two occasions, one far past with one present. The recurrence of experience, of identical stimulus, modified by the severe changes time has wrought in the experiencing subject, permits the simultaneous perception of motion and stasis that has been my concern. As his most acute commentators have pointed out,[17] Wordsworth has himself provided just the metaphor to express this trapping of temporal change: those moments, laden with "a renovating virtue," he terms "spots of time" ("The Prelude," XII, 208)—precisely the union of spatiality and temporality I have been trying to demonstrate. The very word "spot," related as it is here to time's movement, yet brings us to stasis, the arresting of time, by seeming to refer to a place, a permanently defined spatial entity. This notion accounts, in "To the Cuckoo," for the poet's capacity to transcend the limitations of literal reality in order, through a double exposure, to blur time's movements to an identical spot. Conscious, then, of his animistic delusion, he chooses to see the cuckoo as "No bird, but an invisible thing,/A voice, a mystery. . . ." As in other bird poems by Romantic poets, the poet moves from the fact that he hears but cannot see the bird to the self-deceptive synecdoche that the voice *is* the bird, so that the bird becomes a disembodied voice, free of the mortality that attends a single finite bodily existence. Once he has thus transcended the bird as earthly animal, Wordsworth is able to return to his childhood with the claim that this is the very bird he then heard and could not find: "The same whom in my schoolboy days/I listened to . . ./And I can listen to thee yet. . . ." Now, listening still, he must—by the conscious choice of self-deception—willfully create ("beget") that "golden time" which, in his boyhood, he shared instinctively. In this conscious decision to ignore the reality of the babbling bird for the visionary voice, he has created for the now "blessed Bird" the "unsubstantial, faery place" that is its "fit home." Dare we think the place to be his Byzantium and the recreated bird of the mature poet's imagination his golden bird? We could, if it were not that his awareness of the self-induced state of delusion leads him to remember its "unsubstantial" nature. The delusion is not firm enough to construct an object that would perpetuate itself, *realize* itself.

The poet in Keats' "Ode to a Nightingale" also undergoes the fanciful

[17] None more incisively than Geoffrey H. Hartman. See his *Wordsworth's Poetry 1784–1814* (New Haven, 1964), especially pp. 153, 211–19, and his "Wordsworth, Inscriptions, and Romantic Nature Poetry," in *From Sensibility to Romanticism, Essays Presented to Frederick A. Pottle*, ed. Frederick W. Hilles and Harold Bloom (New York, 1965), pp. 389–413.

transformation of reality induced by the song of the bird. He is, even more than Wordsworth's poet, the captive of his trance, so that his fairyland demands the firm denial of the bird's material reality: "Thou wast not born for death, immortal bird!" He so uncritically accepts the magic of the synecdoche as to allow the identity of the sound of the voice to lead to the undoubted identity of occasion: "The voice I hear this passing night was heard/In ancient days by emperor and clown:/Perhaps the self-same song that found a path/Through the sad heart of Ruth . . . The same that oft-times hath/Charm'd magic casements. . . ." Yet even here the reality principle naggingly remains. It reminds the poet that the suspension of chronological time is, for humanity, not an attribute of an aesthetic never-never land, a Byzantium, but an attribute of death's nothingness: "Now more than ever seems it rich to die . . ./Still wouldst thou sing, and I have ears in vain—/To thy high requiem become a sod." Further, the immortality conferred, by contrast, upon the bird is in effect withdrawn when the poet, awakening from the spell, admits his return to empirical singleness, tolled as he is back to his "sole self." He acknowledges the final failure of the delusion sponsored by the song of the bird, now wistfully referred to as "deceiving elf," the failure of his own fancy ("the fancy cannot cheat so well"). And the song is now permitted to depart with the departure of the physical bird:

Adieu! adieu! thy plaintive anthem fades
  Past the near meadows, over the still stream,
    Up the hill-side; and now 'tis buried deep
    In the next valley-glades. . . .

Beyond the "still stream," for the poet it is nothing less than "buried." Keats' poet, aware of man's need for time's movement as well as his need to capture it, has—more than Wordsworth's poet—overdone the extravagance of his earlier Platonic delusions. But he has not managed to find a material object that can contain the still perfection in an earthly form (or an earthen form, if we dare fancy Keats to be searching for an ekphrastic equivalent to his urn). Since he cannot travel to Byzantium and convert his bird to hammered gold, both he and the bird return to time-bound reality to proceed with the complexities of aging. Only the moment, but that moment memorialized, preserved, stilled—and distilled—in the poem, remains. In this well-wrought residue, the ekphrastic principle asserts itself even in the turning aside from an ekphrastic object.

How different are these experiments in synecdoche, with their attempts to hold the turning world as it turns, from the simple postulation by Shelley of the other-than-material nature of his skylark. He begins at once with the flat disembodiment of the "blithe spirit": "Bird thou never wert." But the liveliness of motion is denied together with its status as bird. Its existence in human time is by fiat transcended, so that the collision of movement with movement captured is evaded. All is stilled, and there is no living movement. One thinks, by contrast, of the urging of movement in the pleas to the mistress in "Corinna's Going A-Maying"; the conflict between moving and staying is the very principle of form in the poem. The poet warns against the dangers of staying movement, culminating in the penultimate line, "while time serves, and we are but decaying." Here movement can *seem* to arrest decay and *seem* to make us the master of time, rather than—in decaying stasis—its slave, as the "while" of "while time serves" assures we shall be. This is the foretaste of that masterpoem about time, "To His Coy Mistress" ("Had we but world enough, and time"), and Marvell's invocation to action as the subduer of time, leading to the ekphrastic introduction of the physical, spatial object which is the emblem of his mastery over time even as time works its destructive power:

Rather at once our time devour,
Than languish in his slow-chapped power.
Let us roll all our strength, and all
Our sweetness, up into one ball . . .
Thus, though we cannot make our sun
Stand still, yet we will make him run.

(lines 39–42, 45–46)

Discussion of earthly birds turned legendary, of poems concerning birds that are at once temporal and supernal, must lead to the albatross of Coleridge's "Ancient Mariner." In few other places in literature is the opposition between stillness and motion more central to the structure, and their relation is controlled by the bird as it turns sacramental. The poem swings between the movement sponsored by the breeze and the calm, the curse resulting from its being withdrawn. We are likely to agree with the first judgment of the mariner's shipmates: that he "had killed the bird/That made the breeze to blow." Everywhere descriptions of movement in its varied paces, and of calm as the dread alternative, direct the poem's own pace. The poem moves with and among its movements and calms. The gratuitous murder of the albatross marks the fall that is to stop all movement. And the mariner becalmed finds his appropriate emblem: the albatross instead of the cross is hung about his neck. It is this static, uncreative, decaying state that characterizes the poet of Coleridge's "Dejection: An Ode." The poet, in effect the cursed, becalmed mariner, asks for the airy impulse that "might startle this dull pain, and make it move and live!" (line 20). "Dejection" is a poem that laments the becalming of spirit, that claims failure, the failure of movement, as its subject. Herrick's "Corinna" showed us forcefully the implication of decay in stillness. Far more graphically in the "Ancient Mariner," total stillness is accompanied by decay, the decay that motionlessness permits to set in: "The very deep did rot" (line 123), "the rotting sea," "the rotting deck" (lines 240, 242). The mariner's becalmed life-in-death is a surrealistic paralysis, seven days and seven nights of the unblinking curse in the eyes of his struck-dead shipmates. In his suspended state he yearns for the effortless motion of "the moving moon" (line 263), a still movement not unlike the movement we have marked in a Lena Grove. The gloss to the poem at this point furnishes a moving statement of such a natural, a routine motion as the mariner requires:

In his loneliness and fixedness he yearneth towards the journeying Moon, and the stars that still sojourn, yet still move onward; and every where the blue sky belongs to them, and is their appointed rest, and their native country and their own natural homes, which they enter unannounced, as lords that are certainly expected and yet there is a silent joy at their arrival.

Later, after the partial penance by the mariner and the partial forgiveness bestowed upon him, the return of the beloved breeze and his eventual return are not of this sublime order; he is returned to his native country and to man, but as a wandering stranger among them. And, still doing penance, he must move in ever-recurrent circles among them, ever retelling his tale.

His tale, the poem proper, has movement even in the face of calm; further, as "Dejection" does not, it succeeds at last in conquering—in moving beyond—the state of being becalmed; nevertheless, it remains a "still," even-now movement. For it is framed by a repetitious, unendingly repetitious, ritual action, as the mariner must tell his tale again and again, wandering continually in search of a listener—still, even now as I talk. Thus the archetypal nature of the singular, integral poetic action in its transcendence of the empirical—and thus our assurance of its casuistry, an assurance that permits our aesthetic pleasure in response to what in life would be unendurably painful. The "Ancient Mariner," in its emphasis on the necessity of the endless retelling of the tale, is a paradigm of this aspect in our greatest works. In its rounded completeness, in its coming to terms with itself—in short, through pattern, that which is bent on destroying its simple, linear temporality—the work guarantees its special, its other-than-empirical realm of being. Our despair at tragedy, for example, while preserved as despair, is yet transfigured to comfort in our knowledge and assurance of its still and inevitable movement, of how it has been and will always be—how it must be. Oedipus must pursue his stubborn ignorance identically to the identical catastrophe; Hamlet must make his always identical way to the absurd indiscriminacy of the final sword play; Lear must prance *his* always identical way to the wretched loveliness of the reconciliation scene that ironically lulls him and Cordelia to their deaths. And still they make their inevitable movements, even now as we talk—if I may stick at this point.

This is the final meaning of aesthetic inevitability or circularity—even as the urn demonstrates it; this is the final meaning of Aristotle's probability and necessity that bring poetry and its casuistry beyond history and the empirical world's possibility. The poem as total object has, despite its entrancing *movement,* become the fixed—or rather transfixed—object, its own urn, Yeats' golden bird that has been placed inside the poem to prove that the latter must breathe in its manufactured, artificial perfection forever. But, as the casuistic principle insists, it is always in its unique, contextual singleness that the poem so functions, not as a sign to the universal; in its finitude, its discrete discontinuity from all other poems, from poetry or from language as ideal forms, not as an opening to these.[18] *Ekphrasis,* no longer a narrow kind of poem defined by its object of imitation, broadens to become a general principle of poetics, asserted by every poem in the assertion of its integrity. Is it too much to say that essentially the same principle lies behind the employment of the poetic refrain, indeed behind the employment of meter itself? Such is largely the ground for Wordsworth's and Coleridge's justification of meter: the reduction to the sameness of repetition of that which is disparate, varied, progressive, in motion; the identity of recurrence together with the unceasing change of movement. It is the lack of such minute but systematic guarantees of recurrence that creates some of the handicaps prose fiction has in proclaiming itself a rounded object and that accounts for many of the *ad hoc* devices it invents to make itself into an aesthetic, a still moving, entity.

Every poem's problem as its own aesthetician, and every critic's problem after it, is essentially the problem of Keats with his Grecian urn: how to make it hold still when the poem must move. And the critic's final despera-

[18] Again it is the alternative to Frye's archetypal universality that I am insisting upon.

tion is an echo of the outburst, at once absolute and equivocal, of the last two lines of the poem. There are unanswered factual questions asked through the course of the "Ode" ("What men or gods are these? What maidens loth? . . . Who are these coming to the sacrifice? To what green altar . . . ? What little town . . . ?"). These have guaranteed the poet's exasperation at the inadequacy of empirical data before beauty's archetypal perfection, the inadequacy of fact before artifact. The final two lines confer universal absolution in that they absolve in absolute terms (to press the redundancy) the poet's need to ask such merely informational questions. We are reminded of Sir Thomas Browne's dismissal of a similar series of questions concerning the historical data surrounding his urns, "the proprietaries of these bones, or what bodies these ashes made up," questions further beyond man's resolution than those that ask "what Song the Syrens sang, or what name Achilles assumed when he hid himself among women."[19] The aesthetic of Keats' final lines, then, is the only culmination of still motion's transcendence of unarrested progression.

And so it is with the critic's desperate struggle to wrestle his slippery object to earth. It is the problem of defying the Lessing tradition, with its neat separateness of the mutually delimiting arts, and seeing the time-space breakthrough in the plasticity of the language of poetry. This language, in taking on Burckhardt's "corporeality," tries to become an object with as much substance as the medium of the plastic arts, the words thus establishing a plastic aesthetic for themselves, sometimes—but not necessarily—using the ekphrastic object as their emblem.

But in one sense the tradition from Edmund Burke and Lessing which sees a uniqueness in the literary medium *is* affirmed. For literature retains its essential nature as a time-art even as its words, by reaching the stillness by way of pattern, seek to appropriate sculpture's plasticity as well. There is after all, then, a sense in which literature, as a time-art, does have special time-space powers. Through pattern, through context, it has the unique power to celebrate time's movement as well as to arrest it, to arrest it in the very act of celebrating it. Its involvement with progression, with empirical movement, always accompanies its archetypal principle of repetition, of eternal return. The poem can uniquely order spatial stasis within its temporal dynamics because through its echoes and its texture it can produce—together with the illusion of progressive movement—the illusion of an organized simultaneity.

[19] *Urne-Buriall*, p. 44.

My earlier unfavorable claims about Eloisa's religious firing, like my few words on Shelley's "Skylark," were meant to serve as warning against the Platonic denial of the empirical, the mere stilling of movement. In resistance to the ekphrastic impulse, it cannot too often be urged that the aesthetic desire for pure and eternal form must not be allowed merely to freeze the entity-denying chronological flow of experience in its unrepeatable variety. The remarkable nature of Eliot's "Four Quartets," we must remember, is that the shaping of their musical form into the Chinese jar never deprives existence of its confused multiplicity. For, if we may shift to his other key metaphor, life at the periphery of the wheel never stops moving, even as it radiates from the extraordinary dance at the still center of that turning world. Yet "The Rape of the Lock" reminds us that there is a clear danger from the aesthetic purification of life. We see this danger anew if we return to the urn-jar motif and refer to yet another aesthetic jar, this time in Wallace Stevens' "Anecdote of the Jar":

I placed a jar in Tennessee,
And round it was, upon a hill
It made the slovenly wilderness
Surround that hill.

The wilderness rose up to it,
And sprawled around, no longer wild.
The jar was round upon the ground
And tall and of a port in air.

It took dominion everywhere.
The jar was gray and bare.
It did not give of bird or bush,
Like nothing else in Tennessee.[20]

The jar's roundedness and—in its aesthetic "dominion everywhere"—its grayness and bareness do no justice to the sprawling "slovenly wilderness" that surrounds its hilltop heights. (Indeed, it is only the jar's round presence that forces the formal impulse to attribute the function of "surrounding" to the aimless wilderness.) Only transcendent, the jar has nothing of life—"of bird or bush"—in it.[21] Here is the warning against the deadening of life, the freezing of movement, caused by too simple and Platonic a sense of aesthetic purity, of the jar or urn motif which, in my ekphrastic mood, I have

[20] *Collected Poems of Wallace Stevens* (New York: Alfred A. Knopf, Inc., 1954), p. 76.
[21] For a very persuasive reading, together with a summary of conflicting readings of the poem and of corroborating passages in Stevens' work (especially those relating the jar to the urn), see Patricia Merivale, "Wallace Stevens' 'Jar': The Absurd Detritus of Romantic Myth," *College English*, XXVI (April, 1965), 527-32.

The Ekphrastic Principle

described admiringly only. Time, in its unique empirical particularity, must always be celebrated in its flow even as we arrest it to make its movement a forever-now movement. Or else poetry is hardened into static, Platonic discourse that has lost touch with—indeed that disdains to touch—our existential motions. But as poetry, even Stevens' poem, in its persistence, itself becomes the jar, though more insistently involved with flowing existence than was the hilltop jar it decries. Like Eliot's, it has absorbed a liveliness whose moving slovenliness it must cherish.

Writers on time in the vitalistic tradition of Bergson have commonly claimed that, in its inevitable universalizing, language tends to give death to the dynamism of experience by spatializing it and thus freezing its undemarcated ceaseless flow of unrepeatable and indefinable, un-entitied units. Thus phenomenological literary critics in the spirit of this tradition have tended to anti-formalism, to the neglect of the object and the accentuation of the subjective flow in the transcription of their authors' consciousness of time. However just their charges against the spatializing, and thus the killing, power of language generally, I must maintain—in the tradition of Keats in his "Urn" and Yeats in his Byzantium poems—that aesthetic jars usually avoid the inadequacy recorded by Stevens, that the specially endowed language of poetry frees as well as freezes temporality, frees it into an ever-repeated motion that has all the motion together with its repeatability, through the rounded sculpture-like inevitability that guarantees its endless repetition. For this aesthetically formalized language takes on plasticity as well as spatiality. Through its ekphrastic principle, literature as poetic context proclaims at once its use of the empirically progressive and its transcendent conversion of the empirical into the archetypal even as it remains empirical, into the circular even as it remains progressive.

In this sense poetry must be at once immediate *and* objective: neither the mediated objectivity of the normal discourse that through freezing kills, nor the unmediated subjectivity that our idolaters of time-philosophy would want to keep as the unstoppable, unrepeatable, un-entitied all; neither life only frozen as archetypal nor life only flowing as endlessly empirical, but at once frozen and flowing (like the urn), at once objective and immediate, archetypal and empirical. I would share the interest of the Georges Poulets and the Maurice Blanchots; but I would give the special liberating license to our best poetry, insisting on its ekphrastic completeness that allows us to transfer the human conquest of time from the murky subjective caverns of phenomenology to the well-wrought, well-lighted place of aesthetics. For the poetic context can defy the apparently mutually exclusive categories of time and space to become fixed in the still movement of the Chinese jar that poets have summoned to their poetry as the emblem of its aesthetic, which that poetry's very existence, its way of being and meaning, has implicitly proclaimed. The patterned and yet passing words can, as Eliot has suggested, "reach into the silence," "reach the stillness."

II
THE PLACE OF CRITICISM

9
The Disciplines of Literary Criticism[1]

 Perhaps no area in the English curriculum has undergone more radical changes since the Second World War than has literary criticism; indeed, only since that time has it become an area. Earlier, literary criticism would hardly have been thought worthy of separate treatment in a book of this sort. Surprisingly, this concern with criticism has shown itself most markedly at the two extremes of the university curriculum—in elementary courses and at the graduate level. What *Understanding Poetry* represents in the recent history of courses in the introduction to poetry *Theory of Literature* represents in the new awarenesses that graduate training has recently been seeking to impart. Indeed, the increasing influence of the latter served to increase that of the former: that is, *Theory of Literature* helped indoctrinate theoretically those graduate students who were to teach basic undergraduate courses in literature and indoctrinated them in the very way that would make *Understanding Poetry* their appropriate textbook as beginning teachers.

It was of special importance that the final chapter of the original (1949) edition of *Theory of Literature* was entitled "The Study of Literature in the Graduate School" and that the reforms it so urgently called for were the very ones that graduate schools seemed ready to undertake. It especially illuminates the development of graduate education in English to note that in the paperback reprint edition of 1956 the authors eliminated this chapter as no longer necessary, since its reforms had been accomplished and its complaints might have sounded anachronistic.

[1] Originally written for *The College Teaching of English*, ed. for the NCTE, MLA, CEA, and ASA by John C. Gerber, John H. Fisher, Curt A. Zimansky (New York, 1965), this essay was edited by Curt A. Zimansky, who tried to bring some uniformity among the contributions. Some of his alterations I have restored to their original form; some—with thanks to him—I have happily allowed to stand.

THE PLACE OF CRITICISM

But was their seeming optimism justified, or is it justified even now? Although literary criticism has received increasing recognition and offerings in it have been welcomed into English departments, to what extent has it really become an integral part of the graduate program and, consequently, an informing part of the attitude of the beginning undergraduate teacher? Although this book is directed primarily toward the undergraduate level, in the case of literary criticism this level is almost totally controlled by graduate school attitudes. So we must ask, to answer the questions I have raised, how extensively courses in critical theory and critical method have been inserted into English department graduate programs. To what extent has awareness of critical method affected the orientation of all graduate courses? To what extent has it permeated the orthodox "scholarly" approaches to literature that control the general program? How professional, responsible, and disciplined has the introduction of critical methodology been? Or, to ask this another way, how much have departments really demanded of those whom they have chosen to introduce critical awareness at the graduate level? I acknowledge my own skepticism concerning the reformation of the upper level English program by presumptuously intending this essay to serve the present academic situation as the final chapter of *Theory of Literature* served its more acute situation.

I

The teachers of English of the present middle generation became aware—those that did become aware—of new and revolutionary ideas about the critical interpretation of literature during the 1940's, and most of what they learned came from extra-academic sources. Largely it was the work of those influential "big little magazines" which have since earned their way from the shades of academic unrespectability first to the broad daylight of acceptance and then—unhappily—to the fortress of their own solid respectability. Indeed, academic journals have come to imitate them, to influence them in turn, and, in effect, to forge a common institutional front with them.

It must be admitted that, during these years, the academy also showed occasional signs of a coming change. On some campuses an isolated teacher, like Yvor Winters at Stanford, was gathering about him students who wanted something more discriminating than their courses usually offered. Or an influential scholar-critic, like Joseph Warren Beach at Minnesota, began to gather colleagues whose critical concerns were their primary concerns. Or a scholar of high reputation, like R. S. Crane at Chicago, could reorient the study of literature in a great university. Or an administrator, Norman Foerster at Iowa, could shape a whole English curriculum to a study of values rather than literary history. And there were others. One needs, for example, only to mention the names of Vanderbilt University and John Crowe Ransom. Indeed, as early as 1933, criticism received encouragement from a quarter one would hardly have anticipated when John Livingston Lowes, as President of the Modern Language Association, called for a new direction to literary study:

Our scholarship has tended to move, of late years, from the large to the relatively small. Is it, or is it not, time to return on occasion, *by way of the small*, and with all the new light gained thereby, to the larger ends of scholarship . . . ? Is the time not ripe to apply in larger measure both methods and acquisitions to that formative interpretation which illuminates, and which is after all the ultimate end of our researches? . . . For the ultimate end of our research is *criticism,* in the fullest sense of an often misused word.[2]

Lowes' call went largely unheeded: after all, if one of the most respected and most orthodox scholars chose to indulge himself in a presidential address, what harm could it do? And despite the other heterodox movements in a university here and there, for the most part the establishment—the graduate program in English—continued to defend its own.

By the 1940's the new and iconoclastic claims were red meat to an increasing number of graduate students and young teachers who felt that the humanistic motive for their study was being drained away in philological programming. It was a fresh spirit that for several summers shortly after the Second World War brought graduate students from around the country to a small campus in central Ohio. For these pilgrims the Kenyon School of Letters was a shrine dedicated to the humanistic study of literature. They ran as to an oasis and spent their weeks there; their diligence to the critical task was their tribute of thanks for the brief escape from the aridity that came before and after. The summer teachers at Kenyon were, of course, the writers for those magazines that were then changing thinking about literature within the academic walls. But summer students at Kenyon, if they looked closely, would have observed that their teachers were in increasing numbers also becoming university professors and were moving to larger and more impressive universities year by year. And as the years went by, after the Kenyon School of Letters followed suit by becoming the Indiana School of Letters, the uniqueness of this summer place was gradually lost; increas-

[2] *PMLA,* XLVIII (Supplement, 1933), 1405.

ingly it came to resemble certain aspects of graduate programs that more and more major universities had begun to make room for. There need be no oasis when watering places are everywhere—even though spreading them out causes their shallowness to increase with their number.

Thus arose the peculiar situation in which young Turks, armed more with what they had learned outside the academy than with their doctorates, were teaching the most elementary English courses with a critical sophistication often neither shared nor even understood by their senior colleagues. Since these senior colleagues were in the main defenders of the *ancien régime,* they often sought to perpetuate what seemed to them most valuable—or even sacred—by looking for younger versions of themselves to take over the "scholarly" areas of graduate teaching. Those younger men with less respect for "academic" values were edged into the less prestige-ful, less advanced areas of the curriculum. Occasionally successful publishing records created certain fortunate exceptions even in the most hallowed of historical periods. And some were allowed tentatively to explore new and less traditional aspects of an enlarging graduate program, thus joining those elder statesmen of modern criticism who had earlier been taken into and, to some extent, been taken over by the academies.

Still the irony persisted for a while that elementary courses were being taught at a more mature critical level than most graduate seminars. Even this state of slight fortune could only deteriorate as the revolutionary excitement of those anti-academic days abated, so that the new graduate students, now presumably at one of those watering places that were everywhere but existed in depth almost nowhere, would have neither the fervor nor the extramural guidance. These might manage, in the generation to come, to bring the undergraduate level of teaching down to that of its big brothers. What had promised so much to the institution by being nurtured outside was threatened with the loss of its distinctiveness by being brought inside and absorbed. At best it could only slightly influence the essential form of the institution to which it surrendered. So the apparent incorporation of literary criticism proved to be the shrewdest possible tactic of the establishment: here was the way to smother it by giving it a minor, unassimilated place. Criticism was absorbed, but not digested. What newer scholar-critics there are in important positions at graduate levels—and I have not meant to claim that there are not a goodly number—are still, on the whole, trapped within a framework that has not been transformed in any essential way by the forces I have been tracing here.

The fate of criticism in the learned journals has been similar. It has been invited in, often to be at the mercy of unregenerate editors or readers who have not learned to discriminate among the new scholar-critics whom history now forces them to admit. So these journals have encouraged—sometimes compelled—criticism to deprive itself of much of its vitality as it conforms to their professionalism by turning itself into exercises in explication, as arid as many of the scholarly exercises it replaces or accompanies.

The revolutions that were institutionalized—and thus came to be symbolized—by the accomplishments of Cleanth Brooks and Robert Penn Warren, and of René Wellek and Austin Warren, are indeed far behind us now, and with their victories consolidated. But the problems remain and in subtler form since they give the appearance of having been solved. They are less obviously painful but perhaps harder to cure since our confidence in our catholicity may permit us to mistake conviviality for health.

II

The desire to be modish is hardly a serious justification for instituting or transforming programs. What are the arguments, apart from those of the changing fashions dictated by recent academic history, to support the growing role of literary criticism in the English curriculum? Perhaps in the justification of criticism we may discover its proper objectives. Its primary justification we may derive from those motives that prompted the growth of interest of a couple of decades ago. Through the critical approach to literature, the student can discover the unique subject matter of his field and the unique methods available to him for probing it. No matter what use his particular scholarly interest may lead him to make of a literary work, criticism allows a clear determination of the object he is subduing to his needs—a unified grasp of the thing itself. This grasp can allow him to treat the literary work terminally, thus controlling the instrumental uses of the work; humanely dedicated to the work as repository as well as sign, it can transcend and give purpose to those specialized scholarly studies that radiate outward toward extraliterary subjects through the use of extraliterary methods. Criticism thus presents itself as the one peculiarly literary discipline designed to locate and explore what is peculiarly literary in a national literature.

Thus the interaction between subject and its appropriate method; and from this to the further interaction between the yield of value and the yield of meaning. The concentration upon the literary object as a special sort of entity whose nature is accessible only to special methods can make the student aware of it as the source and container of value, thus restoring to the humanities an area of concern which descriptive or "scientific" interests have sought to undermine and thus *de*-humanize. The student may well find that this value manifests itself in the work's incomparable capacity for meaning, in the special awareness of its moment in its culture's history, an awareness which its aesthetic-thematic organization can generate. For its capacity to function as a sign for meanings indeed follows upon its functioning as a repository of meanings. At this point the circuit of the unique to the unique is closed: the uniqueness of subject is discovered by (and yet helps to create) the uniqueness of the method it demands (and yet will submit to); together the two yield the unique sort of value that receives its ultimate sanction from the uniqueness of meanings—at once aesthetic and thus suprahistorical and yet in another sense historical after all—which the work in the totality of its discovering (and its being discovered) can reveal. The maintenance of this circuit will permit the full-scale study of literature, with its manifold but now subsidiary disciplines, without the danger that the centrifugal force of extraliterary interests and methods will tear apart the heart of the subject and destroy it as a unified entity.

But this view of literature as *a* subject—a view admittedly conditioned greatly by this critic's desire to defend his own—would find literary criticism as the central coordinator of the studies of that subject, as the queen of the literary sciences as it were. It is in accordance with this view that I earlier found the accommodation of the academy to literary criticism to be so inadequate and thus so misleading insofar as it claimed to be humanistically promising.

III

Precisely how much literary criticism has begun to be offered in colleges and universities, what sorts of courses have been initiated, and how do they measure up to the lofty position I have tried to create for criticism? A recent survey by Professor Albert Van Nostrand indicates the answer:

About four out of seven schools of liberal arts offer some course in literary criticism. This figure is based on the catalogues of 350 schools—about a third of those listed in the latest directory of the American Council on Education. As a basis for observation, these 350 schools are a representative sampling of American liberal arts education. They reflect a broad range in enrollment, course offerings, geographical location, affiliation, and the means of financial support.

Most of them offer an undergraduate major in English literature. The catalogues of these 200 schools offering courses in criticism support some further observations.

Regardless of their location, state universities offer more courses in criticism than does any other kind of school. Six out of eight present at least one such course. Characteristically, with their large English departments, these universities provide several—sometimes as many as five—courses on different levels at one time. But this is not necessarily the consequence of enlightened state educational policy. A comparable ratio of courses in literary criticism offered in state teachers colleges makes this clear. Only one out of three state teachers colleges provides a course in literary criticism. Even some of these—called "applied criticism"—turn out to be courses in reading and writing book reviews! That public school English teachers should be kept so innocent of criticism and its attention to the nature of literature is cause for alarm.

According to the catalogues there are varying emphases. Junior colleges show no interest whatsoever in the discipline of literary criticism. City colleges, providing many courses outside of any degree program, have only scant offerings in this field. In the colleges with Protestant affiliations, the subject is more likely to be offered, if at all, by departments of philosophy. In Roman Catholic colleges, courses in literary criticism explicitly emphasize the classics.

As to the courses themselves, the survey is the most familiar. Half the courses in criticism taught each year in the United States are survey courses. From 150 catalogue descriptions, certain standard characteristics of such a course emerge. It is normally a one-semester course (occasionally two). Offered every year, it is taught by a senior member of the department. It is available to English majors, usually in the senior year, but not required. In universities it is a middle group course for both graduates and undergraduates and is usually required of doctoral candidates in English.

This survey may be called a "history" or "principles of literary criticism" or "critical approaches"; in the language of the catalogue these are synonymous. The description of English 462 at Eastern New Mexico University makes the characteristic emphases: "A study of the theory of and practice of criticism from Aristotle's *Poetics* to the New Criticism. The *raison d'etre* of criticism itself; the characteristics of criticism as a literary form; the relationships between criticism and the literary masterpieces themselves." Usually, in catalogues, the title of a course appears without further description. . . .

More specifically, the emphasis is on English criticism from the Renaissance through the Victorian period. Augustana College at Rock Island, Illinois, specifies this: "The classical critics are touched upon, likewise the Renaissance criticism on the continent, though the emphasis in the course is placed upon the development of English critical theory as it relates itself to the prevailing thought tendencies from Sidney to Arnold."[3]

---

[3] This survey was made for this chapter, which Professor Van Nostrand was originally to have written but was unable to complete because of other commitments. I am grateful to him for the extensive researches he conducted, now several years back. I have freely made use of his findings, especially his surveys of courses taught in literary criticism in colleges and universities and of the changing textbook situation in the area of literary criticism.

The Place of Criticism

It is obvious that the number of courses in criticism and the number of institutions offering them have increased considerably in these last years; that a survey like Professor Van Nostrand's, if conducted several years earlier, would have revealed much less going on in this area; and that a survey of the situation as of yesterday would reveal even more going on, with fewer schools going without some coverage. The increasing interest is also reflected in the recent revolution in textbook production and planning for the English department market, as Professor Van Nostrand also pointed out at length in his original version of this chapter. But by now the larger numbers of certain kinds of books are sufficiently evident to us all to require no extended discussion here. The increased variety of anthologies of criticism, of introductions to the critical study of the various genres (either with or without accompanying anthologies of literary works or critiques of them), of glossaries of critical terms, together with the recent invention, and even in these few years the exhausting production, of the textbook genre commonly termed the "casebook"—all these testify impressively to the growing role of literary criticism and its influence on the English curriculum generally.

However, Professor Van Nostrand's survey should alert us also to the unsystematic—if not altogether grudging—manner in which criticism is often permitted its place in the larger domain of the going concern of the institution, for reasons like those I have indicated. On the whole there is a lack of program. What is required, if there are to be more than modish reasons for teaching criticism, is an awareness of how it can be related to the English curriculum. And this awareness is also lacking—thus the predominance, at the advanced level, of the historical survey of literary criticism. There could be no shrewder way for the older vested interests to adapt the newly demanded offerings in criticism to the general organization of offerings in the English department. The criticism course could thus share a common historical method and organization with other period or genre courses. Its impact on these other courses, on the organization of the curriculum, and on the systematic justification of the organization could be minimized; the very idea that it offered a principle of organization could be obscured. On the elementary level there could be an increase in the "how to read" courses in the various genres with little danger that these would interact with those courses in the history of taste, ideas, and literary opinion that were allowed to pass for advanced courses in criticism and critical theory. Here is the split which I lamented earlier between the criticism courses at the two extremes of the curriculum, between elementary courses in applied criticism and advanced courses in critical history and theory. This is hardly a rational arrangement, and fortunately it does not exist everywhere. But the exceptions are fewer than many of us have the right to wish.

And what about the teachers for such courses? I have already discussed the junior level teachers, noting that their critical awareness was frequently superior to that of their seniors. The advanced courses, more often than not, are handed to one of the latter as something he might enjoy doing for a while with his left hand, leaving his major energies free for his proper work in a historical period. In fairness it must be admitted that it may not be easy to find a teacher of literary theory at the advanced level since there is little formal training of an extended sort in this discipline. But there is a disposition to believe that almost anyone trained in literary history and capable of reading the texts in the history of criticism is qualified to teach the course. It is, of course, reasonable to argue that the proper teacher of literary theory must be more than parochially English in his literary concerns since, as a systematic study, literary theory can hardly be restricted nationally. And it is reasonable to argue that the proper teacher of literary theory must have a sophisticated grasp of the theory of the fine arts generally and that this grasp of aesthetics naturally involves a sophisticated grasp of philosophic method at large. These claims would argue that literary theory is a specialized discipline indeed, one requiring a specialized training. The English professor, however, has too often and too easily been thought of as being above the petty cavils concerning philosophic consistency for such stringent requirements to be imposed upon him, so that the conception of literary theory as a discipline or a body of related disciplines is not allowed to inhibit the rather casual introduction of courses in this area into the unaltered, general English program.

IV

What would be a fuller and more systematic conception of a program in literary criticism? To begin with, we would have to recognize that such a program must have a double role. First, as a separate group of courses, it forms its own subdepartmental program training future teachers in such a program; second, it must have an influence on the subject, methods, and values of the department's general offerings and organization of offerings. In its first role, it cultivates its own garden; in its second, it uses its theoretical discoveries to contribute to the arrangement of the department's more

THE PLACE OF CRITICISM

varied garden. This second role is the more difficult, and in the long run perhaps the more important: it means altering the attitudes toward the reading and teaching of literature for all of us as practicing humanists and defenders of the arts. But this role can be performed effectively only if the first, more exclusive role is performed with creativity and systematic awareness.

How can we best cultivate that separate group of areas that constitutes the distinct program in criticism? There would seem rather obviously to be three of these areas: the history of criticism, the theory or theories that allow criticism, and practical criticism—the disciplined application of criticism to specific literary works. It is mainly through this last that criticism can spread its influence to the rest of the department's offerings.

I have already spoken of courses in the history of criticism, those which—similar in method and objectives to courses in literary history—tame criticism by reducing it to a familiar and conventional framework. As advanced courses, usually elective, they do get criticism into the curriculum with the least jarring of teachers' or students' habits. But they do so at the price of foregoing the chance to create a systematic view of literature and, through this, a systematic view of how it should be taught, a view that might alter the attitudes and organization of the department as a whole. Also lost is the opportunity to relate literary theory to the usual courses in applied criticism, those elementary "how to read" or genre courses that I have mentioned several times.

A systematic view of criticism as *a* subject would require that the history and the application of criticism must be related to each other, and it is obvious that they can be so related only by way of a theoretical approach to criticism. Thus the role of courses in critical theory is central: these must give direction to courses in the history of criticism and practical criticism, controlling these so as to allow them to form related areas within a larger, integrated domain. Of course, giving so central a role to critical theory involves the risk of reducing an entire criticism program to inflexible dogma. Only the liberal intelligence can guard against this reduction, and our self-conscious wariness of the possibility must never be lulled. But the alternative danger, that of having no systematic and controlling view of the subject as *a* subject, as a body of disciplines, would so dissipate the potential energy of a criticism program as to make the risk of dogma one worth taking. This theoretical perspective will allow courses in applied criticism to be offered profitably at a higher level, thus reducing the disparity of levels that I have noted between practical criticism and the history of criticism. Further, it can reform courses in the history of criticism so that they need no longer be routinely historical examinations of chronologically ordered texts, which pick up their method from other courses in literary history or from an elementary anthology-text whose theoretical awareness may very well be questionable if not utterly primitive.

Let me pause here to describe the course that I have found most successfully transforms the history of criticism within a framework that serves an objective that is primarily theoretical. It is a two-semester course that could be offered at either the undergraduate-graduate or the graduate level. Although there is much that is historical in its proceedings, its essential organization is intended to be analytical. The first semester is directed toward establishing the central problems of literary theory and examining the solutions proposed to them through the nineteenth century. Reading is mainly in the obvious major documents and the important scholarship surrounding them. Beginning with Plato and Aristotle, the course moves through the mimetic tradition; then, starting again with Plato and Longinus, it traces the expressionist tradition. The teacher should not take these labels too seriously; rather he should show elements of expressionism in the so-called imitationist and elements of imitationism in the so-called expressionist. He might conclude with obviously mixed figures who defy the imitation-expression dichotomy altogether, using them to show what there is about the nature of the problems of poetics that demands something of each of these traditions, and yet to show also that the price of mere eclecticism is higher than one should pay without further attempts at systematic resolution. The semester could close with the impasse reached with the early Benedetto Croce at the turn of the century. If the course has done its job, it should have exhausted the possibilities for solving the problems of literary theory—both individually and as parts of an integral subject—within the terms in which they were set through the nineteenth century. The student should see that they were not solved, perhaps that they could not be solved, within these terms.

The second semester examines those critics in our own century who, moving from the earlier exhaustion of possibilities, put their questions in a new way to evade the impasse to which imitationist-expressionist poetics in their older forms had led. The readings are dominated by new versions of the theoretical problems and recommended solutions rather than by merely new representatives of the older and already fully tried formulations. Yet sufficient voice should be given to discordant notes that challenge the cogency of these new versions. This semester will not yield, of course, any last word or final solution or even final setting of the problems, but rather, it is to be hoped, a sense of some advance over older formulations even if an impasse has been reached again. At least one will have reached higher ground before the impasse: certain theoretical traps will once and for all have been eluded, so that we can claim some advances in critical thinking in spite of those traps that yet remain.

Beyond their immediate substance these courses have a methodological objective: to sophisticate the student's theoretical habits and to make him recognize the relevance of these habits to the daily practice of criticism on individual works. The teacher must continually foster this awareness of the relation of systematic thinking about criticism to the practice of criticism and to actual literary works. Further, despite the theoretical orientation of these courses, the student must learn an essential modesty about the claims of literary theory: he must see the "more things in heaven and earth" in every good literary work than any theory can hope totally to account for, and also the values of the great critics in our literary history despite (or perhaps because of) their theoretical shortcomings. Yet on the other hand, this student must understand the advantages of being aware of theoretical presuppositions behind critical claims, even though a wholly adequate and coherent theory is unlikely to emerge. He can go on to apply his hard-won theoretical awareness to those crucial questions of method that control the courses in the program concerned with the systematic criticism of specific works.

V

This sophisticated awareness of theory, both its necessity and its limitations, is what many departments fail to achieve when they merely add literary criticism to their other offerings. It is what too many English scholars least want and think least worth having. In short, the defence of literary criticism as an organized program must finally turn on the defence of literary theory as a necessary discipline.

The usual argument against literary theory—and it is advanced as much by practicing critics as by scholars—is obvious enough: literary theory, like its parent discipline, aesthetics, has a distracting interest in philosophical abstractions rather than an exclusive interest in discrete works, so that it is just so much baggage imposed from the outside to burden—perhaps to the breaking point—the purity and immediacy of poetic contemplation. This argument springs from a strange form of anti-intellectual snobbery which many critics and scholars of English literature have, in a precious, self-indulgent, and sometimes stuffy way, allowed themselves. It is an academic weakness we can term the man-of-letters complex. The venerable position of the belletrist demands that his sensitive dignity not suffer the trivial hair-splittings of the hardheaded logician, the system-making logomachist. Perhaps, in criticism as in philosophy, this is but the traditional answer of the empirical English way to the German way which, goodness knows, can have an inflated stuffiness of its own. It is a disposition that makes even those moderns who have found Coleridge most useful somewhat distrustful of him inasmuch as he was rather in the German style. Consequently, it has produced a scholarly and critical atmosphere that often prides itself on being unlearned in matters of formal aesthetics. And it shows an embarrassed discomfort when faced by claims for the guiding role of literary theory, although it may be a discomfort springing from the threat not to the acute sensibility as much as to the gentleman's ease (I hesitate to say sloth) that wants to coddle its preciosity. So it is that a professor who would insist most severely on the use of appropriate scholarly disciplines in an historical literary study does not demand the equally appropriate aesthetic and philosophical disciplines in a critical study, indeed can be taken in by the student's *ad hoc* introduction of the shabbiest sort of hand-to-mouth principles of judgment. Scholarship is of course a term broader than history and its disciplines; it relates to any ordered, systematic study and to the mastery of disciplines appropriate to that study in our most demanding conception of it. I am suggesting that the areas required to master criticism as a discipline governed by scholarly responsibility are other than those which English departments usually assume to be the areas most required for a scholarly performance. And I am suggesting that this attitude leads to scholarly irresponsibility in critical study even where historical responsibilities are most carefully met.

It must be granted to the scholar-belletrist that, throughout the history of criticism, writers too dedicated to the philosophy of art have afflicted criticism with the misdirections of what George Saintsbury, borrowing from Pope, disdainfully termed the "high *priori* way." It is the way, often the German way I have mentioned, that moderns have referred to as the imposition of "aesthetics from above." Certainly many such writers have been interested more in theory than in literature and have fashioned Procrustean beds, each to his own measurements, instead of doing the more open and empirical job that is rightly demanded of criticism. In such cases the primary concern with the *a priori* to the neglect of the thing itself does construct too "high" a way for criticism to pursue and still remain *literary* criticism.

On the other hand, it is not possible for criticism to proceed in such utter neglect of theory as a Saintsbury might propose. How humbly and unqualifiedly "low" dare we allow sensibility's empirical "way" to become without endangering the critical enterprise from the other direction? Any interest in the aesthetic presuppositions that, consciously or unconsciously, condition not merely our poetic response but even what we see in the poem is, after all, an interest in theory. None of us can, nor should we want to, come upon the poem with a theoretical *tabula rasa*, without some ideas about what we conceive a poem to be or how we think it ought to serve us or we it. We hope that these ideas will remain flexible and will damage the poem for us as slightly as possible, but have them we must. They will limit us, but if we know what they are, we may be better able to force them into flexibility. Strip our perception as bare as we can, in the unguarded moment the theoretical guard resumes its sway. Or will even the most anti-intellectual of us dare assert—while asserting that he is a critic worth listening to—that among his individual judgments of literary works no faintest pattern can be traced? Can even the historical or biographical scholar, who withholds himself from judgment, claim, in his assertions about the relation of environment or of personal life to what goes on in a literary work, that he has no hidden assumptions about how literature comes to have its meaning as an expression of what has happened outside it? If we must live with the inhibiting presence of theory, then, surely it is sensible for us to examine a theory closely to determine whether it will make us a bearable companion as we journey our way through works of literary art. Surely, too, it is sensible for us to fix it firmly so that it may always show us the same face. In other words, we must examine it to determine whether it accounts adequately for the facts of our poetic experience (even as we acknowledge that this experience is largely conditioned by the theory, whether implicit or explicit), and we must fix it in order to ensure its logical coherence. It is this examination and this fixing that the critical theorist undertakes. If he is acting as a historian of criticism as well, it is this scrutiny to which he subjects the writers under study. The teacher of critical history or of critical practice is the more valuable as he faces up to this theoretical responsibility.

One can insist, then, that every literary critic, and likewise every literary historian, is involved with theory whether he wants to be or not. So the historian of criticism, for part of the way at least, has to take the "high" road. In labeling an anti-theorist like Saintsbury an impressionist and a hedonist, we are attempting to place his theory, his high-road assumptions. And from the standpoint of most modern criticism, in applying these terms to him, we are saying that we do not much care for his theory, that we do not think that it permits him to treat adequately either literature or the history of its critics or their theories. Of course, although we can trace *a priori* principles, and thus a theory, in Saintsbury's anti-theoretical claims for pure sensibility, it must be allowed that Saintsbury's is a theory to end all theories and theorizing. His urgent insistence on the primacy and even autocracy of taste and its pleasures—a taste intellectually unguided—can lead only to an insistence on the irrelevance of aesthetics and its disciplines. Yet it is strange to find a similar anti-theoretical bias among many influential critics in our own day, even though these never dare to claim Saintsbury's theoretical justification for it. In a T. S. Eliot, an F. R. Leavis, an Allen Tate—whatever the differences among them—we often find a sort of absolutism that must and does reject outright the subjectivism and hedonism of Saintsbury's literary atmosphere even as, strangely enough, it shares with Saintsbury the distrust of theory as an unpoetic intruder upon the intimacy of the poetic moment. Still it is as much the case with them as with Saintsbury that, like it or not, they must reckon with theory even as they must live with it. Perhaps, as they sometimes claim, they have no theory. But is it not true that if a critic manages to hold no theory, he does so only at the price of unconsciously holding and presenting two or more theories, and mutually incompatible ones?

It would not seem unwise to be more conscious and thus more critical of the theories we assume. For example, this matter of the incompatibility of theories is a curious one. We have seen that the critic must try for a theory that can most fully accommodate the poetic experiences which, since he is a critic rather than a philosopher, are most precious to him. And, once he recognizes the theoretical problem, his poetic experiences may force him to make changes in his systematic bias. This is only to assert the obvious, that the dictation should not flow in one direction only, from theory to sensibility. But what if all his poetic experience should lead him to what seem to be contradictory theoretical claims—for example, the claim that poetry in some sense represents the world of our experience and, simultaneously, the claim that poetry in some sense is utterly nonreferential, representing only its own contextual world? Must he make up his mind between them and inhibit all future poetic experiences accordingly as he decides one way or the other? If his poetic experience has continually revealed to him the equal truth of both claims, surely he may provisionally hold on to both of them—in full awareness, however, that here is a serious need for resolution which he must try to serve as he goes about future poetic experiences.

It may even be that he will come to feel the ultimate futility of theory in trying to evade the dilemmas provoked by the poetic experiences he dares not forsake. But even so he must earn his right to doubt or even to reject the promise of theory by serving the stern apprenticeship to it. And if he has served well, he will suspect, or at least hope, that in his unhappy conclusion he is wrong—thanks to his own inadequacies. Despite all his trying difficulties, however, how much better off—and how much more useful, too—he is than the critic who, theoretically unaware, moves blithely along through what may ultimately prove to be intellectual chaos, all for the sake of preserving the integrity of a sensibility that in truth is everywhere being badgered by another unknown master.

So much, then, for this attempt to justify those awarenesses that should lie behind an organized program in criticism and each of its courses, whether historical, theoretical, or practical in its emphasis. Is this not reason enough for me to have insisted on the variety of areas of knowledge and discipline that I did? Can any responsible scholar who would be a teacher of criticism afford not to be able to trace the relations of his subject to its parent theoretical disciplines, aesthetics and philosophy, and to its brother areas seen in comparative literature and in criticism of the other arts, where generic literary and aesthetic problems, as distinguished from merely local ones, may be discovered? Clearly what I am arguing toward is the specialist in criticism, a man trained in a graduate field that involves a difficult combination of disciplines. The field is hard to determine fully and, given the available teachers, harder to cultivate, but it is no less necessary for that. Just as it is no longer adequate to speak of criticism as being a matter of private taste, so it is no longer adequate to see its objectives as being less ambitious than what I have been claiming here, even if there is the danger of ambition's being a mask for mere pretension.

VI

If the criticism program can be rigorously pursued, then it can have the diffuse influence on the department's attitudes and objectives that I have spoken of earlier. By restoring a common subject matter to teachers and students of English literature—common to them but unique to a department of literature—it can allow a oneness to what we all do below the diversity of those specializations that radiate outward toward non-literary subjects and methods. Even more important, it can insist—while asserting the differences between critical method and historical method—that these differences rest not on pedagogical claims but on cognitive claims. It is not enough to urge, as some do, that to turn from philological studies to critical studies is to turn from an interest in making discrete "contributions to knowledge" to an interest in teaching the proper object of literary study, the work itself. For this is to limit the critic's function to pedagogy alone. The critical theorist can remind us that, unless we wish to surrender to the positivist's narrow definition of knowledge, literature and criticism can give us what might be called knowledge, even if it is not of the would-be scientific sort at which the philologist used to aim. Indeed, there may finally even be a bridge between criticism and history constituted by the former as it reveals the special historical role that literature and its meanings *sui generis* can play. Criticism may finally move beyond criticism by allowing to the work a peculiarly literary influence on the march of cultural forces and their ideologies.[4] It may view the poet as exerting cognitive influences on his society that are unique and that need probing tools unique to them if we are to see fully how they function as well as how they come to mean. By so doing it may restore broadly cognitive claims to literary study, joining a function that is humanistically philosophical to the pedagogical function that many commentators have recently granted to the academic adoption of critical methods.

This essay would seem to claim a fearfully imperialistic ambition for criticism, giving it an autonomous realm and also authorizing it to mold all other realms to its own objectives. Yet its ambition should be nothing less than this. We must say of the teaching and study of literature what Matthew Arnold said of poetry itself, for the iron time strained him to justify his

---

[4] I discuss this movement in criticism in some detail in my essay "After the New Criticism," *Massachusetts Review,* IV (Autumn, 1962), 183–205. On this occasion there is space to do little more than mention this function as a desirable one for criticism to perform.

mistress as, in its exaggerated form, it strains us to justify ours: ". . . if we conceive thus highly of the destinies of poetry, we must also set our standard for poetry high, since poetry, to be capable of fulfilling such high destinies, must be poetry of a high order of excellence. We must accustom ourselves to a high standard and to a strict judgment." And so it is with our claims for our profession. If, as teachers of English literature, we defend our humanistic group of disciplines by settling only for the highest standards, by discovering for it and cultivating its unique subject matter, methods, values, and the kinds of cognitive awareness all these yield, then we shall have to give appropriate status to that area that can establish and maintain the hegemony of the domain to whose high destinies this entire book is to testify and whose high standards it is to urge.

10
Joseph Warren Beach's Modest Appraisal

No one who knew Joseph Warren Beach well can help speaking personally about him, even on a professional occasion.[1] He was one of the rare ones among us, a member of that disappearing species uncommon enough in its time: the distinguished scholar who was at the same time your complete man of letters. Not because of a zestful, universal, but casual amateurism, which sometimes is all that is meant by this phrase, but because he savored language and letters deeply and seriously all the time, in everything he did—because literature and good talk, committed talk, about it were for him a total way of life. Thus he forces me to humanize even this occasion, the review of his posthumous volume, though it cause me (or especially because it causes me) to break with formality and convention. I am sure the gesture would please him.

Obsessive Images is just this kind of good and committed talk. As such, it is a fitting last book in several ways. It is fitting even that it is and must remain unfinished, for Joseph Beach's humanistic process-philosophy must have regarded all talk about literature—and thus literature itself, written and as yet unwritten, all of it still entering the life of culture and always new—as essentially and happily unfinished. It is fitting, too, that this final work of a long career should be among the first to concern itself at length with the great bulk of poetry written only yesterday. For nothing distinguished Joseph Beach more, or more openly revealed his dedication to literature as an endlessly vital force, than his insistence upon outliving the

[1] For these same personal reasons, if for no others, I could not resist including this combination of book review (of Joseph Warren Beach, *Obsessive Images: Symbolism in Poetry of the 1930's and 1940's*, ed. William Van O'Connor) and tribute in this volume. At the same time I might rationalize its inclusion by pointing out that one cannot justify a master scholar-critic like Joseph Warren Beach—and the masterly modesty with which he served his discipline—without at the same time delimiting, while justifying, the place of criticism.

taste of any period by not confining himself to the confinements of any literary fashion, by growing and changing with the limitless energies of literature—like literature, growing without aging. Always with him it was the elevation of the catholic over the parochial, of the open, empirical transaction with the work over the niggardly, guarded, modish tryst with it; in short, it was the age-old critical task of uncluttering the literary talk that helped give literature its life by purging the cant that could talk it to death.

I met and began to know Joseph Beach only very late in his career, when he was well into his retirement. But from the first he forced me to abandon any idea I might have had that there were too many generations for us to speak across in our personal and literary companionship. He understood all my young man's prejudices—knew them, even in a way felt them—but had assimilated them and put them in their place. If he refused to play Victorian fuddy-duddy, neither would he be so disloyal as to replace old fads with new ones. Miraculously, it sometimes seemed, he could absorb the new without losing all he had and was. And how smartly he could sting the upstart for a modern judgment that issued, not out of thought, but merely out of the mouth of the times. I know, for more than once I felt him do it. No name could be taken lightly, for literary judgment was not a light matter; no name dismissed, for dismissal was not an action consistent with humane enterprise. So no yawning impatiently over a Swinburne or an Edgar Lee Masters, or whom you will. Instead always the call to the alert critical intelligence coupled with a ready sympathetic appreciation. Not that Joseph Beach couldn't make up his mind or even become quite fierce, but not on assumptions that would preclude his having a good look for himself.

Here is the fitting person to write an incomplete history of our recent poetry; and perhaps there could be no more fitting subject for his last task. He had to come to terms with the very latest developments in our (and his) long literary history, so that he had finally, in his retirement, to turn to the poetry—most if not all of it admittedly minor—of the thirties and forties. And would it not also have been the fifties, were it not that he had to choose a decade in which to do the writing and his decades were running out on him? It was as unlikely as it was fitting that one of our oldest critics should undertake this youngest task, and of course uniquely helpful that for so uncharted an area, in which violent partisanship sweeps the field unchecked, we are graced with an incomparably experienced guide who is singularly unembattled. That in his retirement he worked hard at being a poet himself only made it seem more crucial for him to work at this study, although it did not alter his unaging catholic taste, his antique capacity to absorb later and later works by the young world around him without an unconditional surrender to them.

Thus it is that his study is so remarkably inclusive, that he takes serious account of such a vast and varied array of names, not without being aware of a hierarchy of value and influence among them, but with a greater awareness of his primary need to give a rounded report of a fearfully undifferentiated group that offers masses of work for our approval and for the selective memory of history. Actually, however, his method is to draw our attention not directly to the poets themselves but to words and attitudes they share. The earlier and, for me, the most exciting part of the book treats historically and comparatively certain words and phrases that have come into common usage for these poets, who have created rather specialized meanings for them. In effect, he is helping to discover a period diction, a series of verbal conventions for poets whose greatest effort is to avoid the verbally conventional. Thus this procedure is as important as it is difficult, and Joseph Beach carries it out with great tact. He not only must recognize the "obsessive image" that grows into cliché but must distinguish its more original and creative uses from its stale, unfunctional echoes. It is here that his ear, his delicate sensibility, his absolute honesty, serve him well. He discriminates persuasively among his subjects again and again, often unmasking the unconscious imitation behind the pretense at originality. Nor does his candor even spare himself. From how many authors could we expect the following admission, which occurs as the last words in his discussion of *definition?*

So it seems that this word still has its appeal to our poets and they are still capable of giving it a witty or provocative turn. It is not yet clear how long or useful a life it has before it—nor how soon it may come to be shunned by those most in the know as smacking of cliché.

Here the joke is certainly on the writer of this pedantic treatise. He is himself a writer of poems, which he would devoutly hope to be original and as free as possible from affectation and cliché. He had long been conscious of the danger lurking in this word. But what was his horror, on completion of this section, to receive a magazine containing a poem of his own, and to discover that in the course of this one poem (rather long, to be sure) he had twice used the now cliché word *definition!* Naturally, he has tried to persuade himself that there is nothing obscure or strained in his use of the word. But for all that he cannot fail to be red in the face at finding himself in such a box. (page 103)

After this, even his severest word about others must be tinged with too much humanity to have any sting.

As we read these early sections, we discover that we are involved in more than a matter of technical word-counting. Instead the word is seen to take on substance, and language opens out onto thematic dimensions. The author's phrase "Web of Thought and Image" is clue to the way in which the symbolic use of common words transforms them into common awarenesses, indicative of a common existential stance. This intertwining of thought and image is in accordance with modern organic theory that can make what begins as the mere study of diction the key to the poet's entire world. But as the book moves on past the mid-point, we become more directly concerned with concepts themselves, as the interest in the mediating word wanes. In most of the later sections abstract concept becomes philosophic attitude as the focus shifts from poetry to ideology and, unhappily, thought becomes utterly disentangled from image. Our author allows himself to become critic of the age in general and of the extrapoetic notions of a generation of poets in particular. He cannot resist measuring their retrograde opinions against his own secular humanism, and his vigorous anti-religious convictions find them lacking. I believe it is unfortunate that he permitted this, his one predilection, to come between him and the express intention of *Obsessive Images*. It is perhaps in this ideological respect alone that he showed his age in that he remained a child of the late nineteenth century in its post-Darwinian aspects. Where his philosophy most obtrudes, he is farthest from all that is so effective in the first two-thirds of the volume. And the earlier method returns momentarily even to the end. I like to think that revisions and additions would have softened the doctrinal passages and have made the study a more uniform reflection of the critic's sensibility that even now illuminates by far the greater number of its pages.

Joseph Beach has given us an unexpected legacy in this pioneer treatment of a subject perhaps too jumbled in its contemporaneity with us for the courage of the lesser scholar-critics whom he left behind. Perhaps it took the perspective of an older period to view ours with enough objectivity to help delineate it for us—an inversion, as it were, of the normal historical perspective we call for. Or rather, I could believe this if I were not so persuaded of his own continuing youthfulness of perspective that kept him one of us, only a far wiser and more courageous version in that he was also himself alone. One ends by wishing fondly that Mr. O'Connor, devoted friend, could find yet more of Joseph Warren Beach's posthumous papers that would demand his editorial tact. For the true man of letters so keenly sensitive is too rare and too needed, so that one must be forgiven for wishing to keep him an active contributor among us.

11
Contextualism Was Ambitious

Walter Sutton has now offered two essays in this *Journal* in which he tries to dispose of what he terms "contextualist" literary theory.[1] Between the two, Eliseo Vivas published an extensive and impressive reply to the first,[2] although Sutton's second essay, strangely, makes no reference to it and instead seems for the most part merely to repeat his original charges, perhaps with a strengthened tone.

For several reasons I feel compelled to address myself to Sutton's charges, especially to his more recent statement of them. He names me prominently both times as a student of the "contextualists" whose expounding of their position he has apparently found useful. His use of the term *contextualist* as the most distinguishing characteristic of certain so-called New Critics seems to be taken from *The New Apologists for Poetry*; indeed, in view of his quotations from that book, it would seem that the very title of his original essay comes out of my discussion in Chapter Eight of that work.[3] Thus I feel in a way responsible for this attack, having in effect myself offered him the weapons—weapons which I feel he has seriously misused. Having subjected the contextualist aspect

---

[1] "The Contextualist Dilemma—or Fallacy?" *Journal of Aesthetics and Art Criticism*, XVII (December, 1958), 219–29; "Contextualist Theory and Criticism as a Social Act," XIX (Spring, 1961), 317–25. Quotations are all taken from the second of these articles; in each case the page number of the reference will follow the quotation in parentheses.

[2] "Contextualism Reconsidered," *Journal of Aesthetics and Art Criticism*, XVIII (December, 1959), 222–40.

[3] My discussion of the contextualist dilemma appears in *The New Apologists for Poetry* (Minneapolis, 1956), pp. 135–38. I refer to it as "The contextualist's dilemma" in my analytic table of contents for this section of Chapter Eight on p. xiii. So far as I know, I was the first to apply the term "contextualist" in a systematic way to the position underlying much of the New Criticism.

153

of the New Criticism to my own theoretical doubts with as much philosophical candor and rigor as I could muster, I remain anxious about the candor and rigor with which others lay the groundwork for their doubts. It is here that Sutton disturbs me no end, since I fear that, rather than meet the full theory itself head-on, he has, all too often and all too easily, allowed his polemical intent to make the theory be what he would most conveniently have it be in order to dispose of it.

Let me first correct two serious factual misrepresentations of the contextualist position which Sutton uses to make his task easier. Contextualism need not have added to its already considerable burdens the sins either of aesthetic hedonism or of the vulnerable aesthetic of Edgar Allan Poe, since it differs significantly from each of these. Yet Sutton wrongly piles upon it the weakness of both.

From the beginnings, even in the primitive behaviorism of the early I. A. Richards, the contextualist quite self-consciously opposed hedonism, perhaps partly out of a desire to differentiate himself from the aesthete of the nineties with whom careless readers might identify him. In view of this, it is discouraging after all these years to hear Sutton tell us that by the "extreme contextualist" "the realm of art is seen as a kind of haven (or heaven) of unremitting pleasure and gratification, affording an escape from the conflict and tension of ordinary life" (page 318). Nor is this a momentary slip; shortly afterward, while insisting on the incompleteness of the New Critical version of the aesthetic experience, he concedes to their view (that is, his view of their view) that "the imagined world of the work" "is usually pleasurable though it need not be (as in the response to a tale of horror); and it may provide a beguiling escape from persistent tension and conflict" (page 319). But, unfortunately for contextualism, this is truer, he tells us, of the naive than of the sophisticated reader.

Now all this is startling indeed. It has long since been commonplace to attack the contextualists for their single-minded insistence on literary complexity, their unremitting use of terms like *irony, paradox, ambiguity,* and their exclusion from the best in literature of works to which these terms do not apply. And perhaps the one word, introduced by an originator and leader of the group, that has come generically to represent the rest, is the crucial word *tension*.[4] Yet here we find that Sutton has the New Critics

[4] Originally used by Allen Tate in his now-famous essay "Tension in Poetry" (1938), the term has had an important history in modern criticism until the

calling for a literary response that, in the name of pleasure, would afford an escape from tension, in truth the very objective of literature and of the poetic experience for most of them in their most consistent moments. Further, although New Critics have continually rejected the "pretty" in poetry and called for anti-sentimental realism of motive—for a sufficient "objective correlative"—Sutton charges that "this view ignores the fact that an aesthetic experience need not be pleasant and that objects that may be felt to be ugly or revolting—and thus not conducive to a state of rapt contemplation—also stimulate aesthetic responses" (page 318). But who these days would deny "the fact"? Surely not the contextualists. But if there is no argument about "the fact," there can be no agreement about what "this view" is—and the latter is also a factual matter. What induces "a state of rapt contemplation" is for these critics not the mild escapism of a pleasurable object but the all-containing, mutually opposing energies of a tension-filled object that block our escape from its context and thus from its world, which is an intensified, endlessly organized simulacrum of our own. If it is tension that Sutton wants and an evasive hedonism he wants to avoid, then I suggest he join the contextualists who have constructed their system largely out of the desire for the one and the dislike of the other.

Accompanying his charge of aestheticism, quite naturally, is his allying of these critics with Poe—again despite their explicit, unfriendly reactions to Poe's weak aesthetic. In tracing the "authorities" called forth to support their theory, Sutton—masking his own dubious authorities behind the evasive passive, without a footnote—tells us, ". . . Edgar Allan Poe is seen to have a proper New Critical emphasis in his stress upon the need for unity of effect . . ." (page 318). And in criticizing the definition of the aesthetic experience as rapt, intransitive contemplation, he claims:

. . . the line of contextualist argument should lead us back to Poe's dictum that "a long poem does not exist," because for Poe as for the modern contextualist intransitivity and unity of effect are essentials of the aesthetic experience. Poe's proposition is absurd (except as a journalistic attention-getting device); yet the contextualist should support it because it represents the logical culmination of his own theory. Actually the long novel or the long poem cannot be read either as contextually pure poetry or as pure document, alternatives required by theory of this kind. (page 319)

---

conclusive essay by W. K. Wimsatt, Jr., "Poetic Tension: A Summary," *New Scholasticism*, XXXII (January, 1958), 73–88. See also my essay which follows Mr. Wimsatt's, "Recent Criticism, 'Thematics,' and the Existential Dilemma," *Centennial Review of Arts and Science*, IV (Winter, 1960), 32–50.

THE PLACE OF CRITICISM

In attributing to modern contextualism the "absurd" claims of Poe, Sutton gives us the clue to his basic misunderstanding of the position under attack. The above quotations make it clear that he identifies Poe's "unity of effect" with the unity demanded by "modern contextualist intransitivity." But the frequent attacks upon Poe's "unity" by these critics should indicate that the two are anything but the same. Indeed, Poe's kind of unity can be cited as a prime example of what these critics would term "the affective fallacy." Often revealing a mechanistic stimulus-response psychology, Poe then seems to view the work as little more than a push-button manipulator of emotions. Astute students of Poe have recognized that, unlike modern contextualists, Poe finds the primal unity in the response rather than in qualities within the object, that Poe denies the possibility of the "long poem" because he restricts himself to actual readers and their actual attendant weaknesses of fatigue and faltering concentration. Thus he cannot consistently find a locus of unity in relations inherent to the object, relations which can be seen objectively to compel attention even if any one, or all, of us fail for any personal reason to respond. But it is precisely this locating of the unity in the context of the object, regardless of all idiosyncratic responses (and all actual responses are seen as more or less idiosyncratic), that markedly unifies contextualist critics and indeed led me to bestow the term "contextualist" upon them. And the critic who does focus on the objective context, with containing powers that are independent of statistics concerning its actual containing consequences upon readers, can indeed speak of a long poem, of a poem of any length, and never touches the absurd *reductio* created by Poe for himself in his affectivism.

Oddly enough, it is Sutton who is really on Poe's side, at least in one important respect. Like Poe he restricts himself to the effects of poetry in our actual experiences with it, limiting it with our limitations, weakening its chances for an intrinsic unity with our centrifugal weaknesses. In both essays he cannot manage an awareness of the fact that neither the contextualist generally nor Vivas in particular claims that we actually do or must undergo experiences characterized by unqualified intransitive attention. Whether or not we do is irrelevant to Vivas' "definition of aesthetic experience," which is meant to be a normative definition rather than a description of actual experiences. It is theoretically rather than experientially derived; that is, one must predicate these qualities of the experience if he wishes to make it an experience *of* (which is to say, controlled by) an object of a certain kind, of that kind defined by contextualism. This is to say once more that our focus must be turned back to the object from which the response, if it is to be termed "aesthetic," *ought* to be derived. The *ought* here is clearly theoretical —and circular—rather than moral. All this Sutton failed to see in his first essay, in which he attacked Vivas' "definition" on the empirical grounds that it did not describe many actual experiences. Vivas' answer acknowledged as much but insisted at length that, whether it did or not, the "definition," heuristic as it was, could still profitably be made on *a priori,* analytical grounds. In Sutton's second essay, neither Vivas (except as an example in a footnote) nor his response to the first essay is mentioned, although the "definition" and "rapt, intransitive" contemplation are still central points of attack. Here, without specific reference, they are, thanks again to the evasive passive, attributed to contextualism generally (". . . the aesthetic response to literature is often described as an experience of rapt contemplation qualitatively distinct from ordinary perception or contemplation. . . ." [page 317]) though New Critics, except for Vivas, have not to my knowledge used these terms; and the same charges, launched on the grounds of our actual imperfect experiences, appear as if there had been no rebuttal. My complaint is directed not at any discourtesy or lack of candor or even scholarly imprecision so much as at the inhibition of the dialogue upon which philosophical progress largely depends.

Because Sutton fails to understand the position of contextualism in regard to pleasure and in regard to actual aesthetic experiences and their relation to aesthetic objects and a theoretical aesthetic experience derived from them, he continually throws in the teeth of his enemy shattering pronouncements that turn out to be commonplaces which no sensible critic—least of all the contextualist—would dream of denying. We have already seen him proclaim that there must be room in aesthetic objects for what in normal experience would be unpleasant as well as pleasant, that which produces tension as well as that which produces ease and gratification; and we have seen how central these claims have been to the contextualists despite his denials. Or he proclaims our subservience as readers to "cultural conditioning," which no one would deny—except the straw-man contextualist that Sutton is creating. But his crucial pronouncement, one which he hopes will explode contextualism for good, is again one with which all can agree:

In literature there is a necessary interaction between the language of the work and the common language from which it derives, between the events represented by the language of the work and events in the experience of the reader, between the conventions of the individual work and the conventions of a larger body of literature. (page 319)

This claim, he feels, will certainly dispense with the contextualist's attempt to distinguish the language of poetry from normal discourse by insisting on the destruction of language's normal referential operations in the construction of closed, mutually interrelated operations of symbols within a closed context. But how could any critic, contextualist or otherwise, deny the crucial—and obvious—relations between the words in the poem and the words as normally used in the cultural milieu that surrounds and nourishes the poem, between the "life" in the poem and the experiences of all who have to do with it as producer or consumer, between the forms and devices of the work and the received conventions and disciplines of an historically conditioned medium? I should have thought that the many essays from both sides which tried to resolve the dispute between literary history and literary criticism as they dotted our learned journals some years back had at least settled this issue.

Of course there are all sorts of relevancies to our literary awareness of a work, all sorts of information—biographical, psychological, ideological, technical, and in several ways historical—which we can ignore only at our peril. And most of all, perhaps, there is our own mature sensibility as human beings who have experienced. These are all indispensable to our apprehending simply what is going on in that thing which confronts us. Further, I think without question that as we begin to read we read referentially, relating what is inside the work to the world we know, treating the language of the work as we do all other languages, in effect as simple signs. How but in this bit-by-bit, hand-to-mouth way can we possibly approach any language before us? Thus the more we know of the sign through whatever information we can bring to it, of course the better off we are.

But all we have in apprehending extramural sign-relations is still a knowledge and awareness of raw materials only. The test of poetry is whether or not it solicits us to end in another way of apprehending, whether or not it builds intramural relations among its elements strong enough to transform its language into new meanings that create a system that can stand up on its own. Thus for the contextualist the critic's task remains: to transfer us from sign to aesthetic symbol, to show how the work—with what originally seemed to be its atomistic, independently referential elements—manages so to interrelate them, with their clouds of referential meaning trailing behind, as to create that self-sufficient, mutually supporting system that has the capacity to enclose the reader in total submission to it (whether or not in any case or in all cases it does so). But of course we must know where the sign-functionings leave off to know where the symbol-functionings begin, and for this we need all the knowledge of the world behind the signs that we can discover. This means knowledge of the normal world outside the poem, the poet's and ours, and the similarities and differences between them. Still we can allow the work its right to aspire to its own oneness and integrity (and have not almost all critics since Aristotle in their differing ways allowed as much?), although to do so we cannot rest in our knowledge of the signs out of which its oneness can grow but to which it cannot be reduced. If we can find a self-sufficient unity of internal relations out there, soliciting our apprehension—even if in actual experience we can only momentarily transcend the referential relations we grab onto from the start—then we can hope to discover all that the symbols may mean here, in this unique, mutually modifying cluster of them. This "all" can be revealed by no amount of sign-apprehension of all that they have meant elsewhere. The test of a work's poetic value, then, is its capacity to function in this way and thus to persuade the submissive reader *toward* the utterly intransitive, intramural experience even if his experience, in its inevitable waywardness and contingency, never quite gets there.

Now with all this one may disagree,[5] but let us be clear on the facts. Contextualism does not deny the relation of literature to the extramural world; indeed, this relation of its parts, atomistically considered, is indispensable both to producing and experiencing it. Contextualism denies only the reduction of literature to the extramural world in that it claims the poem can grow another self-enclosing dimension as it builds its system—although this dimension cannot be apprehended without a prior apprehension of its extramural relations. Thus it is both true and false to say, with Sutton, that "contextualist theory has tended . . . to deny the reference of [the work's] constituent parts to prior experiences of the reader." While it is true that, according to this theory, the work in its poetic role as a context of aesthetic symbols ought not to have constituent parts that reach out singly to refer, it is false that this theory need deny either that an actual reader does in a

[5] And I have not tried to argue the case conclusively but have only briefly sketched the general objectives of the contextualist's claim since my purpose here is not to prove his claim but only to show that he does not ignore relations between the poem and our world as Sutton maintains. A fuller argument, and one which helps clarify my own use of that confusing term *symbol,* occurs in Carl R. Hausman, "Art and Symbol," *Review of Metaphysics,* XV (December, 1961), 256–70. On pp. 265–67 especially, he seems to back up my charges against Sutton's position.

THE PLACE OF CRITICISM

separatist way refer parts to the extramural world or even that he can originally approach the language of the work in any but a referential way.

Once more the half-truth results from Sutton's refusal to distinguish the waywardness of actual experiences from the prescriptions of a theoretical experience that helps us to predicate certain characteristics of its object. Even if he should not believe in such a distinction, as he obviously does not, faithful exposition of the position under attack would insist he avoid the collapsing which continually traps him. For the theoretical experience is invented by Vivas to discover certain characteristics of the object that solicits it and thus to permit us to correct our own experience with the object. To insist on the autonomy of the actual wayward experience of each of us is to reduce the object to the experience—and, incidentally, to block the education of taste. Yet what better evidence of Sutton's limiting the object with our limitations than the following:

> The form of the work is not a whole the unity of which can be grasped intransitively during the confrontation of the reader by the work. An impression of coherence and unity can certainly be gained sometimes in a single reading. But more often the perception of the interrelationship of the various formal elements of a work is a gradual, tentative, never-to-be-completed process, interrupted by the necessary reference to experience of the language of the work and often by lapses between re-readings of the work. But even during these lapses, sometimes of years, the remembered work remains an aesthetic stimulus, while the reader's conception of its form changes and develops with his changing experience. This prolonged and often fragmented process is a part of the reader's aesthetic transaction with the poem. . . . The aesthetic transaction with such a work as *Hamlet* cannot be limited to a single span of rapt attention. (page 321)

This seems to be on the main an undeniable, if hardly damaging, description of the process. But how untidily (and uncandidly) "the form of the work" has been reduced to and blurred with "the reader's conception of its form." We are really back to Poe who, with a naiveté reminiscent of Castelvetro's notion of "delusion," could define a work's unity in terms of the duration of a sitting by the reader. A telling confession of critical immodesty appears in Sutton's entire doctrine. I like to think the critic is less than the poem, that he learns from it instead of demanding that it tell him what he has known from elsewhere, demanding that it relate experiences similar to those he has had or understands, in short that it become a projection of himself that can be measured by himself.

Fortunately Sutton's consistency fails. Most damaging to his case, if encouraging to me, is his own occasional acknowledgment of just this distinction between the qualities of the aesthetic object and the experience it solicits on the one hand, and the imperfect actual experiences of readers on the other. Conceding that "as an aesthetic object, the work exists as a potential stimulus to any reader," Sutton goes so far as to grant:

> . . . it would be necessary to acknowledge that an uninterrupted span of close attention is aesthetically more satisfying and more conducive to an awareness of the meanings and values of a work in their formal relationship. (page 322)

Here he gives everything away. First, he attributes to the object "meanings and values" and a "formal relationship" among them, all of which have an existence independent of our awareness. Secondly, he grants that this existence can be the more fully apprehended as the reader approaches the aesthetic mode of rapt attention. This, however unwittingly, turns the aesthetic response into a normative affair, allowing for more and less aesthetic responses. He is in effect admitting that, while no uniquely aesthetic experience may actually occur, we can posit one at the end of the line leading to total attention to and total awareness of the object that solicits the attention and the awareness. What contextualist could ask more?

Thus the contextualist can remain unconcerned when Sutton insists on the incompleteness of the reader's attention, of his perception, of his grasp of a unity. For he can be secure that he has Sutton's agreement where it counts, that the only point of attack remaining—calling for the services of a pollster—is based on the mistaken claim that the contextualist refuses to recognize the imperfections of our actual traffic with the arts. Nor need he worry about the historical relativism Sutton uses to prove the inaccessibility of the literary work to any beholder, when in speaking of *Hamlet* Sutton insists that "the conception of the play's form" differs from period to period (page 324). So long as it is only the "conception" that is so unstable—and, again, who would deny this claim?—the object of all the conceptions, as a contextual entity, is not threatened.

But contextualists do not propound the sealing off of the symbolic structure in order to cut the poem off from reality. I have already spoken of the antagonism which contextualists feel toward aestheticism, although I hope that to most readers it seems unnecessary to urge again what I have elsewhere, after many others, urged many times: that contextualism is not identical with the ivory-tower, asocial doctrine of art for art's sake. Since Sutton insists on the old simplification that would identify the two, repeat it again I must. For I wish to bury this false identification once and for all so that we may move on to assess (and, if necessary, to attack) contextualism for views it really espouses. Since I have argued at length elsewhere the claim that the contextualist view *does* intimately relate art to man's other interests, I shall simply assert the conclusion here without support: only by our allowing poems to function as unique objects can the world they present affect in a unique way our vision of our world, and this function makes them not only related to our experience in culture but indispensably related to it.

In view of this conviction I can feel at once weary, impatient, and even suspicious of motives when Sutton writes:

> Politically and socially this theory is conservative, if not reactionary. Many contextualists like to describe themselves as "traditionalists" and in setting forth their political, aesthetic, and religious views tend to identify with an older order of one sort or another. One reason for the denial to literature of referential meaning or of a function in the social process is the contextualist's aversion not only to progressive ideas but to any kind of social change, except possibly in a backward direction. (page 324)

Remembering too well the unfortunate controversy touched off some years ago by the not quite accurate, painful political irrelevancies introduced by violent detractors of the New Criticism who had little else to offer, I am content that I myself tend not to rule on an aesthetic in accordance with its fostering of politically and socially "progressive ideas," backward looks, the status quo, or just indifference. For I suspect that no serious aesthetic directs itself for such placement, just as great literature probably fits none of these. Try, for example, as some have in vain, to prove that the works of Joseph Conrad are "liberal" or "conservative" or neither without confronting denials of your claims by what you have left out.

Given what I take to be the more-than-ideological (and, let me confess, less-than-ideological) density of our best works, I must feel that contextualism can more faithfully relate literature to the affair of living than can a theory more immediately dedicated to this relation. It would seem that those most seriously concerned with literature's role in culture and the history of culture would want to use its contribution *as* literature. Contextualism may lead us to find that literature and the pre-propositional level of felt reality with which it deals if it is true to its nature—far from being unrelated to the surrounding extramural world—may be ahead of frozen ideology in reflecting our most profound cultural dispositions.[6] If there is any chance of this being so, then one can, as Sutton says contextualists do, "deny that the

---

[6] I argue this point at somewhat greater length in "The 'Frail China Jar' and the Rude Hand of Chaos," above.

Contextualism Was Ambitious

poem or novel makes any statement about the world" (page 320), deny that ideas appear *as* ideas, and still (despite his claim to the contrary) assert literature's intimate social and cultural connections, the more intimate for its eluding of the formulae to which our general use of language persuades us.

I hope that my remarks are seen to be of more than personal importance, especially in view of what has come to be open season on contextualist theory. For I would like Sutton to be seen as representative of tendencies in the many recent assailants of this position. It is clearly the case that in the last years literary (and perhaps general aesthetic) theory has turned a corner, that a reaction has set in and has by now firmly consolidated its own position of opposition. But now, as various new directions are tentatively explored, it becomes more important than ever to assess the major doctrine of recent years honestly and accurately, not to allow the zeal for attack to obscure its complexities and its values, so that we may know what to make use of. By this time philosophers, like scientists, should have learned to move through a once revolutionary theory now being discarded—through and beyond it—rather than trying to wish themselves back to where we all were before it came along. But this injunction would mean we would have to give the new enemy its full due, and this is hard and careful work. I have tried to do some of it myself, not only in *The New Apologists for Poetry,* but in all that I have done since, as I try to make my way back to history and existence from the literary object contextually considered.[7] Thus I am sensitive to other attempts, perhaps feeling some guilt about helping to cause them. And I believe we cannot be too demanding about them, even as on the other side we must remain demanding about those latecomers to contextualism who fix it and seize upon it as an unquestioned orthodoxy, thanks to a faulty and unmodish historical sense that doesn't recognize its day is done.

Now that contextualism is decreed dead and one wonders only where to put the presumed corpse, it must of course become increasingly fashionable in literary circles for each to come forward and have his last chance at it. Indeed, Sutton has now had his second chance, without observing that the body, proclaiming its life, in vain tried to speak back. Still the riddled remnant must not be made to carry the burden of every critical sin indiscriminately cast upon it, even if in the name of social-political progress. And so I have stepped forward, perhaps arrogating to myself the role of the

---

[7] See *The Tragic Vision* (New York, 1960) and the essay referred to in footnote 6, above.

injudicious wastrel, Marc Antony, in opposition to his forward-looking, socially conscious antagonist. It was the only way open for me to show not only that contextualism was innocent of many of the sins with which Sutton had charged it, but that it maintains more firmly than he the very grounds from which he launched these charges, that it has explicitly and lucidly avoided them; nay, that it was formulated precisely to avert these charges more systematically than earlier theory could.

Like Antony, I have acknowledged that contextualism was ambitious, perhaps too ambitious, but, unlike Caesar, even more ambitious than its opponents are usually aware of. I have myself been charged with being unfriendly, and even on occasion unfair, to contextualism in some of its purest forms. Perhaps so. But even if it has the difficulties I have suggested, or if it has other and more serious ones, it is not guilty of aesthetic hedonism or of the belief in *l'art pour l'art* or of its corollary, the cutting off of poetry from our moral and social and historical concerns. For contextualism was ambitious in the best way, not to misrule poetry by cutting it off from man's other concerns, nor to abandon it by turning it into a disguised form of these other concerns, but to allow it the sovereignty it requires to flower in the way that can preserve its unique humane function, that of at once reflecting and revealing the human condition through being a total object itself. This is a most delicate way to tread, one that requires theoretical ambition. And I would say again what I have several times said elsewhere: the obvious alternative to contextualism, the yielding to the immediately referential in poetry, the retreat from theoretical daring, would have serious consequences upon the substantial gains made in critical practice these last decades. Consequently, instead of blithely converting its dilemmas into fallacies, any successor to contextualism should be prepared to confront the theoretical complexities that will require the new claimant to be ambitious in the same way.

12
Contextualism and the Relegation of Rhetoric

 Here is a conference dedicated to exploring relations between rhetoric and poetic.[1] Decorum would require that it proceed out of a mutual respect between these disciplines; indeed, academic habit would prompt their mutual inflation. Yet to such a conference I can come only blowing sour notes, even as my sense of the professional occasion leads me to apologize for doing so.

For I come, despite certain reservations that I have several times made in print, as a representative of what I have helped to term "contextualist" literary theory, a dominant theory in recent years. And I must acknowledge—although on this occasion defensively, if not downright blushingly—that this critical tradition can say only negative things about the relation to which this conference is dedicated; indeed, it goes further and builds its pedestal for poetry only by making it all that rhetoric (as this theory defines the term) is not. It makes its criterion for poetic failure the work's falling into "mere rhetoric," and it takes its metaphor ("falling into") literally.

So let me be frank. What can a theory do to help us toward relating rhetoric to poetic when it rests on the need to denigrate rhetoric in order to create the very possibility of poetry? One of the major documents in the formulating of this theory, Allen Tate's "Three Types of Poetry," offers not merely the commonplace that poetry is the work of imagination, but the extreme claim supported by the condescending question of W. B. Yeats, "What is rhetoric but the will trying to do the work of the imagination?" What, then, is inferior poetry or pseudo-poetry (as a work of the will) but rhetoric in disguise, poetry that has—to repeat the metaphor—fallen into rhetoric? In this supercilious strain, the hidden refrain, "Alas, poor rhetoric!"

[1] The University of Iowa Conference on Rhetoric and Poetic, November, 1964.

The Place of Criticism

Of course, all that this theoretical tradition creates as its tactic it can create only because it creates and offers us a card-stacked definition of rhetoric; perhaps it is in an examination of this fact that my sort of essay, propelled from the wrong corner, can be of value to this conference despite the denials on which it rests. What, then, is this rhetoric, as these critics so condescendingly use the term? *Rhetoric* is defined as the use of the available means of persuasion concerning a propositional claim that can be referred to independently of the discourse; which is to say, the claim exists in a complete form prior to the discourse, and it is in no essential way transformed by the discourse. A poem that is termed "mere rhetoric" can be reduced to its means of persuasion, can be treated only as instrument, as device. In short, it is discourse that, however tactically useful, is hardly indispensable. The emphasis on the word *will* as the threat to poetry in Yeats' derogatory definition of rhetoric, with the suspension of the will understood as a prerequisite for the poetic posture, indicates the post-Kantian—indeed almost the Schopenhauerian—sources of this theory. Rhetoric, then, is related to decision and action; poetry, happily, is not. Poetry is related to contemplation and the free play that accompanies it—the contemplation that frees words from their normal semantic and syntactic limitations and that frees our existential world from the contingencies within which our will-driven propensities for action restrict it. Rhetoric is left to employ language in its normal, and normally limiting, way in order to talk about the world within its normally, and willfully, limiting perspectives.

One after another contextualist critic speaks pleadingly of keeping poetry free of the grasp of what is called the "Platonic censor," that which controls non-poetic forms of discourse. And by Platonic they mean pretty much what they mean when they say "rhetorical." It means the directing of discourse toward something extramural, whether a moral imperative, the claim to a moral truth, or to any other sort of truth. So in the dichotomy they draw between poetry and prose or poetry and science—in effect, between poetry and non-poetry as forms of discourse—the techniques of "mere rhetoric" become identified with poetry's antagonist. Wherever there is a separable and transcendent meaning to the discourse, the discourse becomes translation—"mere" translation, to use again one of the favorite adjectives of derogation. All that can distinguish it as discourse—that is, apart from the value of its separable meaning—is its elegance and its effectiveness, "merely" rhetorical properties both, since neither can transform meaning through its ornamental, "merely" ornamental, devices. In such discourse the

Contextualism and Rhetoric

form-content dichotomy is seen as complete. But in poetry—ah, poetry!—there is an organic, ever-transforming quality that renders meaning contextually immanent and untranslatable. Meaning uniquely occurs *in* "these words in this order" rather than being carried inviolately (and indifferently) *through* these words as it might be—or has been—carried through others. If the meaning of a poem can be paraphrased—that is, if it can be reduced to a series of propositions—we must hope that we are oversimplifying its totality in our Platonic haste; for if we are not, if our paraphrase, our reduction, really exhausts the meaning of the poem, then we are dealing with poetry of the will, which is to say pseudo-poetry, disguised rhetoric, "mere rhetoric." And our techniques of analysis should become the more modest ones that concern techniques of persuasion, what R. P. Blackmur called "superficial and mechanical executive techniques"[2] (did he almost mean bureaucratic ones?). I have purposely made the contextualists' distinction broadly and in an oversimplified form to make it unmistakable; and I do not argue for it here since it is rather its consequences upon the study of rhetoric and—even more important to me—of poems that border on rhetoric that concern me.

It goes without saying that the contextualist approach carries with it—and quite explicitly—the downgrading of many poems in the accepted canon, especially the allegorical, the satirical, the didactic. For these are all expressly dualistic, indeed referential in their intention, so that what happens in the poem is largely conditioned by demands of an *a priori* system of meaning—*a priori* in that it pre-existed this poem and has its authority independently of it. Of course, the tactics of argument may lead the contextualist to say not that he is downgrading what may be termed rhetorical poetry *as* poetry, but rather that he is determining it to be a different sort of discourse altogether, one that demands different techniques and standards of evaluation; that as something else in literature it may be splendid even if it cannot create the purely aesthetic occasion that poetry proper can. But this is really no more than a tactical dodge that only mutes the insult if, indeed, it does not aggravate it by an imputation of bastardy.

After I have conceded that entire genres of writing are traduced by the contextualist approach, however, I must insist that this approach often opens our awareness to the other than rhetorical dimensions in a poem which we might otherwise think of as mainly rhetorical—dimensions that can convert

---

[2] "A Burden for Critics," in *The Problems of Aesthetics*, ed. Eliseo Vivas and Murray Krieger (New York, 1953), p. 427.

it into something quite otherwise, a something that rhetorical analysis might never lead us to discover. The persona has been a major device that contextualist critics have used to convert rhetorical analysis to poetic. It has been especially effective in converting the rhetoric of self-righteous satire to the double-edged poetic irony of a satirized world viewed by a similarly, if far more subtly, satirized satirist[3]—thus the revolution in our criticism of Jonathan Swift, most spectacularly of the final book of *Gulliver's Travels,* in which we have learned to treat the Houyhnhnm-loving Gulliver contemptuously, as an imperfect, developing character rather than as Swift's unerring mouthpiece.

I choose Alexander Pope's "Epistle to Dr. Arbuthnot" to demonstrate my point, partly because it is explicitly a verse satire, a traditional—even formalized—satire in general imitation of Horace, and partly because it has received an impressively full analysis as a work of rhetoric.[4] So I choose it mainly because it would seem at the outset to offer so difficult a case— especially when we add the fact that the protagonist and chief speaker in the dialogue is P., obviously Pope, as A., or Arbuthnot, is his interlocutor.[5] Here surely is little room for the fictional ground we would need to convert real author into objectively imagined, dramatically conceived persona. The poet's respectful attitude to his Arbuthnot assures us that we can take his attitude to P. as being equally autobiographical and defensive, as fact rather than as fictive reality only. Biographical facts about Pope and his ancestry, the well-annotated enemies he assails, make us ever more certain. And following the lead of the title and the confessional nature of the prefatory Advertisement, we can expand both initials to the full historical names with

[3] See Robert C. Elliott, "The Satirist Satirized: Studies of the Great Misanthropes," *The Power of Satire: Magic, Ritual, Art* (Princeton, 1960), pp. 130–222.
[4] Elder Olson, "Rhetoric and the Appreciation of Pope," *Modern Philology,* XXXVII (August, 1939), 13–35.
[5] I am assuming, of course, the authority of the Warburton text of 1751, in which the dialogistic attributions to P. and A. are made. There is some question on this point; the Twickenham edition prints the 1739 version, in which the form of the epistle is unbroken except by occasional quotation marks, which often indicate another speaker, sometimes a close friend, with Arbuthnot as a likely candidate. And even its editor, John Butt, acknowledges the possibility that the change from epistle to dialogue was Pope's (Alexander Pope, *Imitations of Horace with An Epistle to Dr. Arbuthnot and the Epilogue to the Satires,* ed. John Butt [London, 1939], pp. 93–94). As a general imitation of Horace, the "Arbuthnot" may be like Pope's "The First Satire of the Second Book of Horace Imitated," which is a dialogue between P. and F., though addressed to Mr. Fortescue. I feel the presence of Arbuthnot is strongly indicated in many of the passages in quotation marks in the earlier version. In any case, the essay by Elder Olson, to which mine is in part addressed, assumes that the poem is a dialogue between P. and A., as in the 1751 version.

equal confidence. Thus the poem can only be Pope's *Apologia pro Vita Sua*, his vindication of himself and his purgative role by his self-righteous condemnation of all enemies.

This is surely the unquestioned assumption of Elder Olson who, in his essay appropriately entitled "Rhetoric and the Appreciation of Pope," treats the poem as an effective demonstration of the prescriptions in Aristotle's *Rhetoric*. Olson defines rhetoric in Aristotle as "that faculty by which we are able in any field of discourse to induce belief or conviction in our audience." Pope's art in the poem is defended as the rhetorician's strategy of establishing himself "as a man of good moral character" assailed by unworthy enemies. Olson engages in an impressively detailed analysis of Pope's tactics, from his manipulation of the dialogue form—of the function of that trustworthy witness and interlocutor, Arbuthnot—to his reassurances to the audience of his own tender innocuousness, despite the attacks that increase in fury (from Atticus to Sporus) as Pope wins the confidence of the audience, now secure in their safety from him. Pope answers the attacks of his enemies by justifying his character even as he assumes the role of attacker himself, though an attacker who has delayed attacking beyond all reasonable endurance. Pure though defiled, he persuades us to understand his own defiling at last, even as Arbuthnot does.

Of course Olson understands that none of this argument proceeds from logic, for the law of its strategy is rhetorical, not logical, as its goal is persuasion, not truth or validity. Thus deception is not only permissible; it is positively to be courted. Every argument in the poem presents us only with circularity since we have only Pope's word for the facts, even for Arbuthnot's presence and for the words that Pope, after all, puts in his mouth. The poem is to establish Pope's good moral character, except that we can trust what he says in it only if we believe, to begin with, that he had good moral character. It is all dissembling, then, but need be no more for its rhetorical purpose of moving "opinions and emotions," rather than creating a proper response to the demonstration of truth. Saying what he would and acting as he would if he were truly virtuous, he circularly persuades us that he is. He gives us a "semblance" of virtue rather than logical proof of it, the "semblance of truth" rather than truth itself. Imitation becomes a cheat that effectively works its intended way.

Olson would have to acknowledge, then, that our persuasion depends on our taking the fiction for the fact, on the illusion that we are overhearing an actual dialogue, not the "imitation" of a dialogue fabricated for his own interests by Pope. We must, in effect, mistake art for nature—surely not the sort of response the neoclassical writer normally expected of his sophisticated reader who cherished art's artifice. It is the sort of demand, however, that the rhetorical intention demands of its reader, as the poetic—proper imitation seen as but an imitation—does not. All this is the price of Pope's creating his "P." as an ego, not as an objectively created, dramatically conceived alter ego; the price of converting poetic imitation to rhetorical persuasion.

Should not this very demand—that the reader be persuaded to forget that he is reading a poem, a free fabrication—put us on our guard against Olson's easy claims that we take the poem for reality in accordance with Pope's strategy? And is it not rather supercilious for Olson to suggest that only a critic as rhetorically wary as he has shrewdness enough to see through the semblance, the deception, and the underlying circularity? As Pope's wit everywhere shows, he was ready to grant wariness to his readers; and any wary reader would surely not be taken in. How many are persuaded by P.'s self-righteous pointing to himself as the injured and the innocent party, especially if we add his contemporary reader's awareness of Pope's reputation for playing a venomous and craftily aggressive public role, a role that Pope would surely trade on? And how many seriously credit the delightful and brilliantly manipulated fiction of Arbuthnot's presence and sympathetic support? To turn A. from character in a dialogue into the breathing reality of Arbuthnot requires as much blindness to the aesthetic fact as he exhibits who would leap onstage to rescue Desdemona from Othello's clutches.

I am not about to invert Olson's claims by saying merely that the poem fails as rhetorical apologetics because of an error in tactics or an underestimating of his reader. Rather I would hold that Pope must have meant to give the game away, that he wanted us to see through the transparent employment of P. and A. and the sometimes painful self-righteousness of P.'s coupling of attacks and self-vindication—to see through these even as we admire the wit that flashes from them. How else to account for what W. K. Wimsatt means when he characterizes the poem as "an exquisite vibration between mayhem and pious professions"? He sees the persona as "a masterpiece of fighting traits justified by benevolent intentions and milky innocence—or mock-innocence (it matters not; in either case, the victims must squirm, and the self-portrait remains in some degree inscrutable)."[6] To

---

[6] "Introduction" to Alexander Pope, *Selected Poetry and Prose*, ed. William K. Wimsatt, Jr. (New York, 1951), p. xlv.

what extent has the poet convicted himself and his role as Horatian satirist, to what extent given evidence of his own irrationality as well as his rational, justifiably self-righteous superiority over his enemies? I see the conventional Horatian role deepen, the humane being in part overcome by the vicious—the vicious in himself as well as in his enemies, even if we grant that his own viciousness has been inspired and even forced by the attacks of those enemies. Still the put-upon poet becomes, in his forced role within the public arena, the violent man.

Our maturest reading finds P. to be a splendid wit and a dangerous enemy, and thus far to be preferred to his antagonists; but he is also self-deluded precisely where he tries to delude us. And I would claim that Pope means to leave his speaker exposed even as that speaker far more damagingly exposes his enemies. The poet's gladiatorial role is seen critically, even sadly perhaps, although P. is given great freedom to play it broadly enough to appease the appetite of his embittered creator. But the creator is also poet enough to keep P. as the object of a case study. He is transformed from spokesman to persona as the "Epistle" is transformed from rhetoric to poem, from apologia to mock-apologia, at least in part.

But the common-sense likelihoods I began with that support the biographical equations are still there, so that evidence of this transformation must be inclusive indeed if our acceptance of these equations and the single satirical thrust is to be shaken. Evidence there is, in the manipulation of both argument and tone: in tactics whose transparency converts them in part to pseudo-tactics and in juxtapositions that shriek their contradictions of motive, compelling our critical awareness of the mixture of violence in innocence.

P.'s primary tactic is to cajole friendliness from his readers through the obvious device of telling them that only the unworthy and the dishonest need fear him: "A lash like mine no honest man shall dread" (line 303); or, earlier, "Curs'd be the verse, how well soe'er it flow,/That tends to make one worthy man my foe" (lines 283–84). We are having a distasteful trade proposed to us: say my verse is righteously inspired and I'll say you are worthy or honest. The very act of dreading my lash is an admission of your guilt; so protect yourself by defending my verse. But P., in his anxious display of self-righteousness, must overstate his case to the point of disingenuous sentimentality. His verse is to be cursed, not only if it makes one worthy man his foe, but, he goes on, if it should "give virtue scandal, innocence a fear,/Or from the soft-ey'd virgin steal a tear!" (lines

285–86). If the reader is not aware that he is being put on in the first of these couplets (lines 283–84), this second of them, with its dead-pan piety, would seem to make it unmistakable.

P. uses the sentimental and the pious in many places to proclaim his sanctity. There is the repeated invocation to "thee, fair Virtue," as his goddess, to whom his satires are at all costs dedicated and who oversees the bitter sacrifice her servant willingly undergoes. And if he must be impolitic even where it is politically dangerous, his goddess prompts the indifferent priggish pronouncement, "A knave's a knave, to me, in ev'ry state" (line 361). Self-satisfied by the "pious professions" Wimsatt spoke of, P. can continue with his justified "mayhem." Where his own person enters, piety and sentiment come with it and together they introduce a cloying self-pity as well. I can cite, as an obvious example, his reference to "this long disease, my life" (line 132), the "being," "preserv'd" by Arbuthnot, which the poet must manage to "bear" (line 134). Another and more extended example is his introduction of his gentle parents, innocent, maligned by his enemies, one dead and the other kept awhile "from the sky" (line 413) only by the poet's dutiful and loving solicitude.

But insidious juxtaposition appears here, as well, to give the game away. P. begins by defending the unslanderous natures of his parents: Why are they slandered? ". . . that father held it for a rule,/It was a sin to call our neighbour fool;/That harmless mother thought no wife a whore:/Hear this, and spare his family, James Moore!" His pious defense of his slandered parents as non-slanderers ends in slander, with P.'s implying the gossip that James Moore Smythe was a bastard. Don't you insult my family, who is innocent and who, in its honest simplicity, would insult no one, not even your family, who deserves the insult I hereby give it!

This device of contradictory juxtaposition is the poet's defense against being taken only seriously by us, his indication to us of his self-critical awareness. He uses it frequently. Often he will join disarming modesty about his poetic talents with implied confessions of genius. The phrase "many an idle song," which he uses to describe his works in a sentimental couplet ("Friend to my life! [which did not you prolong,/The world had wanted many an idle song]," lines 27–28), occurs just two lines after the conjunction of "wit, and poetry, and Pope." This conjunction has all the world's ills blamed on him as the sole incarnation of the twin spirits of wit and poetry. Or where he apologizes for falling involuntarily into the harmless and soothing art of poetry to help him bear this long disease, his life, he lists those distinguished writers whose praise encouraged him. His conclusion is hardly in the soft tones: "Happy my studies, when by these approv'd!/Happier their author, when by these belov'd!/From these the world will judge of men and books,/Not from the Burnets, Oldmixons, and Cookes" (lines 143–46). Here his name-dropping (Granville, Walsh, Garth, Congreve, Swift, Talbot, Somers, Sheffield, Atterbury, and Bolingbroke) has led to a braggadocio awareness of his talents.

The momentary modesty of claims about himself, related to his half-meant retreats to soft sentimentality and like them undercut by a tougher scornfulness, is related also to his protestations of his patient endurance of ill-treatment. And ironic juxtapositions occur here as well. He can proclaim his humility with a sequence of examples that concludes with his charge of plagiarism against his enemy, James Moore Smythe: "So humble, he [P. himself] has knock'd at Tibbald's door,/Has drunk with Cibber, nay has rhym'd for Moore" (lines 372–73). His humility turns into his pride in being copied, his docile nature into an aggressively charging one. Yet the transformations are masked by the parallel order which presents his being victimized by the plagiarist as an act that is graciously voluntary on his part ("has rhym'd for Moore"). The irony in the juxtaposition totally undercuts the soft pretension. Or earlier, answering charges that he has written barbs that were really fashioned by others, P. seems to be at once above reproach, cocky, and arch: "Poor guiltless I! and can I choose but smile,/When ev'ry coxcomb knows me by my style?" (lines 281–82). Here we have his half-meant claim of innocence ("Poor guiltless I!") together with his awareness of his inimitable satiric style and his hidden acknowledgment that his own barbs, well sharpened and directed, have earned him everyone's anxiety—hardly a consequence of innocence, of guiltlessness. Guiltless he is, in these particular cases; but he is mistaken to be guilty—as he implicitly admits—only because he has been so guilty, and so brilliantly and so often guilty, elsewhere. Thus while insisting upon his softhearted endurance of violent opponents, he clearly admits to retaliating in kind: "Were others angry: I excus'd them too:/Well might they rage, I gave them but their due" (lines 173–74). And after describing one after another of his dunces, he concludes with the claim and counterclaim, "All these, my modest satire bade translate,/And own'd that nine such poets made a Tate" (lines 189–90). "Modest satire" indeed!

It is the act of attacking while denying he has the temperament to attack that constitutes the basis for these contradictory juxtapositions.

Can Pope not wish us to ask how the P. who speaks his brilliant and damaging lines in the poem can also characterize himself as "soft by nature, more a dupe than wit" (line 368)? Are you serious? The words burst from us if we have been observing P. at all carefully. As we have repeatedly seen, he represents himself as one who would excuse—has excused—his enemies, although he insults them on all levels, public and private, lightly and gravely, even as he parades himself as resisting the urge to do so. We have observed how the excusing of those who rage (line 173) is coupled with his giving "them but their due" (line 174). Through the use of indirection, the tongue-in-cheek contradiction takes back his claim in the very act of his making it.

The boldest example is, of course, the Atticus portrait in its relation to the disclaimers that precede it. In the preceding verse paragraph P. has been giving the dunces their due, arriving at the summary couplet, whose mixed quality we have noted: "All these, my modest satire bade translate,/And own'd that nine such poets made a Tate" (lines 189–90). His modesty is answered by rage: "How did they fume, and stamp, and roar, and chafe!/ And swear, not Addison himself was safe" (lines 191–92). Is he? Well, P. follows by opening his next line with the unqualified assurance, "Peace to all such!" What follows, of course, is the portrait of Atticus, with its almost unveiled attack on Addison. This daring conjunction of protestation and vituperation is mockery indeed. The wounded innocence of "Peace to all such!" —as if I would touch *him*—joins with the thin disguise of the code name Atticus and with the contrary-to-fact condition of the extended subjunctive construction that follows as the portrait ("But *were* there one . . ."). What makes the disguise not merely thin but utterly transparent is the fact that Pope knew his readers, as followers of the arena of public poets, would know and recall that the Addison portrait had appeared some dozen years earlier without disguise. How in keeping with the complex nature of P.'s satire here that in being assimilated to a new whole the formerly discrete portrait follows so misleading a preamble.[7]

[7] Both the 1722 (perhaps unauthorized) and the 1727 versions of the portrait, printed long before its inclusion in the complete "Arbuthnot" in 1734–35, refer to "A———n" instead of "Atticus." While the first puts the portrait in no significantly broader context, the second ("Fragment of a Satire") not only is very close to the final version in "Arbuthnot," but is also preceded by lines very similar to the preamble we have examined. But one of the differences is crucial—and most helpful to my argument. Just before "Peace to all such" we find "How would they swear, not *Congreve's* self was safe!" How significant to replace Congreve, a respected ally Pope would not attack (see "Arbuthnot," line 138), with Addison, the very figure

P. may indirectly be reminding the reader, through the portrait of Addison and the history of feuding it recalls, that the current poem is hardly the first time that its author, creator of *The Dunciad* (referred to in line 79), has been on the offensive, despite his pious protestations of innocence, of a desire to live outside the arena: "Oh, let me live my own, and die so too!/(To live and die is all I have to do:)" (lines 261–62). These lines of simple and soft retirement lead to others: "I was not born for courts or great affairs;/I pay my debts, believe, and say my pray'rs" (lines 267–68). This subliminal awareness of his prior role as assailant is to qualify the central and continual assumption that the self-righteous P. appears to be urging: that except for the assault he is launching *now*—at the very moment of composing this poem, at the very moment of his claiming not to be launching it, not to be temperamentally able to launch it—except for this one time he has resisted launching it. How, then, this poem, unless he is using the paradox of its being, its curious status, to reveal the uproariousness of his soberer claims, to reveal the fact that he is toying with us and with his satirist's role.

At one of the poem's more naked moments of self-exaltation, P. is describing the ideal poet (guess who), what he avoids and what he seeks. (For example, "Not proud, nor servile, be one poet's praise," [line 336].) What he does, including his satirizing, the moralizing of his song, he does "not for fame, but virtue's better end" (line 342). Are we to believe in this selfless, disinterested service of the goddess? Or are we to recall the more damaging implications of the earlier line 127: "As yet a child, nor yet a fool to fame"? As a self-proclaimed servant of virtue, he still is not a fool to fame, then? My point must be, it should by now be clear, that in playing the game, in writing this very poem as he has written it, he does become one. And the earlier line indicates his half-knowledge of the fact. He proves that he has become a fool to fame by the very act of claiming—in the ways we have seen him claiming—not to be one. But he becomes one necessarily, through the aggressive need to defend himself, to show himself as self-righteous, protector of the role of poet become Horatian satirist-rhetorician in the degrading and self-degrading public arena. But the poet has remained to

---

immediately to be attacked. Could Pope have made such a substitution—from a name that claimed his innocence to one that proved his guilt—without a keen awareness of a changed strategic purpose which the satiric portrait of a poet now a decade and a half dead was in the final version made to serve? For the earlier versions, see Alexander Pope, *Minor Poems*, ed. Norman Ault, completed by John Butt (London, 1954), pp. 142–45, 283–86.

remind us of his saving critical consciousness of that role and its demands, demands that have caused him to be victimized into writing his apologia.

Thanks to his continual tongue-in-cheek qualification of this angry defense, our double view of P. tempers the rhetorical with the poetic, so that the element of mock-apologia ends by leading to a far profounder apologia, one based on an understanding of the pressures, the appeals, the temptations of the public poet's arena, its rivalries and hatreds, its inhumanities, and the human response to it as well as the rationalizing—if transparent—defense of that response. He may be the best of poets (and surely he is trying to persuade us of this as well, I am free to admit) but as *The Dunciad* tells us, it is the worst of times. There is, then, a final sense in which the flight from rhetoric or transcendence of rhetoric leads to a rhetorical purpose after all, so that poetics may be seen to have its rhetoric or rhetoric its poetic. This possibility opens the way for—indeed demands—a new and far subtler, far more flexible and even poetic, definition of *rhetoric* than Aristotle's. But that would be the subject of another, and a far more difficult, essay than this one—one that would be friendlier and more fitting to the union of disciplines that is the proper objective of this conference.

Let me admit, by way of epilogue, that, partly out of my engagement with polemic, I have meant somewhat to overstate my case for the persona, thus rendering clearer than they are the confusing, and probably confused, elements in a poem that is too much a collage. In my own defense I point out that I have tried throughout to insist upon the doubling of our rhetor-poet's voice, his bitterness at others as well as his self-awareness, except that I have not sufficiently pressed the unsystematic, sporadic nature of this doubling. My further methodological confession, then, is that I have meant to follow Pope's lead, learning tactics from his tactics, as in my employment sometimes of the first and sometimes of the third person in speaking of the contextualist. For, like Pope, I have meant to insist upon the limitations of my perspective even as I have tried to exploit it for all the advantages it could provide, thus rendering myself attack-proof even as I deepened my attack—by including myself in its swath. But such confessional candor in motive-hunting is the subject for yet a third essay.

13
Critical Dogma and the New Critical Historians

We may have to begin speaking officially about the Yale group of critical historians. For some time, I suppose, academic literary men have been aware of a group of critical theorists there—René Wellek, Cleanth Brooks, William K. Wimsatt, Charles Feidelson—who were pursuing a common direction. But now the first three of these, not content with searching out the theoretical basis for a significant area of recent literary criticism, have been constructing—or would their opponents say "reconstructing"?—histories to lead up to it.

The present volume[1] is appropriately dedicated and, admittedly, is heavily indebted to Wellek, who with an impressive start on his more ambitious project has preceded Wimsatt and Brooks onto the fearfully undifferentiated field of past literary criticism. Wellek has tempered his four-volume confrontation of such multiplicity by calling an arbitrary beginning around 1750, while Wimsatt and Brooks qualify their effort only with the modest adjective "short." Both undertakings ask no further concessions from their endlessly complex subject as they seek to reduce it to order while not trimming it more severely than order demands. Hence the crucial and obvious question: to what extent should order justly demand the simplifying sacrifices of the subject, or, rather, to ask the less austere converse, to what point should one respect the integrity of a difficult subject, at whatever cost to order?

I have recently had occasion,[2] in reviewing the early volumes of

[1] William K. Wimsatt, Jr. and Cleanth Brooks, *Literary Criticism: A Short History* (New York: Alfred A. Knopf, Inc., 1957). All quotations are from this edition.
[2] "Critical Theory, History, and Sensibility," *Western Review*, XXI (Winter, 1957), 153–59. Some of these arguments are reproduced in "The Disciplines of Literary Criticism." See above, pp. 142–46.

The Place of Criticism

Wellek's history, to defend at some length the primacy of theory as controlling agent in the writing of critical history. Otherwise I would be tempted to use my arguments here, since the Wimsatt-Brooks volume, however different in scope and intention, invites the same kind of defense even as, with its theoretical preoccupations, it may invite many of the same antagonists. In treating Wellek's work I claimed that, however basic his theoretical assumptions, his was still essentially a faithful history even though it carried an argument with it, one that necessarily modified his inclusions and judgments. For once we recognize the historian's obligations to theory, we must see the effective history as occupying that precarious middle position between theoretical argument historically documented and mere neutral, objective chronicle—the kind of history which, mercifully impossible to achieve completely, makes a work the more unreadable as it is approached. In effect I was accepting Wellek's claim that, despite the necessary intrusion of his theoretical point of view, he means still to write a history; that is, to treat history "in all its complexity and multiplicity, in its own right" and not to present "a thesis about the origins of modern criticism."[3]

The present volume, necessarily so much more skeletal in its coverage, may seem to move more openly and purposefully toward historically documented argument, away from history for history's sake. But this is only what the authors have warned us about in their Introduction. Consequently, even if one would charge them with unfaithfulness to the scope and method promised by their title, he could not justly claim that they have betrayed in their execution what they explicitly intended in suggesting the more accurate, if more unwieldy, alternative title, *An Argumentative History of Literary Argument in the West* (page vii). Still we must note their insistence that, despite the qualifiers, it is a history they are writing.

One might, with even more cause, claim, as has been claimed in the case of Wellek, that their history goes wrong where they become deluded by the easy Hegelian trap which leads them to accept a present position as that horizontal meeting point toward which centuries of seemingly chaotic and on occasion even capricious variations have been converging. But this is what they perhaps think of as their good fortune—and history's: that they have read history aright and have dialectically found their position under its guidance, not that having arbitrarily seized upon a position out of the prejudices of their era, they have created a history *ex post facto*. Brooks may find himself an especially likely target of such charges since it is this sort of

[3] *A History of Modern Criticism 1750–1950* (New Haven, 1955), I, 5.

distortion that his approach to poetic analysis has sometimes—and sometimes semi-hysterically—been accused of. Now, his opponents may wish to argue, he has with Wimsatt compounded the sin of using theory to misrepresent the nature of our poetry and its history with the sin of using theory to misrepresent what others have said critically about this poetry. Or since Brooks and Wimsatt, like members of their critical school generally, are attacked as "absolutists," their offense may be seen to be churchly, using the typical strategy of establishing precedent and tradition for a claim to new doctrine. And in our day this is the height—or depth—of offensiveness.

Such capital charges need not for the most part be taken seriously, for we may be rightly suspicious of the premises from which they spring. But they may indicate, at least for tactical purposes, likely points of approach to a work of such magnitude and diversity as the present volume. I suppose one can understand why these impressive historical undertakings stir the resentment of historically inclined anti-new critics (and it is only they who these days use the term "new critics" with any confidence about its referent). They must view this writing of history as the latest move in a bid to take over our academic culture. Having begun with an anti-historical approach that insisted upon the discrete analysis of the isolated poem, critics like Brooks then urged a *rapprochement* between criticism and history, a policy of peaceful coexistence based on criticism's need for the facts of history and history's need for the judgments that criticism alone could supply. Now these critics, the distrustful soul may fear, not content with so reducing the realm of the literary historian, are trying to take over the writing of history themselves, but of course always with an eye out for the advantage of their theory.

It must be conceded that the apportioning of space in the *Short History* would seem to give comfort to such accusations of parochialism. The reader must observe with some surprise that he is finished with all of literary criticism through the eighteenth century when he is only half finished with the book, that as much remains on the last hundred and fifty years. This general disproportion is aggravated by the space allotted to our minor contemporaries—some of them with not yet a substantial body of literary work—as compared to that allotted to some distinguished older critics with extended and productive careers. Thus an Arthur Koestler, a Leslie Fiedler, a Richard Chase, is given a fuller treatment than a Hazlitt or a Lamb. We should thank the authors for guiding us through uncharted territory instead of only retracing old ground more safely: thus we should welcome the careful exposition and sound, unflinching judgment of such recent movements as, for example, that of the "myth" critics. But it comes at a heavy cost to justice. There may seem to be a provincialism of place as well as of time, so that after the chapter on sixteenth century themes, in which the Italians are treated so thoroughly, the early cosmopolitanism of the book is replaced by a concentration on English and American critics, even in periods when other nations assumed critical leadership, with a major and unavoidable continental figure or theme intruding only occasionally. But the authors faced severe limitations of space and thus, despite the promise of their title and of their all-inclusive earlier chapters, were forced to restrict themselves—as they admit in their Introduction—and "to follow the main lines of critical heritage and then draw in the story toward the end to the immediate arena of the modern English-speaking world" (page x).

Whether their detractors like it or not, these theorists have become our most serious and ambitious historians for now—at least of literary criticism. And very able historians they are. It is a matter for congratulation rather than for mistrust that Wimsatt and Brooks have made themselves so profoundly fit for their scholarly task. In the pursuit of this task they everywhere reveal a breadth and penetration, a learning that is never unused or misused in deference to their theoretical affiliations. If their work differs from that of the orthodox historian, then, it is surely not on the score of erudition. Rather, where their work does differ, it differs by reason of the humane and witty quality of their writing, their acute responsiveness to actual poems, and their professional awareness and depth of understanding—most uncommon to professors of literature—in all matters of philosophy, technical and otherwise. For such differences as these we must indeed be thankful, since for men with so rare a combination of gifts to dedicate themselves to so wearying a drudgery as an almost universal critical history is a gracious act of public service which we could never dare ask of them.

It is especially surprising, in view of their candid acknowledgments in the Introduction, to see how little their critical assumptions seem to interfere with their presentation of the vast array of critics, especially through about the middle of the eighteenth century. This group, of course, makes the severest demands upon their scholarly resources (or at least upon Wimsatt's, since he claims "substantial responsibility" for this portion), but the demands invariably are brilliantly met. Occasionally the narration is momentarily interrupted in order for us to be told where our authors stand on a given issue, as, for example, at the close of their treatment of Aristotle on tragedy and comedy (page 53), where in an admirably balanced statement they at once affirm the act of criticism as a rational procedure and accept its limitations in the face of the ultimate mysteries of poetry. But for the most part the flow of the narration is continuous and left pretty much to run along on its own. Or so, at least, it appears. However, though the unwary reader may not suspect it, there is a planned recurrence of certain themes which are later to emerge out of the maze of utterances to build toward the authors' theoretical pronouncement.

Several leading themes return again and again for further development. And these are not just the usual, indeed the inevitable, subjects on which critical historians dote: literary form and content, the moral and hedonic functions of poetry, the authority of rules and classical models, the purity of dramatic genres. To be sure, these important problems are extensively considered, as they must be. But this undertaking is truly original as critical history: refusing simply to follow the older lines with their stereotyped characterizations of various periods, our authors join to the treatment of such subjects new materials—sometimes of purely antiquarian interest, it may at first seem—not before considered the sort of thing to be a functional part of the history of criticism. And thus they add new themes to fill out their account, carrying along—especially in the earlier sections where there is such an expanse of time and space to be covered—an awesome multiplicity and diversity of them that challenge but never overcome the flexible organization.

For example, we would expect especially lengthy and valuable discussions of the history of rhetoric since Wimsatt has distinguished himself as a student of this field. But we might not expect them to function so importantly in his development of the role language must be assigned by poetics. For we needed this treatment to make us aware of it. From the beginning Wimsatt sees in statements about rhetoric the need to resolve the problematic relation between word and thing in literary art. He casts Plato as the defender of philosophy who asserts reality over its pale symbolic imitation and, on the other side, casts Isocrates and Aristotle as those who, defending poets and orators, "affirm the power of the word" (page 71), its creative role in wisdom. Moving from the latter to the even more forceful Stoic doctrine of the *Logos* and summoning to the aid of the word the eloquence of Cicero, Wimsatt later leads us to the Middle Ages, where the emphasis on allegorical meaning, being an emphasis on things and ideas rather than on the language that lightly veils them from us, subverts the primacy of the word. Then, with the introduction of what he views as a new and even more austere Platonism—the doctrine of Ramism with its absolute separation of dialectic from rhetoric—the fortunes of the word are dealt a nearly mortal blow for the glory of thinghood. As Brooks later shows, it is only with the recent symbolist-expressionist philosophers that it has been restored to its former place, indeed has even had that place heightened. For frequently, even in the more enthusiastic encomiums to the word in our ancient past, there was the uncomfortable suggestion of "ornamentalism" when its function was being described. But Brooks makes it abundantly clear that its role as prime mover is completely unquestioned by our symbolic idealists.

Yet we must notice that, while the contemporary theorist must deplore the concept of ornamentalism and thus make Plato's partly the villain's role, our authors do not press their views in a doctrinaire way. Wimsatt has a full and sensitive treatment of neoclassic "wit," one in which he attends with arresting clarity to the shifting, all-important differences between concept and term. This discussion—normally, one would expect, a candidate for a self-enclosed exercise in the history of ideas—is converted into yet another aspect of the relation between thing and word which, as we have seen, is at last shown to be the controlling, if often neglected, aspect of the never neglected relation between poetic form and content.

Finally Wimsatt reaches and dares pause upon the notorious couplet

True wit is Nature to advantage dress'd;
What oft was thought, but ne'er so well express'd.

While properly insisting that this aphorism hardly "describes the 'meaning' of Pope's own poetry in its fullness," he acknowledges, as he must, that it "has seemed to the post-romantic mind an all-too-apt expression of the superficiality of neoclassical rhetorical practice. The statement, both as specific theory of Augustan poetry and as general theory, is in fact disappointing" (page 242). But disappointing, we may assume, again to the post-romantic mind, Wimsatt's and ours, so that the fault may be ours rather than Pope's. He pushes a bit farther when he adds, "The element of 'dress' (so repugnant under that figure to the romantic mind) is never quite squeezed out of poetic theory except by a rigorous extreme of idealistic symbolism" (page 242). Thus he asserts the almost unavoidable dualism inherited by the available language of criticism; and an awareness of it may cause one to concede that Pope's couplet is "a sort of token, or temporary expression" for an idea that is better than it sounds, that Pope may be trapped by the very nature of critical terminology as well as by that of his own rhetoric. Thus, too, Wimsatt can conclude his section, after quoting prosaic and more blatant examples of neoclassic ornamentalism,

> An expression of ornamentalist theory when it takes a form like Pope's couplet means something a little different from what a less guarded expression means. And the general theory of ornamentalism means one thing when applied to the verse of Blackmore and another when applied to that of Pope himself. (page 245)

Now one must find this sort of commentary liberal, even generous, in the extreme. Surely there should be no objection to this attempt to allow sympathetic reasonableness to rule over the merely dogmatic and thus the flexible historian over the rigid doctrinaire.

And yet Wimsatt's is not exclusively a bland acceptance of Pope's phrasing; there does remain something in it that bothers him. Perhaps this combination of reactions, even in this single minor instance, pinpoints his special value to us. He has come through recent critical theory, and with enough sympathy for it to worry about Pope's couplet, while making himself—at least for the occasion—historian enough to see beyond its most obvious meaning and the theoretical antagonism it perhaps ought to arouse. If a more hostile view of his presentation sees in it merely a ruthless attempt to get Pope—with whatever distortion—into the modern theorists' club, it has missed the obvious fact that the rigors of modern critical theory have been made to give way at least as much as Pope has. And as if to reward our author for his flexibility, Pope proves his point for him by furnishing the quotation with which he can conclude his chapter: the closing lines of *The Dunciad* that startlingly reveal a profound awareness of the *Logos*, of course along with a fear, or at least a stark mistrust, of it.

Lo! thy dread Empire, CHAOS! is restor'd;
Light dies before thy uncreating word.

Other discussions too that in other contexts might have had their scholarship as their sole justification are here pressed into valuable service. There are many views given us about the imitation of the ancients—not only as a practice to be followed or scorned, but as a precise genre—and about the related genre of translation. We move from the obvious advice of Horace and Vida to a sensitive description of Ben Jonson's imitative theories and practices. Later we pick up the subject with Dryden, who not only redefines the same issues but adds the delicate and special problems of imitation involved in translation. From there to the new techniques of imitative verse in Pope and Dr. Johnson. Then the principle of neoclassic imitation is seen shading off also into that of parody before the notions of the Longinian sublime and original genius bury the entire question, and neoclassicism as well. But this recurrent issue is made to shed new and striking light from a familiar but unexpected source on the still unresolved problem of poetic creativity or, to use the well-worn phrase, of tradition and the individual talent. And we are prepared for the crucial theories of imagination that follow.

One can trace also the continual return to discussions of tragedy and comedy, as our authors follow the varying extents to which past theory has intermingled the two or has kept them discrete. Thus they work their way toward a conception of genres that neither obliterates them, Crocean fashion, nor so respects their integrity as to create a theory of classes; for the latter would multiply the single poetic principle toward which the volume is directed (pages ix–x). But no matter how ingeniously handled, these and other major themes cannot give us a full idea of the variety of subjects involved in past criticism. And our authors are too dedicated to their materials in their complexity to impose a rigid scheme upon them. Thus the narrative pauses for special chapters—almost digressions, they may seem at times—which treat a single problem, one most prominent in the particular period, by running it back to its roots and projecting it forward to its consequences. If some of these chapters, like those on poetry and the other arts and on poetic diction, seem somewhat wayward, threatening momentarily to transform the book into a collection of miscellaneous theoretical essays, they enrich the book immeasurably. By maintaining so flexible an organization the authors manage to give us a far fuller sense of the diversity of critical interests than could the professional historian's over-schematized, routine recital.

I should like, however, to return to the authors' major themes, since I am troubled by their treatment of one of them—the development of the expressionism that follows from idealism. This is for them a key theme since it emerges—out of what they say about Plotinus, Coleridge, Croce, and finally the recent symbolist-expressionists—as one of the two or three "radical ideas" which they try in their Epilogue to reconcile into a workable theory. The difficulty did not arise for me until I arrived with them at the late eighteenth or early nineteenth century and at the problem of imagination, perhaps because it is not until that point that the volume seemed to get more seriously argumentative. We have already seen that pre-nineteenth-century criticism is somehow compressed into the first half of the volume. Further, this earlier portion requires exacting scholarship in explication. It may be that Wimsatt was just kept too busy to allow himself much leisure for theoretical dispute. Or it may be that these earlier materials seemed less urgently demanding of judgment, that the need to speak out increases as we approach our own time and its peculiar problems. Wellek suggested that the mid-eighteenth century was a good time to begin his critical history since what was said earlier was largely of "antiquarian" interest and "unrelated to the problems of our day."[4] While Wimsatt and Brooks begin their book pretty much at the beginning, it may be that they are, perhaps unconsciously, agreeing with Mr. Wellek—much as their brilliant early sections ought to persuade them otherwise—in that they do not pursue the argumentative aspect of their work very consistently until after the time he specifies.

Wimsatt approaches the romantic and idealist conception of imagination from the associationism of the latter eighteenth century. With a characteristic brilliance of historic insight he shows an essential continuity between the power, permitted by associationism, of recombining fragmented sensory experiences and the uniting power of the creative imagination that was shortly to be asserted. The earlier, still associative faculty at rare times even had attributed to it the power of fusing—not merely adding together—ideas into a new and unique object (page 305). Indeed, we are almost led to ask what need there was for German idealism or for the Coleridge whom it spawned except, perhaps, to announce and take credit for an innovation already achieved. I found myself asking whether all this was not too brilliant, with a facility that beguiled us into moving too quickly.[5]

The passage from the associative to the Coleridgean imagination calls for a leap from one epistemology to another, from a mechanical passivity to an organic creativity, from the concept of a mind limited by what it takes in to one whose spontaneity creates beyond its materials—in short, from what Coleridge termed "fancy" to what he termed "imagination." This kind of

---

[4] *Ibid.,* p. v. See also p. 1.
[5] Elsewhere too we find Wimsatt perhaps over-anxious to establish historic continuity. For example, in his desire to connect Croce with the aesthetic movement, he calls Croce's "a master theory of art for art's sake" (p. 500). Shortly after, he more correctly calls his theory "the most resolutely cognitive of all modern art theories" (p. 508). This hardly suggests autotelism.

leap ultimately defies the mediating claims of historic continuity. Its effect upon literary theory is as radical: the empirical doctrine of association, for all its seeming subjectivity, could still, through its notion of the mind's essential passivity, permit of a theory of imitation—validating it from the other end, as it were. Only expressionistic doctrine could do justice to the literal creativity bestowed upon the new imagination. In Wimsatt's passage an awareness of the full impact of the organicistic revolution seems to be lacking. There may well be hints in this direction in the later writings of associationists, but logically they have no business there so long as these writers remain associationists. Our author should have more explicitly instructed us that one will have to do better—or at least differently—epistemologically and metaphysically, to earn his organicism.

This is no mere quibble. For I believe Coleridge does not come out very favorably in the chapter on imagination because Wimsatt does not give his doctrine of organic creativity its due. He refuses, for example, to see all it can do for a general theory of poetry and instead finds it "slanted very heavily toward a particular kind of poetry" (page 398), obviously a poetry romantic in style and ideas. Like D. G. James before him,[6] he even equates Coleridge's theory with the rightly unpopular one of Ruskin, not only in its identifying the imagination with the serious and the fancy with the playful, but also in its dedicating the imagination to the "pathetic fallacy."[7] One must grant, especially in the face of Wimsatt's impressive mass of quotations, that Coleridge was too immersed in the romantic milieu not to share in its fondness for the serious, the emotional, the vague. But I have elsewhere argued extensively[8]—in dealing with T. E. Hulme's similar condemnation of Coleridge—that it is its organically creative aspect which gives life to his concept of imagination just as this concept has given life to recent theory, even as espoused by those who disparage Coleridge. I was, in effect, asking for the latitude and generosity of treatment which we have seen Wimsatt, with perhaps less reason, accord Pope, but which a literalism

---

[6] *Skepticism and Poetry* (London, 1937), pp. 47-49, 83-87.
[7] One must ask whether this "theory of 'animating' imagery, of romantic anthropomorphism" (p. 400)—the investing of nature with human qualities—begins to do justice to the kind of interpenetration, of union between tenor and vehicle that the Coleridgean imagination provides for. Does the "pathetic fallacy" leave nature *as* nature at all, or rather is not nature being ruthlessly used, to the neglect of its intrinsic qualities, in order to be assimilated to the human ideas it is to embody? This is a one-sided affair certainly.
[8] *The New Apologists for Poetry* (Minneapolis, 1956), pp. 32-45, 65-68, 180-81.

seemingly invoked for the occasion prevents him from according to Coleridge. I did concede, however, that only by rooting the creativity of his imagination in the creative resources of language more deeply and firmly than Coleridge did, can one even partly avoid the romantic extravagance of his theory. And this describes the sort of thing many recent critics after I. A. Richards as well as those like Cassirer whom Brooks calls "philosophers of symbolic form" (pages 700–8) have been trying to bring about.

It is rather surprising that in his development of the defense of the word over the centuries, as I have already traced it, Wimsatt divorces the notion of the primacy of the word in cognition from the idealist and expressionist tradition. Surely there is something monistic about the desire to destroy the antinomy between word and thing. Nor do I think we ought to be completely comfortable to have so notorious an "ornamentalist" as Aristotle cast as the word's early champion and Cicero as his successor. The defense of rhetoric, though it ministers to the user of words by asserting the desirable union of wisdom and eloquence, is still not a proclamation of the word's creative power. It was this I had in mind when I spoke earlier of the "ornamentalism" that seemed to hover about most of Wimsatt's proposed word-centered tradition.

It is not that we can deny Plato's activities against the word, although we must remember, too, that there is a somewhat different Plato who passes down to us from Plotinus through modern idealism and expressionism. But we may wonder whether, in his desire to make the Platonic-Aristotelian opposition too clean-cut[9] and to put Aristotle on the right side, Wimsatt has not erred in excluding expressionism from the stream of verbalistic theory. He seems uncertain himself about how purely Aristotle is to serve as the representative of "the power of the word" (page 71). For he acknowledges

[9] There are some other too hasty distinctions drawn also. Wimsatt blandly accepts poetry as "truth of 'coherence,' rather than truth of 'correspondence' " (p. 748). But how can he, when he is so deeply concerned about poetry's imitative and cognitive function that poetry for him must have to do with "seeing and saying" as well as with "making" (p. 755)? Or, in an admirable attempt to classify exhaustively certain nineteenth-century tendencies, he uses for one of them a phrase that approaches oxymoron—"autonomous didacticism" (p. 425). He clearly means by this that while poetry is to teach, it is to do so in its own right, no longer as a surrogate for philosophy or religion, which it is to replace. Still it is an unfortunate phrase, forced on him by the nature of his classificatory distinctions, especially as applied to Matthew Arnold. Later Wimsatt admits that in Arnold's famous definition of poetry as a "criticism of life," "the criticism would obviously have to be somehow faithful to, or limited by, its object" (p. 491). Surely faithfulness, limitation, and an external object do not seem convincing evidences of autonomy. Nor does Wimsatt's implication that Arnold did not approach "a distinct concern for literature" (p. 451).

Aristotle as an "ornamentalist" who sees words as the attractive coloring of the poem's outline, of its soul, its plot (page 264). He uses Aristotle also as representative of the mimetic principle, "which does justice to the world of things" (page 750), although this function would seem to set Aristotle on Plato's side against the Aristotle we were told of who champions the word. And yet there would appear to be a fourth Aristotle against the world of things and words, one who represents pure formalism, the notion of structures "devoid of any meaning" (page 752). While Wimsatt is surely aware of these differences and while there is that in Aristotle to justify each of these interpretations so that reference to him is, in the context of these passages, understandable, nevertheless the contradictory nature of some of them may make one question the wisdom of using him so crucially and unqualifiedly in the early defense of the word. Wimsatt should have lined up his teams more tentatively. It seems especially unfortunate that the kind of theoretical tradition that is ushered in by Aristotle, who is after all most influentially an imitationist, must be one that is inimical to the philosophical orientation that can do most for the word—the idealistic and expressionistic. For the latter produces thinkers who are Platonic in their lineage, although theirs is not the austere Platonism that Wimsatt seizes upon to allow his early dichotomy—the Platonism of Ramus. There is a need, then, to supplement his version of Platonism, though I cannot answer it here.

Since Wimsatt does not separate some degree of ornamentalism from the verbalistic tradition, his leniency toward Pope's notion of thought and its verbal "dress" may not be so striking as I have suggested. He has told us, "The element of 'dress' . . . is never quite squeezed out of poetic theory except by a rigorous extreme of idealistic symbolism" (page 242). Since this is clearly too rigorous an extreme for him, he must be willing to put up with some degree of this "element." Apparently since he cannot go all the way with organicism (and who can?), he would like a theory part "ornamental," part "integrational." Would that it were possible to take organicism by degrees or to have words serve even slightly as decoration without destroying the uniquely cognitive possibilities of poetry. But what we saw before as generous historical breadth in Wimsatt's acceptance of Pope's couplet may from another view appear like theoretical timidity.

There is a central difficulty in idealism that concerns Wimsatt deeply, as it well ought to. When discussing it in connection with Coleridge, he says it "has haunted all idealistic theory of art from Plotinus to Croce and Susanne Langer" (page 399). If all perception is creative, in what way is poetic creation differently creative? In more contemporary terms, how can one differentiate aesthetic symbolization from the universal symbolization needed in every mere act of human knowing? Either poetry is assimilated to non-aesthetic activity or everything is made poetry. In either case it in effect ceases to exist. If idealists cannot extricate themselves from this puzzle, it is because they have not fully enough insisted upon the need for language, the highly disciplined and formalized medium of poetry, to bring a special creative power to life, through its restraining as well as its enabling powers. A freely ranging symbolizing power cannot manage this kind of creation on its own. Only in art is there this kind of medium and thus this kind of creation. It may be that this is to call on idealists to yield somewhat to realism and to see less creativity in ordinary perception. But what is more important to us here, it calls on them to assert even more strongly the principle of the *Logos* with which their expressionism has led them to identify themselves, as Wimsatt should have more clearly pointed out. But his initial setting of the problem of the word prevents him from tracing their connection with this principle.

Wimsatt's own theoretical orientation seems too antipathetic to the idealistic notion of creativity for him to appreciate its complete meaning. The pre-Kantian language of epistemological realism gives him away. Thus he can speak of such extreme idealists as Schelling and Friedrich Schlegel as having "a lofty view of the artist's power of reshaping reality" (page 491) without recognizing that "reshaping" is far too weak, is not sufficiently creative, since it suggests only the shuffling of a full deck. Or at the end (Wimsatt is responsible for the Epilogue also) he extends himself to include expressionism in his final synthesis by using, to satisfy it, the term "seeing" (page 753). But "seeing," with its suggestion of a something there to be seen, of mere discovery, is more a realist's—indeed an imitationist's—term than an expressionist's. This is not to quarrel with realism but only to criticize this realist's inability to give us a full sense of so important a recent theoretical strain as idealistic expressionism. Perhaps we find at least a partial source for his realist bias when we read the following in a quotation he uses from Jacques Maritain: art "transforms, removes, brings closer together, transfigures; it does not create" (page 497).

Oddly enough, it is in Wimsatt's collaborator, Cleanth Brooks, that the idealist-expressionist doctrine receives a sympathetic exposition which conflicts at times sharply with the kind of attitude we have been observing at work. Early in his portion of the book we find Brooks opening the all-important and impressively synoptic chapter on symbolism with the pronouncement, "The doctrine that words create knowledge is a part of the romantic theory of imagination." He follows this immediately with a quotation from Coleridge who, in defending poetry as the mediator between subject and object, says, "I would endeavor to destroy the old antithesis of Words and Things; elevating, as it were, Words into Things and living things too" (page 584). Brooks then connects Croce, Cassirer, and Mrs. Langer with this tradition, even as he later traces the "emphasis upon organic form" back to Plotinus (page 653). At this point he includes Augustine, too, in this line of thinking, although we may remember that Wimsatt rather ranged Augustine on the anti-Platonic Aristotelian team (page 72). These identifications suggest that Brooks has a very different, and I think a more correct, sense of the relation between idealism and the belief in the primacy of the word. Surely there is little implication in Wimsatt's treatment that Coleridge had so important a verbal interest or that his organicism has had such revolutionary effects. And where Brooks sees the local romantic weaknesses of the Coleridgean imagination, he corrects them with notions drawn from the more essential aspect of the same theory of imagination, thus testifying, as I have, to the concept's far-flung theoretical value:

> Marvell's poetry, with its serious wit, challenges Coleridge's distinction between the fancy and the imagination, for many of the devices in Marvell's poetry that Coleridge would have to range under fancy are actually used to achieve effects that show the full power of the imagination. (pages 666–67)

But would not Brooks be the first to admit that his second use of *imagination* in this passage, as well as his first, is Coleridgean in its derivation, so that he has corrected Coleridge with Coleridge?

If in his earlier publications, however, Brooks has seemed to be somewhat unrestrained in his advocacy of organicism, complexity, poetic inclusiveness, we find him here qualifying his claims considerably, thanks either to the subduing effects of confronting history, to the influence of his collaborator, or simply to his own theoretical development. Let us note some passages:

> . . . if there are no fixities and definites at all but only symbolic fluidity, then there would appear to be some danger that everything will disappear into froth and bubbles. (page 587)

And, citing Yeats as a corrective, but one still operating within the framework of idealism:

Indeed, we have had few poets in history who have stressed more powerfully the density and hard particularity of the objects of the external world. In celebrating the power of words, as all proponents of symbolist-expressionist doctrines must, Yeats did not lose thereby his grip upon things. Or, if we were willing to suppose with the symbolists that we could get at things only through language, then we would still have to say that in Yeats's poetry, language is not denatured and diluted into a common gray "wordiness." Words retain the sharp outlines and individual profiles of "things." (pages 604–5)

While Brooks believes Yvor Winters goes too far in the other direction, he pays this tribute to him:

Winters' bias toward the logical, the definite, and the unequivocal gives him a certain corrective value. He has refused to be imposed upon by misty and vague meanings, and he has been able to put his finger on tendencies toward incoherence that have escaped the notice of many other modern critics. (page 673)

In his retreat from a pure organicism and its unlimitedly romantic consequences, Brooks seems to carry a nostalgia for the systematic consistency it would allow. While his theory is now broadened and eased, as a result he must with other modern theorists confront the dilemma that a partial organicism is impossible, is in effect no organicism, and that the alternative to organicism is destructive of all that recent theory has taught us about poetry. He seems to be not so far as he might like from the position in which he finds Susanne Langer:

If Mrs. Langer avoids [Emerson's symbolistic] monism, as on the whole she does, it is because in practise she uses more referential criteria than she is perhaps aware that she is using and more than her theory strictly entitles her to use. (page 708)

If, despite the differences remaining between them, Brooks has moved closer to Wimsatt, when the latter returns for the Epilogue he also appears somewhat more moderate, as for example in the following concession:

Thus the authors of this history find little difficulty in explaining to themselves a strong sympathy for the contemporary neo-classic school of ironic criticism and for what it has in common with the theory that prevailed in the time of Coleridge and the Germans. (page 742)

At the end there is a stirring note of triumph, sounded metaphorically in terms borrowed from another and higher sphere of age-long battle. The authors reject the all-exclusive, too spiritual monism symbolized by Platonism or Gnosticism and the all-inclusive dualism and unresolved conflict symbolized by Manichaeism in order to embrace the final affirmation that can come as a miraculous, all-reconciling grace only after an *almost* total abandonment to conflict—metaphorically "the religious dogma of the Incarnation" (page 746).

This soaring conclusion carries us in the direction of aesthetic order beyond the dramatistic theory of endless struggle, the dualistic or pluralistic—if not chaotic—theory of unresolved irony which was for some time associated with Brooks. It is now repudiated as the aesthetic equivalent of Manichaeism. If this religious metaphor could be as convincingly translated into aesthetic terms so that we could have both the internally multiplied complications of organicism and yet, somehow, finally, the responsibility to order and to the world, poetic theory would have been granted a miraculous gift indeed. But perhaps literal translation is more than we dare ask even of a metaphor used in argumentative discourse. When Wimsatt and Brooks make their only attempt at translation at the very close, they come forth with the claim that poetry unites the notion of *making*—the Aristotelian—with the notion of *saying* and *seeing*—the Platonic (which, be it noted, now includes the romantic and expressionistic). We cannot help noting that these twin definitions of the poet as seer-soothsayer (*Vates*) and as maker (*Poeta*) are precisely the two that Sir Philip Sidney began his *Apology* by coupling and distinguishing. And we may wonder whether, in their desire to do right by all that their history has revealed to them and to us, our authors have really carried us beyond those older and unsatisfactory formulas which called for the unity of form with content, of the *dulce* with the *utile*.

Perhaps the best way to tame those who pursue any divergent theoretical course that threatens to become narrow is to force them to confront the multiplicity of history. It makes for sanity, for tolerance. In transforming their anti-historicism into a desire to write history themselves, recent theorists seem as likely to be touched by history's catholic spirit as they are to alter the interpretation of history's facts. Surely our authors, for all their philosophical rigor, have been chastened by the lessons history, with its distance, gives of other doctrines and by the diversity it so prodigally displays. Indeed, confronted with the historian's task, we all are likely to give way to the temptations—yes, even the virtues—of an all-embracing eclecticism. We have heard much in recent theory about the "poetry of inclusion." Perhaps now, if the attraction to history writing continues, we are to be heading toward a similarly inclusive poetics. In their Epilogue our authors urge us to "a theory of multiple focuses," leading to "an indefinitely variable criticism of *all* poems" (page 750). Speaking of the unfortunate division of aesthetic value into sensory and conceptual values, they urge us to learn "how to embrace them both and thus have a double or paradoxical theory" (page 752). But being discursive, theory may not do so well with the paradoxical as poetry can. Our authors would be the first to insist that to confound criticism with poetry is to commit again the error of the critical impressionists. How, except by moving beyond the rigors of system, is the theorist, who is philosophically aware but is newly broadened by history, to reconcile with his concern for consistency the several incompatible traditions he now feels the need to accommodate? All of this is perhaps only to say that if the critical theorist is enabled to range more freely by turning critical historian, this latter role is not likely to solve for him the problems set by the former. This critical history, then, even in its Epilogue, cannot finally show us the theorist's way, much as it opens avenues. It is not to be expected, nor would our authors, in their self-awareness, pretend to it. It may after all be necessary once again to turn away from history, to assert its limitations with its breadth, and to head—now more wisely as more knowingly, thanks to our authors—back into the narrows of theory in search for the meaning of poetry.

14
Platonism, Manichaeism, and the Resolution of Tension: A Dialogue

 It seemed worthwhile, even in this collection of my own work, to assemble the essential passages of a debate that proceeded for several years between W. K. Wimsatt and me beginning with my essay on the Wimsatt-Brooks critical history, immediately above. I have meant fully to share the pages that follow with his voice of opposition, to present the dialogue between us honestly, and not merely to use his counterclaims to present my own claims the more forcefully. I feel that I have succeeded in this attempt since, in addition to granting his permission to reprint, Mr. Wimsatt kindly consented to look over this collage and has approved it.

These materials are presented, then, not because I want the last word in this debate—indeed the reader will find that it is Mr. Wimsatt who is given the last word in this grouping (although I must confess that my own final essay in this volume in a way grows out of these issues). Rather I am anxious to present this debate as one that has crucial theoretical indications for recent criticism, its dilemmas and its muddles. Yet the debate seems to rotate about an ineluctable *either/or*, as old as criticism, concerning the meaning of poetry. Can poetry finally have a meaning of a different kind from non-poetry? Can poetry maintain *its* order even as it retains as its subject the disorder of conflict, a conflict to which the poem as an orderly object can never surrender but whose density it dare not thin? To what extent do these questions—and, in consequence, the very nature of modern poetics—depend on an irrationalist phenomenology, on an existentialist view of experience as *not* being grounded in reason, on what Mr. Wimsatt, in the title of his recent book, refers to as "hateful contraries"? But to ask further or say more would anticipate the pages that follow.

I have tried to tailor the following excerpts within the bounds of economy without making them seem too piecemeal. The materials I have assembled, besides "Critical Dogma and the New Critical Historians," are the following (and I list them here in the order in which they appear so that in the text I may simply begin each entry by referring only to the author):

1. From Murray Krieger, *The Tragic Vision* (New York, 1960), pp. 235–48;
2. W. K. Wimsatt, review of *The Tragic Vision, JEGP*, LXI (January, 1962), 141–44;
3. From Wimsatt, "Horses of Wrath: Recent Critical Lessons" (1956, 1958, 1962), *Hateful Contraries* (Lexington, Ky., 1965), pp. 24–47.

From *CEA Chap Book* (Supplement to *CEA Critic*, XXVI [December, 1963]):

4. From Wimsatt, "What to Say About a Poem," pp. 18–19;
5. From Hyatt H. Waggoner, "A Poem is Just a Part," pp. 21–23;
6. From Wimsatt, "Responsio Scribleri," pp. 32–33;
7. From Robert B. Heilman, "A Postscript on 'Appreciation,'" p. 30;
8. From Wimsatt, "Responsio Scribleri," pp. 35–36;
9. Krieger, "Every Critic His Own Platonist," pp. 25–28;
10. From Wimsatt, "Responsio Scribleri," pp. 34–35.

I am grateful also to Mr. Waggoner and Mr. Heilman, who have allowed me to use their brief excerpts to advance the dialogue.

1. *Murray Krieger.* [Of the so-called New Critics] only [Cleanth] Brooks seemed for a long time to be holding out against any slightest surrender of the inviolable context to the demands of the referential or the propositional. He appeared rightly to understand that, like uniqueness, organicism is an all-or-nothing affair and that to qualify it was, theoretically, to yield completely. And so he held out even under attack by new-critical colleagues like Ransom who found him unmitigatedly romantic. But his recent association with William K. Wimsatt in their *Literary Criticism: A Short History* seems finally to have brought Brooks around as well. He now speaks of the need for "fixities and definites," of "the logical, the definite, and the unequivocal," as the antidote for "incoherence" and "symbolic fluidity.". . .

The difficulty of [contextualist critics] arises not so much from their

Platonism, Manichaeism, Tension Resolved

own indifference to theoretical consistency as it does from the very real nature of the dilemma they face. Some considerations demand that the poem be seen as a closed system; some considerations demand with equal persuasiveness that it be seen as opening outward to the world and to externally imposed laws of rational order. Yet it cannot be partly closed, partly open. If we want poetry to be more than a pleasing and pretty version of another form of discourse (one which, if less pretty and less pleasing, is more exacting), then it must have a different way of meaning. And since poetry is distinguished by its highly wrought internal relations and by its powers to do and say so many things at once, it would seem that whatever claims can be made for it as a special form of discourse that has a special way of meaning must be made in consequence of its special contextual characteristics. Organicism and inviolability of context being matters of kind and not of degree, poetry must be seen as a form of discourse in some sense nonreferential even as it must be in some sense referential to be a form of discourse at all. It must be seen as in some sense a closed world of meaning even as this many-faceted world is created largely to open onto and illuminate the facets we would miss in the outside world of every day. . . .

In the conclusion to their recent history of criticism, Wimsatt and Brooks try their hand at resolving this dilemma by suggesting how we may preserve the valuable conclusions recent critics have reached about the several opposed voices with which the poem can speak without encouraging aesthetic chaos and outlawing all moral commitment. While their suggestion is finally no more than a metaphorical one and is, I suppose, to that extent unsatisfactory, the metaphor is a most provocative one—one that will put us a long way toward drawing thematic implications from the aesthetic we have been examining. They are again contrasting the Platonic conception of poetry that sees a single transcendent meaning and the organic conception that sees an organized and complex opposition of immanent meanings. They again find both inadequate, the Platonic because it destroys the role of poetry by thinning it and thus trimming it down to other discourse, and the organic because it contains no final return to order, no final affirmation of a cosmic controlling principle. Indeed, by definition the ironic view can nothing affirm. Translating these alternatives into theological terminology, the authors believe

> that the kind of literary theory which seems . . . to emerge the most plausibly from the long history of the debates is far more difficult to orient within any of the Platonic or Gnostic ideal world views, or within the Manichaean full

dualism and strife of principles, than precisely within the vision of suffering, the optimism, the mystery which are embraced in the religious dogma of the Incarnation (page 746). . . .

The leap to the Incarnation represents their rejection of an all-exclusive intellectualism and an all-inclusive [tensional] density as they embrace the final affirmation that can come as a miraculous, all-reconciling grace only after an *almost* total abandonment to conflict.

It is clear that in this kind of formulation the final reassertion of aesthetic order becomes a reflection of the reassertion of moral order. After all, we have seen not only that the tensional version of contextualism, in the extreme form that is its only consistent form, seems to forego any aesthetic order externally imposed upon its self-complicating dynamics, but also that this theory, in its ironic posing of counterclaim along with every claim, seems to forbid any final thematic resolution, any final moral commitment, in the name of experiential complexity, which readily supplies the skepticism that comes of a total awareness. Yvor Winters may have been more correct than many of his detractors, in their anti-didacticism, have credited him with being in his insistence that rational poetic form exerted upon recalcitrant materials is a reflection of the poet's moral control of his disturbing experience: to forego one is to forego the other. Consequently, we begin to see how completely this aesthetic would seem to depend on a metaphysic or even a theodicy. In a recent essay that pursues the implications of the concluding chapter of the history of criticism, Wimsatt turns more explicitly in the thematic direction himself. Again he at once attacks the Manichaean implications of unresolved thematic tensions and defends the dramatic need to give full due to the mixed and imperfect nature of the human condition. He ends by exhorting the Christian writer and the Christian critic to recognize the need for a clear moral commitment in literature, but only a commitment that has been earned through an *almost* total dramatic submission to the forces of opposition.

But can *anything* be withheld if the test is to be complete, if the ironic, self-contradictory nature of moral experience is to be allowed full sway? Is not even the slight rational, philosophic control of the stuff of drama infringement enough to ensure the stacking of the cards, the intrusion of an abstract order that pre-exists the poem upon thematic oppositions, even as we earlier saw the slight concessions by our critics to referential and propositional discourse to be enough to open the organic context irrevocably? For Wimsatt, and probably Brooks, the need in poetics to find an order that somehow does full justice to the internal complications of the context not only is analogous, but is intimately related, to the need in the realm of theme to find a moral order that somehow does full justice to the fearful paradoxes that inhere in experience. But can the pleasantly eclectic compromise satisfy in the one realm any more than it can in the other? . . .

Following the more organic aspects of the new-critical poetics . . . we can define *thematics* as the study of the experiential tensions which, dramatically entangled in the literary work, become an existential reflection of that work's aesthetic complexity. Thematics thus conceived is as much beyond "philosophy"—and in the same way beyond "philosophy"—as, in pure poetics, an organic, contextually responsible form is beyond a logically consistent system. There can be occasions on which the author means to be conceiving his work dualistically, as an embodiment and a demonstration of a "philosophy," except that he has been more faithful—dramatically and existentially faithful—than he knows, so that a fully thematic analysis would reveal that significant opposition is engendered when this philosophy enters the total poetic context, with the consequence that an objective hierarchy of values and the poet's full sympathies are not so easily identified or, thanks to the endless qualifications, perhaps not identifiable at all. . . .

This way of conceiving thematics as a *literary* method, and as the only method capable of dealing with meanings in literature, would seem to predispose the moral-theological—indeed finally the metaphysical—issue toward the irresolution of Manichaeism. It would seem to argue against any cosmic resolution, however ultimate and however qualified, since this would reduce the complexities of theme (in my sense of the word) to the single-mindedness of "philosophy" and thus reduce poetry to its "Platonic" conception as a form of propositional discourse. . . . But what is being insisted upon here as Manichaean is not the ultimate nature of metaphysical or noumenal reality so much as the existential nature of that reality which makes itself dramatically available to the poet whose only commitment as poet is to experience and to the dramatic exigencies of his art. . . .

It is really a commonplace to say that every poet must, at least provisionally, be something of a Manichaean. This is but a way of our asking him not to stack the cards, but rather to give his drama full sway, always to allow his opposition its argument a fortiori. But if he does no more than this—if, that is, he submits his thesis to the hellfires of antithesis with no doubt of the issue and only to allow this thesis to be earned the hard way—he is no more in danger of heresy than is any profound version of

Christianity that is willing to take into account all worldly imperfection without reducing the extent or the goodness of God's sway. Once more let me repeat that this is Wimsatt's position in the essay to which I have referred several times, and once more let me repeat also that this position, however mature and qualified, cannot finally make literature more than "Platonic," bearing its propositional thesis, any more than it can finally allow the dominion of God to be shared.

As we know from Augustine, the attractions of Manichaeism are disarming. For one struck by the ubiquity of evil it can be an assurance that he is not compromising with reality in order to appease an optimistic need for order, for cosmic meaning. A Christian as sensitive and mature as Wimsatt fights this temptation by distinguishing his view from the Pollyanna view that C. S. Lewis termed "Christianity-and-water" and by accepting the all-affirming grace only after a not quite total submission to the Manichaean face of reality (just as he is willing to have aesthetic reconciliation in literature only after a not quite total submission to contextual tension). . . .

It is, however, not really accurate to speak of the contextually poetic or of the existential as involving self-contradiction. Or rather it is not relevant. For in neither are we dealing with propositions. It has been suggested, for example, that new critics are inconsistent when they speak against the "heresy of paraphrase," that they actually are not against all paraphrases as being inadequate to the poem but are only against oversimplified paraphrases that do not take into account the nuances and the paradoxes. In this case all one has to do is to elaborate and extend the paraphrase in order to satisfy them and exhaust the poem of its meaning. But I believe one discovers as he elaborates upon the paraphrase that, after a certain point, the work begins to slip through his over-solicitous fingers and to sound like capricious, self-contradictory foolishness. For what is likely is that just as the confining terms of any "ethical" system—the universals of the "ethical" stage itself—are inadequate to the raging existential world, so the world of propositions is simply inappropriate to it, although, viewed from the standpoint of propositional procedures, this existential world and the poetic discourse that reflects it may well *seem* to be filled with contradiction. This world is not, then, a propositional world with all coherence gone. . . . It is rather an extra-propositional world, of another order, a pre- or post-propositional world—as you will—even if it seems to be contradictory when, using the only discourse at our disposal as critics, we try to talk logically about it, so that we come out with a confusing proliferation of would-be propositions. . . .

Yet for the literary work there is still the need for aesthetic wholeness. Literature may deal with the experientially full in avoiding the single, thin line of system; but to the extent that it remains art it must claim to have some kind of aesthetic system all its own, a system still, though so different from a philosophical system.

2. *W. K. Wimsatt.* This book is a twin "structure," or a "sequel," as Mr. Krieger says (page ix), to his earlier book *The New Apologists for Poetry* (1956). In the earlier book he was concerned to inquire whether an organistic and internally "contextual" criticism of poetry could really protect poetry from reference to and contamination by the outside world. And his answer was that it could not. Now, pushing his inquiry to a further level, which he calls "thematics," and which means in effect the confrontation of opposite principles, good and evil, order and disorder, in a poem, he is concerned to inquire whether the dramatizing poet (and by implication the analyzing critic) can actually do justice to the ubiquitous occurrence of evil in the "existential" world (the felt, given, or really experienced world) and at the same time confer upon the poem the saving grace of any reconciliation, any ultimate moral meaning or order—the cognitive counterpart of any catharsis. And Mr. Krieger's answer is, just as earnestly and emphatically as before, that the poet (and by implication the critic) cannot. To attempt any such harmony is a "platonic" resort to an unknown noumenal order, a fiat of miraculism. It is untrue to the "existential" absurdity of the world and hence invalidates the poem as a revelation of reality.

Mr. Krieger's argument here and there seems to recognize that this has not always been true—that in the old days there were poems which did assert and earn a moral order (e.g., page viii). The existential absurdity of which he is talking would on this recognition be a special truth of our own times, a product of the "crisis mentality" so precious to one kind of modern literary criticism. Near the outset he utters a modest disavowal: "For a work not to qualify as an example of the tragic vision is hardly a mark against it" (page 2). But far more often Mr. Krieger talks as if the existentialist truth of absurdity were the ultimate and only thing. Characteristically, he explains that many authors (presumably many of the older ones) have supposed that they were writing poems in support of this or that Platonism, but "fortunately the best of these have failed to be as exclusive as their more

201

committed and less aesthetic selves may have wanted" (page 260). (Milton, of course, was of the Devil's party without knowing it.) Just how far back he would push this—or how pervasively—to include Milton? Shakespeare? Dante? Virgil? Sophocles?—may not be quite clear.

Near the end of the book, by some very fine shaving of M. O. Percival's interpretation of *Moby Dick,* Mr. Krieger contrives a momentary or apparent saving grace in an argument that the poet *can* have his acquiescence in cosmic order (must have it in order to produce the ordered whole of his literary work) but can do this only in an "illusory," detached and reflective way, which Mr. Krieger here calls "aesthetic"—as distinguished from the deeper, more existentialist "thematic" way, which would involve the actual choice, commitment, action, "earned" vision of a major character. Ahab, the demonic Manichaean, is the existentialist force, or assertion, of the story. Ishmael, the reconciler, is passive, absorptive, reflective, a mere "perspective" projection of a narrator's uncommitted mind. But then Mr. Krieger, in a reverse flip, following a repeated pattern of his middle chapters, shows he can have it both ways. The blander vision is equally susceptible of being called the more inclusive, the uncommitted, the "Manichaean." The historically and technically Manichaean Ahab can be seen as actually the fanatic, the abstractor, the chooser—albeit negative and demonic. Mr. Krieger is just short of invoking the term "Platonic" here: see especially pages 258-60.

It is apropos of that juncture in the argument that I can perhaps most conveniently express my dissatisfaction with the term "thematic" as Mr. Krieger employs it. This term can fairly enough I think be used to refer to the *method* by which a critic seeks to get at or define the principles of opposition implicit in a work of literary art. But Mr. Krieger seems also to use it frequently to mean the actual immanence of such principles in the work itself. And this I think is not only pivotal to his whole way of reasoning, but highly misleading. It is a central mechanism in the constant slide back and forth from art work to critic which is a necessary part of his rationale. Thus Ahab's violently active demonism is called "thematic"— where it would be more usual in literary discussion to call it "dramatic" and hence "poetic" and hence "aesthetic" if one wished to move this far into the metaphysical. And on the other hand, Ishmael's more tolerant perspective on the world, which is mainly a kind of editorial reflection (as Mr. Krieger stresses), is called "aesthetic." And thus the usual values of "thematic" and "aesthetic" are reversed. Surely it is Ishmael here who is the "Platonist," and it is the "Platonic" values of the story which Mr. Krieger seizes and appropriates to his own cause in a paradoxical attempt to demonstrate that even in this example—so disastrous actually to his thesis—the Manichaean noncommitment does prevail.

Obviously we are caught here in a tricky sequence of reflexive, self-consuming distinctions. The critic, standing between the mirrors, is unable to count all the images of himself. Mr. Krieger's endlessly elaborative and qualificative style (which in this book takes on moments of wan brilliance, sad lyric grace—"Darkened so, yet shone the Archangel") is an admirable vehicle for traversing any given short stretch of the labyrinth which he inhabits. Within the span of a single page or paragraph he can be painstaking, fair, subtle, relentless, luminous. He is an extremely fair, a courteous and considerate, controversialist. The opening pages of his last chapter make as neat a capsule of the American organistic school of criticism and its ultimate difficulties as I have yet seen. Mr. Krieger is a master of the terms and the relations for constructing such a capsule. But he knows also that the difficulties arise not merely from the weakness of the criticism—that they are deeply inherent in the literary problem itself. And so Mr. Krieger will not be surprised if a "Platonist" (a Platonist who is thought capable of having corrupted one of the once stauncher Manichaeans among the new critics) should see over-all projections of the same difficulties in the Manichaean arrangements and, while admiring the argument in parts, should not believe that it makes a really consistent or viable whole.

In his opening chapter (page 19 especially) Mr. Krieger has set up the notion, stacked the cards to the effect, that "vision" means the "tragic" view of things, the recognition of stark absurdity in the universe. Vision is hence the opposite of ethical system, of moral commitment, and presumably of any ideas about physical or metaphysical order. The vision of absurdity is supposed to have in it something direct, felt and self-proving, and hence earned and honest. But ideas of order are miraculous, Platonic, unearned, probably dishonest. Here, to say the least, is an abeyance of ordinary verbal usage. In the classic account, the reconciliation at the end of tragedy is both structure *and* vision. "Vision" normally means a seeing of something, not of nothing.

One may wish to stop and argue a little with Mr. Krieger that it is impossible to formulate any "vision" of absurdity without its becoming to that extent a vision and hence an order. It is impossible for anybody to theorize in so ruthless a way against "Platonists" without becoming just as Platonic as they are. Maybe we shall have to distinguish between bright

Platonists and dark Platonists. But they will enjoy exactly the same footing with respect to the literary object. There is a question, not whether a poet (or his critic) has or has not committed himself to an idea, a "stance," but whether he has committed himself to this one or that one. Mr. Krieger himself is quite frank about his own stance (I mean in this book and for the end of writing this book). One must assume that the speaker in the book is one of those "sadder" people mentioned on page 21.

I acknowledge that, in support of this view of thematics, I must deny that the existential world—the world of felt human experience—can be anything less than a bewildering complex of seeming contradictions . . . how can any more systematic view of it . . . avoid, in its inadequacy, doing this world a grievous injustice? (page 242)

Formalized and doctrinal Manichaeism in a poet or a critic means, I take it, that he wishes evil to be fully and deliberately opposed to good and given a *just* chance against it. But now appears the joker in the Manichaean philosophy—no other than the figure of Ahab. Mr. Krieger seems to suppose that in Ahab, the Manichaean who matures into a Demonist, he is dealing only with a special, subversive instance of Manichaeism. But Melville's vision is more universal than that. The truth is that Ahab looks a good deal more like a type instance. For evil *is* strife, division, disorder. And the deliberate opposition of disorder to order *is* disorder. Demonism is not only the usual and plausible—it is the metaphysically entailed—upshot of Manichaeism. "The existential," as Mr. Krieger says, "takes its revenge by plunging the protagonist into the demonic" (page 262). Even "inaction" can serve "totally and fatally" as a "most committed form of action" (page 266). Mr. Krieger himself, sweetly and lucidly reasonable in each successive phase of his tortuous course, is perhaps as difficult to pursue as the white whale. But he is revealed in the denouement as the violent Ahab of his own book and universe. I would not put on the superior mask of seeming to say that Mr. Krieger himself does not know this.

In my desire to stress Mr. Krieger's ideas, I have delayed saying that the book has eight chapters. The first weaves themes of tragic opposition and irony from Hegel, Kierkegaard, and Nietzsche toward that equation of ethics with falsehood and of vision with chaos to which I have alluded. Chapters Two through Seven use this perspective to discuss novels of Gide, Lawrence, Malraux, Silone, Mann, Kafka, Camus, Conrad, Melville, and Dostoevsky. I am far from being evenly qualified to comment on these chapters, and I doubt that the proliferation of detailed counter-essays on so many special topics is desirable in a review. There is much brilliance and interest here which may well enough harmonize with the over-all philosophy, but which need not be conceived as demonstrating it. The eighth and last chapter proceeds from that gemlike synopsis of "Recent Criticism" which I have already praised to the perplexities of "Thematics" and the "Existentialist Dilemma" with which I have been mainly concerned.

3. *W. K. Wimsatt.* Let us ask ourselves a blunt question: Is a theory of literature as tension of opposites a theory of literary autonomy? or a didactic theory? A charter of literary freedom? or a directive of moral choice? Richards the psychologist with his tenderly balanced scepticisms and his norm of "sincerity," Eliot with his "demon of doubt which is inseparable from the spirit of belief," and the New Critics, with their repeated major premises of "interest," "drama," and "metaphor" advancing often enough to an emphasis on "inclusiveness" and "maturity," have tended at moments unhappily toward the didactic.

Murray Krieger, in his book entitled *The New Apologists for Poetry* (1956), asked some difficult questions about the "self-containment" of the poetic "context" and its relation to the world of reality. Krieger has always made a strenuous effort, and perhaps more successfully than anybody else, to sharpen the dilemmas of critical dialectic to a feather edge. In the final chapter of a later book *The Tragic Vision* (1960), he persists in his earlier line of inquiry, carrying it this time to the level of what he calls "thematics"—the philosophic commitments of poetry. And thus:

> It may, of course, seem at best silly and at worst heretically presumptuous for a critic to argue for an intolerable world view just to satisfy the needs of an aesthetic and a literary method. But . . . it is really a commonplace to say that every poet must, at least provisionally, be something of a Manichaean. This is but a way of our asking him not to stack the cards. . . . But if he does not more than this—if, that is, he submits his thesis to the hellfires of antithesis with no doubt of the issue and only to allow his thesis to be earned the hard way—he is in no more danger of heresy than is any profound version of Christianity that is willing to take into account all worldly imperfections without reducing the extent or the goodness of God's sway. . . . this position, however mature and qualified, cannot finally make literature more than "Platonic," bearing its propositional thesis.

This is making things about as difficult as they can be made for either a poet or a critic who wishes to retain, along with his aesthetic noncommitment, the feeling of a practical human being. And perhaps it will have to be conceded that within the pure literary perspective the claims of belief and action are difficult enough. But larger offstage questions do make a clamorous demand and will be heard from the wings. . . .

The Manichaean, the Dionysian, the Nietzschean note which creeps into so much criticism can be listened to much more thunderously (and perhaps more instructively) in certain chapters of Russian fiction.

> . . . you must go and deny, without denial there's no criticism and what would a journal be without a column of criticism. Without criticism it would be nothing but one "hosannah." But nothing but hosannah is not enough for life, the hosannah must be tried in the crucible of doubt. . . . I . . . simply ask for annihilation. No, live, I am told, for there'd be nothing without you. If everything in the universe were sensible, nothing would happen. . . . Suffering is life. Without suffering, what would be the pleasure of it? It would be transformed into an endless church service; it would be holy, but tedious.
>
> I know, of course, there's a secret in it, but they won't tell me the secret for anything, for then perhaps, seeing the meaning of it, I might bawl hosannah, and the indispensable minus would disappear at once, and good sense would reign supreme throughout the whole world. And that, of course, would mean the end of everything.

These words are spoken, of course, by the Devil—the alterego of Ivan Karamazov—the night before his brother's trial for murder, as Ivan lapses into a brain fever. Through pride, perversity, and ironic mistrust of self, he will sabotage his own testimony and thus bring about the notable "miscarriage of justice" which is the grotesque climax of that terrible story. . . .

Let us say that we recognize the fact of material concreteness in human experience, and though matter itself be not evil (as in the Persian scheme), yet it does seem the plausible enough ground for some kind of dualism, division, tension, and conflict, the clash of desires, and evil and pain. Spirit and matter, supernatural and natural, good and evil, these tend to line up as parallel oppositions. Even so rarefied and geometric a material concept as that of symmetry has its danger for the concept of beauty in unity. How *could* symmetry be part of the definition of beauty? Think, says Plotinus, what that doctrine leads us to: "Only a compound can be beautiful, never anything devoid of parts" (I. vi. 1). But parts and composition (and decomposition) seem to be inescapable in the human situation, and on the modern view, art, especially verbal art, confronts this fact. We say that art ought to have the concreteness of recognition and inclusion; it ought to have tension, balance, wholeness. Anybody can see that there could never be any drama or story, either comic or tragic, without evil. Nor for that matter (though this may not at first glance be so obvious) could there be any pastoral or idyllic retreat, any didactic or satiric warning, any lyric complaint—or any lyric rejoicing—so far are the springs of human rejoicing buried in the possibility, the threat, the memory of sorrow. About hallelujahs in Heaven we know next to nothing.

Of course, we will say that we don't call evil itself, or division, or conflict, desirable things. We only call facing up to them, facing up to the human predicament, a desirable and mature state of soul and the right model and course of a mature poetic art. And I think there is some comfort in this answer—though again, with a certain accent, it may sound somewhat like telling a boy at a baseball game that the *contest* is not really important but only his *noticing* that there is a contest. The great works and the fine works of literature seem to need evil—just as much as the cheap ones, the adventure or detective stories. Evil is welcomed and absorbed into the structure of the story, the rhythm of the song. The literary spirit flourishes in evil and could not get along without it. And so, unless I am mistaken, we face here some kind of problem concerning *The Marriage of Heaven and Hell*.

If we take the relatively cautious course of saying that in poetry there has to be an ironic balance of impulses, rather than clear Fourth of July choices and celebrations, it will sound, and I fear with some reason, to a moralist like Yvor Winters as if we entertained only wavering beliefs and purposes, no moral commitments. And if we talk more boldly about evil being "reconciled" in poetry, we are going to sound to a commentator on T. S. Eliot like Marshall McLuhan, and I fear with some show of reason on his side, as if we were propitiating evil, giving some dark earth spirit its rightful place in the scheme of things. Mr. McLuhan will call us, along with Eliot, a generation of Manichaean dualists, split personalities, pagans trying to stand on tiptoe. At this point no doubt Faulkner's *Fable* ought to be interrogated. It appears that a critic ought to inquire whether in Faulkner's *Fable* reconciling good and evil has not taken the form of making God Himself something capacious enough and something ambiguous enough to *include* both good and evil and to make atonement for his *own* evil—as in the last reveries of the humanist philosopher Paul Elmer More.

So far as I am pushing any thesis in this part of my essay, I am trying to suggest that the inveterate desire of the literary theorist for some kind of substance, as opposed to either Platonic idea or Platonic semblance, is closely tied to, and may even be a cover for, a deeper desire that literary art should embrace something which we cannot very well imagine human substance as being free from, the fact of evil, both as suffering and as destruction. This kind of embrace may very well be a thing that is more necessary to verbal art than to any other. I think there may well be certain truly Platonic forms of fine art—notably drawing and carving, arts which Plato himself was apparently concerned to purify in the geometric direction. But verbal art can scarcely be interesting in that way.

And I have been touching on the idea that if verbal art has to take up the mixed matter of good and evil, its most likely way of success, and its peculiar way, is a mixed way. And that means not simply a complicated correspondence, a method of alternation, now sad, now happy, but the oblique glance, the vertical unification of the metaphoric smile. To pursue the ironic and tensional theories in the way most likely to avoid the Manichaean heresy will require a certain caution in the use of the solemn and tragic emphasis. Dark feelings, painful feelings, dismal feelings, even tender feelings move readily toward the worship of evil. . . .

The question which the technical moralist or the poetic theorist with a moral and theological concern (Murray Krieger or his orthodox opposite, for instance) seems most likely to keep asking will run about as follows: Just how is it possible for the poet to give ample and fair play, not only to faith and control, but to the contagious opposites which prove and intensify those virtues—how possible, that is, without either adulterating a pure philosophy about these matters or creating at least moments of imagery which are a yielding and a seduction? The Knight of Temperance in the second book of Spenser's *Faerie Queene* breaks up the bower of the enchantress Acrasia, but the feat requires his first getting safely past a few stanzas of very superior pinup girl art. The requirement, moreover, is hardly accidental to the poetic needs of the passage. If these stanzas were not at least potentially seductive, it may well be questioned if they would constitute the necessary poetic features at that place in the plot. This example is conveniently allegorized for us by the poet himself into something like a type of what we are talking about. Much more natural and exciting examples might easily be multiplied. It may be said, with as much certitude as anything about literature can be said, that the poet does not write even a moderately good poem about sheer control or about sheer indifference—any more than about sheer sensate experience. . . .

Not that the poet can deliberately or professedly move toward conflict itself as a goal. This is as much a self-defeat as any other direct move on a poetic goal. But the man speaking in the poem will move, toward whatever his goal is, honestly, with a sense of the obstructions and drags, the limitations, in a word, the wholeness of the experience. Poetry is not a direct mimesis of any pure kind of human value, either positive or negative. Rather, the literal drama of the mixed human experience is a kind of intensity and depth which is the opportunity for the poetic reality, the poetic objectification. . . .

But to present the argument of the critic in its necessary and I believe correctly guarded form: He will say that the human condition is intrinsically a material and mixed condition, where faith and love of God and fellow man can scarcely occur except in a milieu that is full of the possibility of their opposites. And this possibility, however it is minimized and pushed to one side by the discipline of the saint, the austerity of the cell, the devotion of the ritual (or the laws of the party), is still a tensional element that is part of the moral quality of the experience. Religious philosophy recognizes this fact clearly enough in its account of faith as an act of the intellect, but directed by the will.

4. *W. K. Wimsatt.* One of the attempts at a standard of poetic value most often reiterated in past ages has been the doctrinal—the explicitly didactic. The aim of poetry, says the ancient Roman poet, is double, both to give pleasure and to teach some useful doctrine. You might get by with only one or the other, but it is much sounder to do both. Or, the aim of poetry is to teach some doctrine—and to do this convincingly and persuasively, by *means* of vividness and pleasure—as in effect the Elizabethan courtier and the eighteenth-century essayist would say. But in what does the pleasure consist? Why is the discourse pleasurable? Well, the aim of poetry is really to please us by means of or through the act of teaching us. The pleasure is a dramatized *moral* pleasure. Thus in effect some theories of drama in France during the seventeenth century. Or, the pleasure of poetry is a pleasure simply of tender and morally good feelings. Thus in effect the philosophers of the age of reason in England and France. And at length the date 1790 and Immanuel Kant's *Critique of Judgment:* which asserts that the end or effect of art is not teaching certainly, and not pleasure in anything like a simple sensuous way—rather it is something apart, a feeling, but precisely its own kind of feeling, the aesthetic. Art is autonomous—though related symbolically to the realm of moral values. Speaking from this non-didactic point of view, a critic ought to say, I should think, that the aesthetic merit of Blake's *London* does not come about because of the fact that London in that age witnessed evils which cried to Heaven for remedy, or because Blake was a

THE PLACE OF CRITICISM

Prophet Against Empire, or a Visionary Politician, or because at some time, perhaps a few years after he had written the poem, he may have come to view it as one article or moment in the development of an esoteric philosophy of imagination, a Fearful Symmetry of Vision, expanded gradually in allegorical glimpses during several phases of his life, into a quasi-religious revelation or privilege which in some sense, at moments, he believed in. Blake's *London* is an achievement in words, a contained expression, a victory which resulted from some hours, or days, of artistic struggle, recorded by his pen on a page of the Rossetti manuscript.

Between the time of Immanuel Kant, however, and our own, some complications in the purity of the aesthetic view have developed. Through the romantic period and after, the poetic mind advanced pretty steadily in its own autonomous way, toward a claim to be in itself the creator of higher values—to be perhaps the only creator. Today there is nothing that the literary theorist—at least in the British and American-speaking world—will be more eager to repudiate than any hint of moral or religious didacticism, any least intimation that the poem is to measure its meaning or get its sanction from any kind of authority more abstract or more overtly legislative than itself. But on the other hand there has probably never been a generation of teachers of literature less willing to admit any lack of high seriousness, of implicit and embodied ethical content, even of normative vision in the object of their study. Despite our reiterated denials of didacticism, we live in an age, we help to make an age, of momentous claims for poetry—claims the most momentous conceivable, as they advance more and more under the sanction of an absolutely creative and autonomous visionary imagination. The Visionary imagination perforce repudiates all but the tautological commitment to itself. And thus, especially when it assumes (as now it begins to do) the form of what is called the "Tragic Vision" (not "The Vision of Tragedy"), it is the newest version of the *Everlasting No*. Vision *per se* is the vision of itself. "Tragic Vision" is the nearly identical vision of "Absurdity." (War-weariness and war-horror, the developing mind and studies of a generation that came out of the Second War and has been living in expectation of the third may go far to explain the phenomenon, but will not justify it.) Anti-doctrine is of course no less a didactic energy than doctrine itself. It is the reverse of doctrine. No more than doctrine itself, can it be located or even approached by a discussion of the relation between poetic form and poetic meaning. Anti-doctrine is actually asserted by the poems of several English romantic poets, and notably, it would appear, though it is difficult to be sure, by the "prophecies" of William Blake. The idea of it may be hence a part of these poems, though never their achieved result or expression. Any more than an acceptable statement of Christian doctrine is Milton's achieved expression in *Paradise Lost,* or a statement of Aristotelian ethics is the real business of Spenser's *Faerie Queene*. Today I believe no prizes are being given for even the best doctrinal interpretation of poems. (The homiletic or parabolic interpretation of Shakespeare, for example, has hard going with the reviewer.) On the other hand, if you are willing to take a part in the exploitation of the neuroses, the misgivings, the anxieties, the infidelities of the age—if you have talents for the attitudes of Titanism, the graces needed by an impresario of the nuptials of Heaven and Hell, you are likely to find yourself in some sense rewarded. It is obvious I hope that I myself do not believe the reward will consist in the achievement of a valid account of the relation between poetic form and poetic meaning.

5. *Hyatt H. Waggoner.* I have just two points to make in criticism of William Wimsatt's lecture. . . . *Explication,* as Mr. Wimsatt defines and exemplifies it here, is not enough. It is fine, it is needed, I wish it were always done as well as he does it. . . . In section eight Mr. Wimsatt adds to it somewhat gingerly, *appreciation,* but this is not really adding to it, it is changing the subject. What is needed at this point is an enlarged conception of explication itself. What is needed is a recognition—or a much fuller recognition than I find in the lecture—that a poem is just a part of the total body of poems the poet wrote. This body of work is the most immediate and essential part of the context in which the poem exists and from which it gets a part of its meaning. . . .

For my second point, only this: I find myself wishing Mr. Wimsatt had written either much more or much less in his last paragraph. Treating the area where criticism becomes philosophy and theology, he has time here only to hint and suggest, where openness and explicitness are essential if discussion is not to be shut off. *The Tragic Vision,* for example, is a fine book, even if its author does think that life's ambiguities cannot be resolved. (The tone of the lecture makes me uneasy at this point). Kierkegaardian existentialists and Catholic essentialists must part company somewhere, to be sure, but both can, and do, write good criticism. Fortunately, good practical criticism does not require a correct metaphysic, though it always ultimately implies some sort of metaphysic. Anti-doctrine turns out, Mr. Wimsatt says, to be itself a doctrine. Precisely. But as critics we must guard the rights of this "doctrine" just as we guard those of the doctrines it rejects. Instead of rejecting this late version of the New Criticism at this point for having formed an unholy alliance, I should prefer to see criticism opened up earlier, at the stage of method, as I suggested in my first point.

6. *W. K. Wimsatt.* In reply to Mr. Waggoner's . . . dissatisfaction, concerning my summary treatment, in a closing paragraph, of the new "tragic vision," I will plead only that my review of Mr. Krieger's book can be found elsewhere, and that in another essay, now two or three years old, under the perhaps too cryptic title "Horses of Wrath," I have touched the same theme. To be consistent with my argument above, I ought to admit that this plea does not relate to my present essay as a composition. I am saying only that my mind can be found a little more fully in other places. There I give a few more reasons why "anti-doctrine," though it does itself have a kind of shadow status as doctrine, should enjoy no privileges and is entitled to no guardianship. Doctrines are entitled to respect and protection not simply for being doctrines, but for *what* they say. They are entitled on general principle to tolerance—but this refers not to the doctrine itself but to the author. I am not advocating any kind of censorship.

7. *Robert B. Heilman.* What precedes has to do in some way with Mr. Wimsatt's last topic, "appreciation." I might paraphrase his "Only poems which are worth something modify awareness." What is appreciable, what has assignable value, alters consciousness; i.e., quality qualifies. In his words and mine there may be a touch of question-begging or circularity. Does not Mr. Wimsatt distantly acknowledge this by not stopping at section VIII and by adding section IX on two "attempts at a standard of poetic value," the pre-romantic doctrinal and the post-romantic anti-doctrinal? He is saying, if I read him correctly, that you can't throw out the former without throwing out the latter too, for both are didactic and lead to a sidetracking of art. There is an alternative possibility, and it may be, indeed, that Mr. Wimsatt would not foreclose it: that there are doctrines and doctrines, and that some may be transmuted into more spacious art than others. The trouble is with *doctrine,* of course, which is a view of reality in its instructional aspect; a dream trimmed into bylaws; the vatic tidied up for tutoring. We would do better to stick to "view of reality" and propose that the wider and deeper it is, the more it *can*—given a mediating artist with enough tools—the more it can elicit a plenitude of the "artifices" that constitute art and, through these,

modify consciousness. It would then follow that if we simply shared in the "exploitation of neuroses" and in the "attitudes of Titanism" we would be too little "rewarded," that is, would be deprived of too much of reality and would hence be confirmed in the restricted awareness of the age.

8. *W. K. Wimsatt.* In [Mr. Heilman's] closing paragraph he rightly surmises that my brief exposure of anti-doctrine as itself a masquerade for a kind of doctrine would not for me preclude a recognition that some doctrines, or views of reality, are more spacious than others and will inform more plenary and sounder poems, which work more important "modifications" of "consciousness." This, it will be intimated by the new visionaries, is a stage in the dialectic which was reached by Eliot in his essays of the 1920's and is hence no longer available to me. But I revert to its truth, and I repeat that anti-doctrine not only makes false pretenses to not being doctrine but that it is enabled to do this because in its actuality as doctrine it is indeed small and miserable.

9. *Murray Krieger.* It may be inappropriate to convert this occasion to a personal one. However, in view of Mr. Wimsatt's open and uneasy concern for my notion of the "tragic vision" in his concluding pronouncement, I cannot resist making my comments somewhat personal, but only because I believe that doing so will serve to illuminate the issues as no other tactic would.

In limiting these few remarks to Mr. Wimsatt's final paragraph I am being woefully neglectful of his lucid enumeration and analysis of the steps to literary understanding. With this description of what we can say about poems (and when and why and on what grounds) I can only utter my admiring agreement; and his demonstrations call forth only my wonder and my envy. So I restrict myself to the far-reaching claims with which he closes since here, as Mr. Wimsatt makes clear, there is significant difference between us. That these claims are important to him is indicated by the fact that, in his radical abbreviation of this paper for *College English* (February, 1963), the lengthy final paragraph appeared intact. Nevertheless, this paragraph tries to say so much for its size that it has telescoped its full import in a way that may make it seem cryptic to some readers. Fortunately Mr. Wimsatt has addressed himself to these issues elsewhere. I am indeed pleased that on this occasion he has seen fit once more to lay bare those differences between us about which, for some years now, we have most respectfully agreed to disagree—after having first agreed about the long path we travel in harmony. These differences have seemed inescapable to us both, and we have both hoped that airing them would clear the critical atmosphere as we try to force it to accommodate new-critical analysis within the larger human concerns that relate poetry's meaning to philosophy's meaning and history's.

The issue between us revolves about the relation of "doctrine" or "anti-doctrine" to poetry. If we see—as Mr. Wimsatt so persuasively leads us to see in his "explication"—the meanings evolving within the fully empowered poetic context, if we see these meanings as comprehensible only as the aesthetic system creates them out of the workings of its internal relations, then how can we reduce this unique body of intra-systematic meaning to any transcendent propositional meaning (or "doctrine") when the latter can be found behind a variety of language constellations? Clearly we cannot do so without surrendering its uniqueness. And the critic who does we call a "Platonist."[1] For if the critic finally sees the total meaning of the poem to be a version of the doctrinal (and translatable) statement—no matter how densely qualified with experiential contingency this version may be—then, for all his effective "explication," he has kept the form and meaning of the poem from fusing: he has kept the poem from becoming its own system of discourse, from taking on its own life. And this even when—as with Mr. Wimsatt's breathless demonstration from Blake—the persistent brilliance of the critic's perceptiveness forces us to see that nothing less than the boldest, most ambitious claims dare be made for the "artifice" that becomes "art." But we remain still, where Mr. Wimsatt wants us to be, with the Roman critic and his *dulce* and *utile:* and this is but another way of putting the older Greek's view. But how can the critic avoid Platonism? How can he have organicism—that is, how can he have the poem take on a unique, contextual meaning—without accepting the consequences?

The consequences seem subversive, however, in that they seem to lead to "anti-doctrine." And, as Mr. Wimsatt wisely and shrewdly insists, such

---

[1] Of course *Platonism* has become a rather confusing term, for critics from John Crowe Ransom to the neo-Aristotelians have been using it in so many ways these last years that the only point their various uses have in common for certain is that this is a term to be used for castigating one's opponents. And then invariably someone has come along to insist the namecaller, in the very act of namecalling, shows himself to be a Platonist. But there is a common sense about Wimsatt's and my use of *Platonism:* it is what characterizes the claims of the defender of doctrine in poetry, as Wimsatt presents him here. And, as he knows I must, I attack this Platonism and this defense of doctrine as destructive of the special powers of poetry—even if I must, and with good reason, be called down for a Platonism of my own.

anti-doctrine is itself a doctrine. If we measure the work's uniqueness as discourse by its resistance to being absorbed by any single doctrinal claim, then we are at least suggesting that the full literary "truth" can deny nothing except the truth of any doctrine, that it insists we see such doctrine as too simple, too experientially thin. And this is to threaten the very possibility of a rational conception of our world, to invite the chaos that Mr. Wimsatt sees as regrettably Manichaean, the product of the Titanism that leads to Satanism. Of course, even if the contextual view of poetry were to lead to all this, it should be clear that it is not the universe itself which is being denied a rational structure, but only that distorted version (or vision) of the universe which, at our experiential level, it is given us to see and exist in. That is, poetry would speak to us phenomenologically, not metaphysically.

Nevertheless we must persist in asking whether the *fully* organic and contextual method (and how can such a method be partial?) necessarily leads to the philosophic irrationalism that causes Mr. Wimsatt, like Plato, to worry about the subversion by the poet of man's rational capacities and responsibilities. If the poem really spoke in this way, it would indeed be anti-doctrinal in a doctrinal way, which would characterize it as an inversion of Platonism, but as a Platonism still. But is it the poem or merely the critic who speaks this way? In the contextual view, the poem can no more *say* anti-doctrine unequivocally than it can *say* anything else. Through its very *being* the poem may provoke the enraptured critic to believe that it is saying this, but its *meaning* cannot be reduced to it. The critic who carries the anti-doctrinal vision out of the poem as a doctrine to be imposed upon the world is indeed a Platonist, though an inverted one. But this is the critic, not the poem. And the critic is so victimized by the poem and by himself because it is the critic's role to be victimized. That is, he is required to use the propositional dialect—the Platonic language of doctrine and anti-doctrine that non-poets and lesser poets must settle for—as he tries to capture for the rest of us the unique language-system whose inexhaustible powers depend on its power to elude the Platonic grasp. The anti-doctrinal critic, then, is the Platonist who tries vainly but faithfully to speak the pre-Platonic language of poetry. It is the fable of Orillo all over again, in Robert Penn Warren's improved version, as he tried some time ago to remind us that, finally, the critic must fail and must want to fail.[2] The terms of the anti-doctrinal critic may make the poem sound like the perverse

---

[2] In the opening two paragraphs of his well-known essay "Pure and Impure Poetry" (1943), quoted above (see pp. 12–13).

denial of philosophic truth which is itself philosophic in its range and claims (or anti-claims). He is, it is true, not a non-Platonist or non-doctrinalist but a propounder of an alternative Platonism or doctrine to Mr. Wimsatt's. I may admit to believing that the anti-doctrinal critic's vision is closer to, or less inconsistent with, the vision of poetry than is that of the more positive Platonism; but since the anti-doctrinal critic also must distort the achieved vision which the poem creates as its own form, this belief does not alter the methodological issue. For there is not, *above* or *behind* the poem, *any* "vision" which is "autonomous," as Mr. Wimsatt puts it, or which any critic, aware of his role and its limitations, would claim to be so. There is only the vision which the poem struggles in its manifold ways to create by creating itself as poem. By doing this it does, in a sense, make itself and its vision autonomous—and inaccessible to all critical languages though so accessible to the critic's experience as to make him put *his* language to the trial.

The visions of modern man may be dark, but even the darkest vision, if it is to be transformed into material for art, must—like Ahab by Ishmael—be controlled and given form by being created within an aesthetic object. Thus the order of art answers the chaos that challenges it. So the visions outside the poem—in the poet or in the audience of his critics—are not the vision of the poem, and existentialist critics must know this as well as non-existentialist critics. Mr. Wimsatt would not, I have reason to be sure, accuse me of not knowing it. If, as Mr. Wimsatt suggests and as he knows I agree, none of us can hope for the reward of achieving "a valid account of the relation between poetic form and poetic meaning" as these create the vision of the poem, we can hope, through experiencing this relation, to approach the vision and try to pass it on. The awareness that, despite the extent of our failure, we can sometimes know we are nearer rather than farther must be reward enough.

10. *W. K. Wimsatt.* Mr. Krieger's careful and informative polemic would have made unnecessary or inappropriate one or two of the things I have already said. But it has reached me last, after my response to the others has been written and sent.

In his present emphasis on the critic's inability to reduce the poem to his formulas, or absorb it into them, perhaps Mr. Krieger does something to show that the difference between us is not so wide as might be supposed. The opposite idea, or the too-zealous attempt to restate the poem, was known to the "new" critics as the "heresy of paraphrase." And I too said: ". . . the technique of the lemon-squeezer is not . . . an ideal pedagogic procedure. It is not even a possibility." The critic, if one likes, must fail, and he must want to fail—or at least he must be content to fail. A difference between Mr. Krieger and myself, however, is that when he says things like this, he means that the critic's utterance is a mere faltering trial, something lame and impotent. And in this it is but the honest counterpart of the poet's own honest refusal to assert anything. (Mr. Krieger's present last paragraph makes, I believe, considerably greater claims for a "vision" worth "passing on" than are really permitted by the rest of the argument or by the book.) On the other hand, my own view is that the critic though he surely cannot render the whole poem, or re-enact its life, in his abstractions, still can make, and must try to make, central, significant, and accurate statements about the poem. He can say accurate things about the poem which preclude other and contradictory things from being said. And within such limits he *can* give "a valid account of the relation between poetic form and poetic meaning." (To say with Aristotle that the son of Diares is a man is not to exhaust the substantive life of the man, but it is to make the important denial that he is an octopus—or a god.) Thus I have asserted, and will reassert, that Blake's *London* does not herald a social revolution to be accomplished by the weapon of venereal disease. I am not sure that Mr. Krieger's critic as critic could assert this—though doubtless as a man he might believe it, for both the words of the poem and the world of human reality supply good reasons. (Clearly, on the other hand, he could not defend the opposite—the battle-cry. Here let Mr. Krieger and Mr. Bateson confront each other.)

Mr. Krieger wants to insist on a complex cluster of distinctions: between the poem and the critique, between the critic as critic and the critic as practical man, between the world of ordered reality (unknown) and the apparent world of chaos, between any world at all prior to or outside the poem and any world inside it. I do not think, however, that here, any more than in his book, he really keeps these ideas apart sufficiently to save appearances. What he seems to want to say is that a man as a man can believe in some unknown order of reality, but that he cannot really and honestly see any such order, and that neither as poet nor as critic ought he to speak as if he did. As poets are supposed to be the most honest and accurate-speaking of all men, the implications of this doctrine must be plain. I believe it is not possible to face these implications, and yet to continue to theorize as Mr. Krieger does, without involving oneself in contradictions. And thus the wavering between poem and critic and between sheer poetic vision and responsible life-views which I noticed in the book. And thus in Mr. Krieger's present dialectic of fact and value a delicately shaded creep which produces within two pages: (1) "... it is not the universe itself which is being denied a rational structure, but only that distorted version (or vision) of the universe which, at our experiential level, it is given us to see and exist in. That is, poetry would speak to us phenomenologically, not metaphysically." (2) "The visions of modern man may be dark, but even the darkest vision, if it is to be transformed into material for art, must ... be controlled and given form by being created within an aesthetic object. Thus the order of art answers the chaos which challenges it."

The basic truth of the human predicament which Mr. Krieger illustrates is that seeing and affirming are indeed beset with difficulties, but that in the choice between seeing something (no matter how incompletely and obscurely) and seeing nothing, there is only one way that permits a consistent discourse. A man can affirm his faculty of knowing and talk consistently. He cannot deny it and do so. And to say that all that he really knows is an "experimental" or immediately sensed and "existed-in" disorder *is* to deny that he really knows anything.

Think of poetry, dear B———, think of poetry, and then think of—Dr. Samuel Johnson! Think of all that is airy and fairy-like, and then of all that is hideous and unwieldy; think of his huge bulk, the Elephant! and then—and then think of the Tempest—the Midsummer Night's Dream—Prospero—Oberon—and Titania!

(Poe, "Letter to B———")[1]

---

[1] I am indebted to Frank Lentricchia of the Department of English, University of California at Los Angeles, who pointed this quotation out to me after becoming acquainted with the essay that follows. Thus only while this volume was being readied for the printer did I become aware of a passage whose polemical relevance might well have inspired my title and my approach to Northrop Frye had I come upon it earlier. Can Poe on Johnson fail to remind us of Frye's model, Blake, on Johnson's colleague, Reynolds?

15
Northrop Frye and Contemporary Criticism: Ariel and the Spirit of Gravity

 The three essays which follow were originally conceived and written independently of one another, and within only a most general format.[2] They could be expected only coincidentally to make up a total consideration of their subject. Consequently, it seemed to me that I might best introduce and organize them by creating a context for them: by commenting both on the theoretical situation upon which that extraordinary volume, the *Anatomy of Criticism*, made its extraordinary impact and on the aftermath of that impact.

Whatever the attitude toward Northrop Frye's prodigious schemes, one cannot doubt that, in what approaches a decade since the publication of his masterwork, he has had an influence—indeed an absolute hold—on a generation of developing literary critics greater and more exclusive than that of any one theorist in recent critical history. One thinks of other movements that have held sway, but these seem not to have depended so completely on a single critic—nay, on a single work—as has the criticism in the work of Frye and his *Anatomy*. For example, pervasive as was T. S. Eliot's influence, it joined almost at once and indistinguishably with that of a number of followers who tried to systematize the master's casual essays drawn together from here and there. But with Frye, there is no difficulty disengaging master from disciple, nor even Frye's own later and lesser works from the masterwork. His followers and his ensuing works produce in the main simplifications and extensions of—even footnotes to—the *Anatomy*, the Word propagated and translated, thinned in order to be spread.

[2] In *Northrop Frye in Modern Criticism: Selected Papers from the English Institute,* ed. Murray Krieger (Columbia, 1966). Mine is the introductory essay to that volume. The three essays here mentioned are referred to later as the work of Angus Fletcher, W. K. Wimsatt, and Geoffrey H. Hartman.

The Place of Criticism

The unequalled sweep with which the *Anatomy* has gathered to itself our theoretical imaginations is largely due to the unequalled sweep with which it claims to embrace our entire conceptual world. Frye's incomparable power among many of us may well be traced, as Geoffrey Hartman suggests, to his universalism, his system-making daring, his unmitigated theoretical ambition, his unlimited reach—even where some would say it has exceeded his grasp. His power may be traced also, as Angus Fletcher and Hartman both suggest, to his revitalizing the flow of a romantic sensibility and vision that the critical tradition after Eliot, with the austerity of its would-be classicism, had too long congealed. Fletcher well reminds us that Frye terms himself an *Odyssey* rather than an *Iliad* critic, and Hartman credits him with the recovery of romance for us all as well as with the recovery of the romantic arrogance that strives for the universal completeness of a man-centered, man-created *logos*. There is a satisfying lack of inhibition in the cosmic pretension with which Frye permits the imagination to chart the galaxies dreamed of by human desires. And this pretension, in its very recklessness, has seized the imagination of the rest of us, long inhibited by the unyielding finitude flung upon us like a blanket by the critical tradition of T. E. Hulme and Eliot. The audacity of Frye's mythophilia is an alternative appealing through the very assertion of its autonomy. Responsible only to itself and, thus, to our dreams of wish-fulfillment, the free-ranging mythic universe shifts its galaxies at will to answer every need. It freely rotates in patterns beyond the fixed sublunary purposes of our pedestrian interests which require the universe to stand still. As pedestrians, we persist in hunting for equations, echoes, parallels, or just analogues among Frye's schematic groupings; and we do find some—or *almost* do, but not quite. Shifts in axis give each of his constellations a different center. Together they elude our two-dimensional spatial need to systematize and thus assimilate them.

Such diagrammatic attempts to freeze the dynamic fluidity of Frye's categories account for the simplifications and reductions that Frye's followers and opponents have worked on the original grand mythic scheme in order to make it hold still either to be applied or to be attacked. And his followers have been at least as guilty as his opponents. Indeed on occasion his own more popularly directed essays have as seriously sacrificed the earlier shifting fullness of his entire scheme. It is true, of course, that critics who tried to take Frye whole could not then put him to their uses; they could only apprehend him aesthetically as having the unusable completeness of a poetic entity. So it must for the most part be said that we have not been responding to the totality of his modes in their own deceptive movements so much as we have been, as followers, adapting his work or, as antagonists, disposing of it for our own more parochial purposes. However we have been using him by putting him to *our* tests, we have not paused sufficiently to accommodate ourselves to him or him to the total march of critical theory. Few except the most faithful (and these therefore too uncritically) have selflessly tried to uncover the source of his power, together with the cost—the expense in theoretical soundness—which that power exacts. We must attempt that critical search, however, with a daring that matches his daring if not, alas, with a wit that matches his wit.

The educational concerns of Frye and the educational possibilities of his work have been largely responsible for the reduction of certain isolated aspects of his theories into fixed and simplified programs. His large-scale categorizing, the tendency to outline, the invention of a nomenclature—all have misled the pseudo-scientific among his followers into making of him a framework for teaching and for literary study. Programmatic applications have begun to appear in places like *College English* and in textbooks, and we can expect more of them. Frye's admitted propensity to spatialize literature has led others to spatialize him, to flatten him into the firmness of diagram. But often there is too little awareness that his space can be Einsteinian, its relations defiant of the two-dimensional page, its categories as slippery as time itself. Frye is far more difficult and deceptive than others have often made him or than he has often made himself in writings after the *Anatomy*. Too frequently, then, the swirling galaxies of Frye's autonomous universe have been fixed in a single position, as by geocentric man, in accordance with the terra firma commanded by pedagogic interests. And what made that universe so uniquely provocative—its elusive, free-swinging character—is lost.

The sublunary concerns of rival theorists have led them to be similarly partial. Without his dedication to an autonomous projection of a universal schematics,[3] his antagonists have had to reduce him to the traditional terms

---

[3] Originally I thought of using *systematics* instead of *schematics* here. But, as Frye points out in his respondent essay to this volume (which I took the editor's privilege of reading before my remarks went to press), his categories and modes might better be thought of as schematic than as systematic creations. The word *system*, used effectively by Hartman at the start of his essay, suggests too regular and philosophically consistent a structure for the bold, imaginative, often system-defying structures of a poet-theorist like Frye.

that have guided the history of more modest critical theory.[4] The essay by W. K. Wimsatt amply and effectively demonstrates the several varieties I shall enumerate of the traditional theorists' impatience with Frye. With their traditional theoretical criteria, they have manifested their distrust of what they see as his too great trust in an eccentric and arbitrary pseudo-*logos*. There has been the general complaint that Frye's shifting categories produce not the brilliant dynamics of dialectic but the sloppiness of inconsistency; but the complaint is accompanied by admiring bafflement at his sleight-of-hand, at the way he evades the reductive and spatial impulse that wants to "place" him. More specifically, there has, first, been the complaint that he neglects, and at times flatly denies, the critic's task of evaluation; but the complaint is often accompanied by the acknowledgment that he sometimes speaks effectively about taste and judgment. There has, secondly, been the complaint that, in centering upon the *literary* relations of literature, he irrevocably separates literature from its relation to life, from its mimetic responsibility; but the complaint is often accompanied by the admission that he, sometimes uneasily, wants it tied to life, even in the name of *mimesis*. It has thus been charged that, while he emphasizes now one and now the other of these desirable opposites, he cannot fuse them systematically, that he has not shown how, "the actual being only a part of the possible," "literature . . . neither *reflects* nor *escapes* from ordinary life."[5] There has, thirdly, been the complaint that Frye's archetypal interests cheat the individual work of its uniqueness by seeing it only as another translation of the universal story, but this complaint should be accompanied by an awareness that Frye does attend to detailed meaning-functions in the more minute levels or "phases" which he attributes to the many-leveled literary symbol. Or, to move in the other direction, we should remember that the archetypal gives way to the all-involving anagogic phase which carries in itself the potential identity of every part of man's myth, both before and in the individual work: the microcosm become macrocosm, but—as always in the

---

[4] My own earlier treatment of Frye (*A Window to Criticism: Shakespeare's Sonnets and Modern Poetics* [Princeton, 1964], pp. 42–49, 207n) is representative of this partial view of Frye's multiple schemes, a view that limits him to what one's own limited position would make of him. I am not confessing to being wrong so much as to treating him only insofar as this treatment was relevant to the fixed concerns of the modern critical tradition. Since his is a revolution against this tradition, both in substance and in attitude, against its conception of the very nature of critical discourse, my terms could not be meant to be relevant to *his* totality.

[5] Northrop Frye, *The Well-Tempered Critic* (Indiana, 1963), p. 155 [my italics].

circular pattern—only as the converse is also true. The movement from literal to archetype and from archetype to anagoge, as it swirls, deprives us of these complaints. Still it allows us, in our sublunary language, to complain now about what we insist on terming inconsistency, discursive irresponsibility, even if our Blakean poet-critic claims, in his lunar dialectic, to soar beyond our downward pull. For example, we find Wimsatt condemning Frye on the one hand for being too Chicagoan in his multiplication of differentiated categories, on the other hand for being too Platonic in his archetypal universals that blur all distinctions and all particulars, and, beyond both, for allowing the two jarring inadequacies to become inconsistencies as well. But what we learn we are learning about Wimsatt and the habits of the traditional theoretical intelligence as well as about the will-o'-the-wisp imagination of the poet as theorist or theorist as poet.

To reckon honestly and totally with Frye, then, to uncover the source and the cost of his power, we must for the occasion soar with him to his lunar universe with its modes that change their faces and shift their places in accordance with a reckless dialectic of dream that shades every point we focus upon and slides across our sober, sublunary, daytime complaints. It is precisely the opposition of the lunar to the sublunary that characterizes Frye's flight from the dominant critical tradition—from Hulme through Eliot to the New Critics—that preceded the fervent revolution he perpetrated. His departure accounts for the true basis of their resistance to him and his sway. About no claim are those I once termed "the new apologists for poetry" more constant or even dogged than the claim that poetry should reveal, and should be limited by, our worldly experience: what Dr. Johnson called "the real state of sublunary nature," product of what Keats called "the dull brain [that] perplexes and retards." These theorists speak as with one voice for the true poet's capacity to respect the drag of material reality, to convert the handicaps of a finite existence and a finite language into victories of an imagination that never forgets or rejects its basis in common experience.

Their early spokesman, Hulme, may have been their most intemperate in his attack on romanticism by way of his defense of classicism:

> What I mean by classical in verse, then, is this. That even in the most imaginative flights there is always a holding back, a reservation. The classical poet never forgets this finiteness, this limit of man. He remembers always that he is mixed up with earth. He may jump, but he always returns back; he never flies away into the circumambient gas.
>
> You might say if you wished that the whole of the romantic attitude seems

to crystallise in verse round metaphors of flight. Hugo is always flying, flying over abysses, flying up into the eternal gases. The word infinite in every other line.[6]

We can see his nearly violent scorn translate what I have been calling Frye's lunar universe of swirling galaxies into "circumambient gas." But in Hulme's extreme statement we can see the basis for the theoretical antagonism to Frye's romantic creativity—a classicist might call it romantic escapism—by the critical tradition he has pretty well supplanted. The antagonism can be traced to the unromantic doctrine of the fall of man which leads the Hulmean to call for earthbound man to recognize and even celebrate his limitations and to avoid the humanist's arrogance that, denying the Fall, disdains the earth for the arbitrary heavens of his own creation. (Clearly in this essay and in the one with which I conclude my volume, I am trying to account for two opposed concepts of the literary imagination: one that relates it to the limiting world in which it finds itself and another that relates it to the unlimited world it would create for itself—thus the downward spirit of gravity that binds and the upward spirit of Ariel that loosens.)

One after another of the New Apologists pays tribute to the poet's capacity to dedicate himself to his material finitude. We can recall that John Crowe Ransom related the unique power of poetry to the rich contingency of the world's body in its earthy density. Poetry for Ransom shows its power by devoting itself to—not evading—the furniture of our world, its dull, burdensome obstacles to our will to flight. We can project what would be his opposition to Frye from his early attack on "Platonic poetry," where he joins the battle for *Dinglichkeit* against a disembodied utopia. Or Allen Tate makes his doctrine of "tension" begin at its lower end with literal reality, no matter how transcendent the symbolic levels into which it opens. In his later work "tension" becomes the "symbolic imagination," which, beginning from the "common thing," "carries the bottom along with it, however high it may climb." The inadequate alternative to the symbolic imagination is the "angelic imagination," which bypasses the earthly, overleaps and cheats the condition of man, "in the illusory pursuit of essence." This "angelism of the intellect," performed by a Frye-like creature too anxious to renounce his sensuous being and to become angel instead of man, can be seen as the poetic weakness deriving from Gnosticism. Or we can recall Eliseo Vivas' constant insistence on the poet's chief obligation to the

---

[6] "Romanticism and Classicism," *Speculations*, ed. Herbert Read (London, 1924), pp. 119-20.

"primary data of experience" or my own claim that the ultimate function of a contextual poetry is to provide existential revelation.

The dedication to the existential is often accompanied, in the modern critical tradition, by the interest in the tragic and the ironic. The difference in Frye's emphasis can be seen point by point. He condemns "existential projection" as the false attempt to destroy the autonomy of the literary universe by reducing it to our lowly experiential world. For literature to pursue a relation between itself and the existential would be, for Frye, an abdication of its high destiny, of its obligation to minister to the creative human desire rather than to open for us the destructive realities of the human condition. Literature is made out of prior literature, not life; it yields poetic, mythic categories, not existential ones. The relation of a central tragic concern to our existential sense seems clear enough from what has been said; this concern can be followed as a major theme in recent criticism before Frye. That his own work centers on comedy and romance, spring and summer, rather than the autumn of tragedy, Fletcher and Hartman, as I have said, make abundantly clear in their essays. Frye dwells on rebirth and not death, not on the descent to the underworld but on the return and the upward movement within the circle which man uses to construct his sense of his destiny. Similarly, irony, which became so conclusive a literary (and existential) quality for critics before Frye, is by him seen as the lowest reach of the downward movement of displacement from pure myth, to be gone through almost before we arrive at it; for irony derives its major excitement for Frye from our capacity to see in it, paradoxically, the beginnings of the upward movement that can return us to the undisguised gods.

Frye and the modern critical tradition, then, should, in their opposition, come to be recognized as utter alternatives, indeed as very little less than mutually exclusive. In spite of my earlier worries about the inadequacy of diagrams in dealing with Frye, let me try the accompanying diagram as an immediate indication of this opposition between him and the modern critical tradition.

In traditional modern theory the critic is seen as viewing the individual work in its relations to the actual world of experience (including the world of art) even as that world is in part defined by the work in its internal relations. The endless variations among such theories depend on how these relations achieve their definitions and their priorities. According to the revolutionary theory of Frye the critic is first seen making a downward movement to the work and the world. This movement is an echo of the downward movement toward displacement and the reality principle that literature makes in its historical movement from unencumbered myth through mimetic forms to irony, although with the latter's promise to return. For myth, like a god, enters history's downward path, marching through history in a variety of displaced forms before the eschatological return to oneness. The critic, too, moves through the lowering displacements of the individual work, the limitations placed on its meanings and movements by its discreteness, its persistent attempt to become a unique self-enclosure. As man, the critic makes a similar downward movement through the unresponsive realities of the unelevated sublunary world. But there is an answering upward movement and return, as in the archetypes of rebirth and of the quest myth: the critic moves from the individuated work, as man

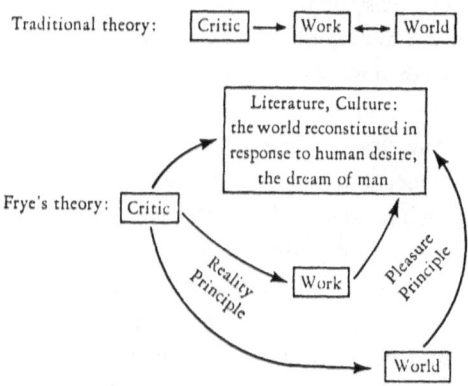

moves from the unenlightened world, upward to his imaginative home, which is their (the work's and the world's) imaginative transposition. This is the world as remade by human desire, man's dream, which as creative act makes a world in which man chooses to live. If the critic's downward movement is made in accordance with the reality principle, the upward movement is made in accordance with the pleasure principle—pleasure rendered innocent as the creation of unfallen man. Thus Freud's development and hierarchy, from pleasure to reality, are reversed. The critic moves from displacements, in their variations seen in multiple singleness, to the pure revelations of the oneness into which all single variations empty. It is as if the work and the sublunary world, suffering similarly under the curse of the Fall, the curse of individuation, were—with critic as midwife—reborn as the Platonic One of which all human experience and all art are in quest.

But the other arrow from the critic indicates that he has also moved directly to this world-as-dream, in an upward movement of unmediated vision. I have warned earlier of the spatial inadequacies of diagrams applied to Frye's schematics. In my diagram of the critic's movements we also find space betrayed and deepened by time. For the critic has had his world of culture—created by himself as poet—prepared all the time for the ascent from the individual work and the world. Until this point we have described the critic as making two movements. The first is downward: he has, as critic, descended to the work and, as man, he has descended to the world. (Indeed, he has descended to what, from the view on high, seems to be the underworld.) But, preparing to make his second movement, which is the upward return, he need not relate work and world to one another since both are to be dissolved into something higher. At this stage the literary work is seen only as it is related to the world of literature, of culture, of dream—only as it evolves out of literary causes. For the fallen world must be raised rather than allowed the praise of art; it must be transformed and not transcribed. Neither subject nor object, the fallen world is what poetry—in its creation of its properly human subject and object—must leap across. But now we discover that there has also been a third movement all along, made prior to and independently of the others, even as it is also made simultaneously with them. The downward and upward movements arrive at the place where the critic has always been, a place to which he must always immediately move. Out of the work and the world, out of the downward movements made by both critic as critic and critic as man, both critic and man make the return to the imaginative world, to the world as man wills to have it, although it is the very world which, as Blakean poet, he has already created from the beginning.

In contrast, then, to the careful distinctions among entities, functions, subject and object drawn by traditional modern theory, in Frye's theory subject, object, and universal—critic, man, poet, work, world, and literature or world-as-dream—all merge into the One that receives all, the One that the world-as-dream becomes even as it becomes the all-transforming creative act of man. No wonder critics in the wake of Frye have devoted themselves increasingly to "vision" and visionaries, to romantic and utopist poet-philosophers. Further, since his notion of epiphany does permit Frye to leave open the possibility of a momentary breakthrough of the desired into the real, of utopia into the resistant world of things, his position can—like an earlier romanticism—have immediate political consequences for those who are in earnest about the egalitarian possibilities of the "classless" society. In all these respects, a vision is being pressed that apparently seeks to define, in the extremest terms possible, the humanist and romantic attitude which Hulme so bitterly denounced in the name of the classic and Christian traditions. It is as if Hulme's too simple caricature of romanticism had truly created itself out of his projections and now reached back to haunt the tradition he so sternly sought to protect. As Hulme saw it would have to be, the romantic attitude is born with the denial that the Fall can touch the human imagination; and this denial leads to the arrogant assertion that man creates, *ex nihilo,* like a god, out of his desires.—And he saw everything that he had made, and, behold, it was very good.—For in that creation man has eluded the traps of the fallen world of experience which would desecrate the innocence of imagination. This imagination is enabled to dream its golden dreams in its transcendence of the brazen world that, in its spirit of gravity, exerts a downward pull.

If the words *golden* and *brazen* recall us to Sidney's *Apology for Poetry,* it is as it should be, since Frye's use of Sidney's opposition of the golden world to the brazen world has been with us from the beginning. Frye's multiple schemes have sought to enclose nothing less than the entire history of human culture as the history of the forms created by man's imagination; and the forms, as archetypal, are seen to be controlled by the principle of eternal return. Therefore, what could be more fitting than to approach the center, the *primum mobile,* of these multiple schemes by way of Frye's own archetypal image? I find this image most clearly in the *Apology* of Sidney even as it came to him from Plato and passed from him to Shelley, though with less precision of adaptation than we find in Frye.

We can begin with Sidney's noted definition of the poet as being in no way limited to created nature but creating his own: ". . . onely the Poet . . . lifted up with the vigor of his owne invention, dooth growe in effect, another nature . . . so as hee goeth hand in hand with Nature, not inclosed within the narrow warrant of her guifts, but freely ranging onely within the Zodiack of his owne wit." The word *Zodiack* should bring us at once to the area of imagery I have been pressing in Frye,[7] that which

[7] In view of my own insistence on Frye's swirling galaxies and my attempt here to relate them to Sidney's "Zodiack of his owne wit," I must record the coincidental title of an essay by John Holloway, "The Critical Zodiac of Northrop Frye," in *The Colours of Clarity* (London, 1964), pp. 153–60. This essay does not refer to Sidney or to the theoretical context of the *Apology,* and I came upon it after my own essay—largely grounded in the Sidney reference—was well under way; but I did find the Holloway title comforting. I am indebted to my colleague and this volume's bibliographer, John E. Grant, for pointing out this review of the *Anatomy.*

Wimsatt reminds us of when he quotes Frye's vision of man's imagination building its "cities out of the Milky Way." But a bit later we find Sidney, in freeing the poet from subservience to fact (he need "borrow nothing of what is, hath been, or shall be"), frees him to "range onely rayned with learned discretion, into the divine consideration of what may be, and should be." To range freely within the zodiac of one's own wit is apparently the same as ranging into the divine consideration of what may be and should be. Clearly wit, as imagination or invention, must be connected to the transcendent world of the ought-to-be. And so it is, in a quotation which comes between the two that I have cited and allows one to be transposed to the other. Anxious lest his reader, in a Hulme-like mood, accuse him of elevating man and his wit to God's level, Sidney tries to account for creative man in a fallen universe:

Neyther let it be deemed too sawcie a comparison to ballance the highest poynt of mans wit with the efficacie of Nature: but rather give right honor to the heavenly Maker of that maker: who having made man to his owne likenes, set him beyond and over all the workes of that second nature, which in nothing hee sheweth so much as in Poetrie: when with the force of a divine breath, he bringeth things forth far surpassing her dooings, with no small argument to the incredulous of that first accursed fall of *Adam:* sith our erected wit, maketh us know what perfection is, and yet our infected will, keepeth us from reaching unto it.

In this properly Platonic concession, our wit is exempt from the Fall, although our will is thoroughly subject to it: our *"erected* wit" which can apprehend perfection and our *"infected* will" which cannot attain it. The brazen world of things as they are, the coarsening individuation of God's world, is the product of our infected will even though our erected wit can within its zodiac range freely, imagining the archetypal perfections of the golden world, the world before the Fall, Platonically governed by the divine considerations of things as they should be. For the erected wit, the free range within its zodiac can never be arbitrary but must automatically bring it to range within its archetypal home, where the perfection of things as they should be works heavenly alchemy on the baser metals wrought by our sublunary will. For in its erect, upward-reaching state, the wit's zodiac is that of the Platonic heavens. The freedom from the Fall granted to wit is like that granted by Frye to his imagination. And it is like that which is found in Hulme's hostile definition of romanticism.

Sidney's elevated world of wit is the world of the poem, as high-flying and as anti-existential as Frye's. The world of things as they should be draws the zodiac of the poet's wit to merge with its own: it thus becomes the free creation of that wit. This world produces "in *Tantalus, Atreus,* and such like, nothing that is not to be shunned. In *Cyrus, Aeneas, Ulisses,* each thing to be followed. . . ." We seem to be in Frye's world of attraction and repulsion in accordance with desire, the wish-fulfillment that produces *his* things as they should be: the "demonic imagery" as "the presentation of the world that desire totally rejects" and its supernal opposite, the "apocalyptic imagery," "the categories of reality in the forms of human desire."[8] Further, as Sidney insists that the poet's should-be world is merely a "figuring forth," that "for the Poet, he nothing affirmes, and therefore never lyeth," that the stage "Thebes" is not the geographical "Thebes" because the poet speaks "not affirmatively, but allegorically, and figurativelie," we sense his closeness to Frye's insistence on the supposed, *as-if* world of literature: "Literature is a body of hypothetical thought and action: it makes, as literature, no statements or assertions" (*The Well-Tempered Critic,* page 149).

It should please Frye for us to have uncovered *his* archetype in some passages of Sidney.[9] Indeed, he should welcome our finding this early source as evidence of his claim that in the history of the human imagination all is new only as it is old, the new word but a new version of the old word, in the spirit of his own essay "New Directions from Old."[10] He should, of course, be quick to point out two serious differences between Sidney and himself. First, Frye can go all the way to the golden world of man's wit and remain

[8] *Anatomy,* pp. 147 and 141. The golden world, for Frye as for Sidney, must always be defined by negative as well as positive fiats, by what we will not have as well as what we must have. Thus, in *The Educated Imagination* (Indiana, 1964), pp. 98–100, as Frye extends literature beyond "only a wish-fulfillment dream" by turning to tragedy as well as to "romances and comedies with happy endings," it is only to show how literature deals with the negation of desire as well as desire, what we reject as well as what we want, nightmare as well as bliss. He can justify the horror of the blinding of Gloucester in *Lear* as "not the paralyzing sickening horror of a real blinding scene, but an exuberant horror, full of the energy of repudiation . . . as powerful a rendering as we can ever get of life as we don't want it." The "most vicious things" presented in literature produce an "exhilaration" from the fact that "they aren't really happening." Here we are—even in tragedy—in full flight from the world of experience to the world as we would have it or as we refuse to have it. The world of the literary imagination, Frye says in *The Well-Tempered Critic,* "is the universe in human form, stretching from the complete fulfillment of human desire to what human desire utterly repudiates . . ." (p. 155).

[9] Of course I am not claiming that Sidney is a unique source or that these doctrines are original with him. Further, one finds similar images in many places, if not within so similar and extensive a theoretical framework. One should notice, for example, that the development in America, in the nineteenth century, of the theory of fictional romance—as in many passages in the writings of Hawthorne and Henry James—is filled with heavenly and, more specifically, lunar imagery.

[10] In *Fables of Identity: Studies in Poetic Mythology* (New York, 1963), pp. 52–66.

in it, while Sidney cannot systematically sustain his gesture to imagination since he is pulled back to the dully imitative by the conservative Italian critical tradition that claimed him. Frye has no Scaliger tugging at him to keep him from the total embrace of his grandest claims. Secondly and more basically, Frye explicitly and continually divorces his humanist-romantic attitude from all metaphysical claims, so that his golden world is the product only of the human imagination and has no other sanction.[11] Like Sidney's Platonic realm, Frye's zodiac of man's wit is related to the world as it should be. But this world has nothing of the metaphysically divine in it as it does for Sidney; the wit creates its zodiac which, responsive only to its creator, has no true home in the sky. So if one believes he can term Frye a Platonist, he must confront this crucial qualification to his claim, a qualification that might suggest Freud as an alternative influence. Freud rather than Jung, since Jung's archetypes also demand a metaphysic that Frye must reject. Frye's mythic gods, like Freud's neuroses, are related to our wishes and the frustration of these wishes, and in each case their displacement can give rise to literary creation. However, while displaced meaning is private for the Freudian poet, in response to secret wishes and secret frustrations, for Frye displaced meaning—like the wishes that create it—is universal and shared, the public property of the common human imagination which created and always recreates those gods.[12] In this departure from Freud, Frye joins Sidney in celebrating the universals of the should-be world, despite his rejection of the metaphysical sanction for them as they are derived from Plato.

The relation of Frye to Plato, however incomplete, should recall us to Ransom's charge of Platonism and Tate's charge of "angelism" or Gnosticism against those who bypass the world of sense for an unmediated

---

[11] Frye himself distinguishes the romantic humanist from the Renaissance Christian humanist in terms of the latter's invocation of the Fall. See the important essay "The Imaginative and the Imaginary," in *Fables of Identity*, pp. 151–67, especially pp. 159–60. He seems, however, less aware of the metaphorical similarities between himself and Renaissance Platonism than he is of the metaphysical difference between them.

[12] Frye can try to make his "desire" something more than either whim or the Freudian wish. Speaking of the imaginative in "The Imaginative and the Imaginary," in *Fables of Identity*, he can say, "The drive behind [the imaginative] we may call desire, a desire which has nothing to do with the biological needs and wants of psychological theory, but is rather the impulse toward what Aristotle calls *telos*, realizing the form that one potentially has" (p. 152). But this introduces a metaphysical dimension that he dare not develop, so that for him "desire" usually seems to carry its normal meanings and implications. He can urge but he cannot earn a distinction between "the creative and the neurotic."

admission to the world of essence. Wimsatt's essay speaks similarly and with disfavor of Frye's "Gnostic mythopoeia." It is worth remembering that, in his conclusion to the *Literary Criticism: A Short History* (1957), on which he collaborated with Cleanth Brooks, Wimsatt spoke against both "the Platonic or Gnostic ideal world views" and "the Manichaean full dualism and strife of principles." The thirst for essence made the first too airy a flight from gravity, while the over-absorption in the evil of the fallen world kept the second too unelevated, too trapped in gravity's downward pull. As orthodox Christian, Wimsatt would resolve the two critical heresies by way of the divine-earthly mystery of the Incarnation. His polemical writings that have followed this statement have pursued this double assault. Wimsatt has attacked existential critics like me for Manichaean tendencies, and now his linking of the anti-existential Frye to Gnosticism reveals him turning against the opposed critical (and theological) heresy. Further, Frye's humanistic liberation from Plato's metaphysic, the self-authentication of Frye's Gnostic tendencies, only compounds his error in Wimsatt's eyes.

We have seen that, in contrast to the dark archetypes of Jung, the archetypes of Frye have no metaphysical sanction. They are a humanistic construct of common man in search of his dream which he creates out of his need for wish-fulfillment. Thus the democratic universality of mythic structures is dependent on the universality, the commonness, of the structure of human desires—even to the ultimately universal dream of man, the "classless" civilization. But this would seem to be an empirical claim, subject to empirical evidence, and in need of an agreed-upon upward reading of the stories of our literature in the direction of spring and summer, as the quest for rebirth. In citing these two dominant archetypes of Frye, quest and rebirth, I suggest that unromantic readers are more convinced by death than rebirth, more convinced by the poverty they find than the pot of gold to which the rainbow promises to lead them in quest. Since obviously the history of our criticism has allowed many alternative readings of literature, we must realize that, far from meaning an empirical claim, Frye is rather creating, within the zodiac of *his* wit, galaxies that respond to his own poetic vision, even as his vision responds to Blake's. It is a vision, gorgeously complete in its dizzying schematics, that can be responded to by all celebrants of man in his spring and summer mood, the romantic singers of the golden world, the utopist questers for an Eden that nostalgia will not permit them quite to forget or forego and that irony will not permit them quite to attain for the fallen daytime world.

Frye's vision must then be seen as his own construct of the world of our literature in terms of his desires, as he would like it to be. What he gives us is the authorization, indeed the licensing, of what earlier positivistic theorists and philosophers disparagingly used to call the "emotive," as they worried about the primary role of wish-fulfillment in the structures of poets and of too-ambitious philosophers. In the fashion of the early I. A. Richards, they used "emotive" to outlaw poetry from the realm of meaningful discourse, and apologists for poetry protested by trying to demonstrate how poetry did give meaning to life. But Frye rather insists on the emotive as poetry's only content and would not have it otherwise; he celebrates poetry precisely for the characteristic that its old enemies proclaimed as its weakness and that its old friends sought to deny. And his licensing poetry according to this definition is also the licensing of his own way of theorizing—so revolutionary in its relation to the theoretical tradition—and of his theory itself as a massive poetic vision with all its swirling galaxies.

The lunar sweep of vision—beyond "Dull sublunary lovers' love,/Whose soul is sense"—must prevent Frye from claiming, with many modern critics, that literature in the narrow sense has a unique role in creating that vision. For him the power of vision must be one with the power of the human imagination to create its structures, poetic or otherwise. The romantic imagination, in search of unmediated vision, must transcend the finite body of the poet's controlled precision in language just as we have seen it transcend the world's body itself. This my earlier diagram was designed to show. The philosopher, the critic—social-political as well as literary—must be admitted with the poet, so that, like Arnold before him, Frye is led outward from literature to culture and civilization at large, all of them products of imagination, nature (science's nature) given human form:

> But it seems clear that Arnold was on solid ground when he made "culture," a total imaginative vision of life with literature at its center, the regulating and normalizing element in social life, the human source, at least, of spiritual authority. Culture in Arnold's sense is the exact opposite of an elite's game preserve; it is, in its totality, a vision or model of what humanity is capable of achieving, the matrix of all Utopias and social ideals. (*The Well-Tempered Critic*, page 154)

If Frye must liberate literature from sublunary experience, if, further, he must liberate the poet's imagination from bondage to the sublunary language allowed it by a Hulme-like critic, so he must liberate the critic from the stringent procedures of a sublunary critical discourse. For the critic

The Place of Criticism

also is an imaginative creator of a lunar world. As Frye—in deference to the ubiquity and primacy of vision—permits the literary imagination to expand to a culture's or a civilization's imagination, as he allows literature to expand to include all structures of thought, so he clearly must include the critical imagination within the literary, within what Blake termed the "poetic genius." The fidelity of the critical imagination must be first to its own free creatures, even before its fidelity to the creatures of others, of the poets, and surely before its fidelity to the bounds of critical discourse as agreed upon by the theoretical tradition from Aristotle to—shall we say—Wimsatt. To the last, Frye seems to demand systematic irresponsibility, a willful recklessness. For his is not only a revolutionary conception of the poet and of criticism, but a revolutionary conception of the nature and function of critical discourse. Whatever may be the accuracy of Wimsatt's assault on Frye's discursive methods, we must ask whether it is appropriate to Frye's elusive disdain for the methodological presuppositions which underlie all such assaults; whether it "is like trying a man by the laws of one country, who acted under those of another," as Pope said of neoclassical attacks on Shakespeare. Unlike traditional theorists, Frye means to leap the barrier between discourses: between criticism and poetry, between himself and William Blake. To do so, he must tear criticism free of those very encumbrances that constitute the measure of Wimsatt's critique.

I have struggled myself with the limits of critical discourse, its conflicting fidelities to its poetic object, to theoretical procedure, and to its own nature. And I respond, if only fleetingly, to the impulse to throw over all but the last of these fidelities in an autotelic defiance. But every critic has always had to concern himself with that in poetry which makes it more than mere transcriber of the world even as it retains the need to reflect the world. His criticism, a part of the sublunary world, has had to creep along in its circumspect way and yet to soar, to share the common world of non-poetic language and yet to ape—however feebly—the sublime world of the poet's tongue. In its long history, the circumspect practice of criticism has hardly led to theoretical resolutions that leave us with the satisfactions of a final revelation. Its failures may be seen as reflecting this fallen world's gaps, its yawning discontinuities. Which of us has not wished to rise to a total vision of our task? Those won over by Frye indicate the risk some of us would run in hope of such a vision. As circumspect critics and theorists bound to this world, the others of us, after our long history, cannot point to such success as to allow us to reject Frye's radically alternative procedure with much assurance—even if our circumspect habits force us to worry about what we must view as theoretical irresponsibility fully licensed and theoretically urged.

Every critic, then, whether before or after Frye, has had to find in poetry some kind of mediation between sublunary nature and the high seriousness of its own lunar world. Every critic should respond with sympathy to Frye's reading of the close of *The Tempest* with its rebirth of innocence and Eden. The genial artist-magician has given substance to his vision in the world: "out of the cycle of time in ordinary nature we have reached a paradise . . . where spring and autumn exist together." "When Prospero's work is done, and there is nothing left to see, the vision of the brave new world becomes the world itself, and the dance of vanishing spirits a revel that has no end."[13]

No wonder Frye sees *The Tempest* as clearly his play. I therefore find it appropriate to conclude with figures borrowed from it. In what has preceded I have tried to account for the resistance to the flightiness, the unearthly irresponsibility of the poet—and the critic after him—as Ariel. But we must remember that the stubborn earthly pull can lead downward to the poet and critic as Caliban, who in his earthbound darkness worshipped false gods. Clearly any critic or poet should prefer to be master of both Ariel and Caliban, to be Prospero, dedicated to the world, but to the world so transformed aesthetically, so commodious, so fit for human habitation, that he can abjure the magic that was the agent of this transformation. Here indeed would be a marriage between the poet-critic's heaven and our hell, the marriage that Frye has radically sought to perform.

---

[13] *A Natural Perspective: The Development of Shakespearean Comedy and Romance* (Columbia, 1965), pp. 158–59.

[The secondary imagination] is essentially *vital*, even as all objects (*as* objects) are essentially fixed and dead.
(*Biographia Literaria*, Chapter XIII)

16
The Existential Basis of Contextual Criticism

There has for some time now been little need to argue for the influence of the Coleridgean imagination on those I have called the new apologists for poetry. But the above closing sentence of Coleridge's famous definition is usually overlooked both for itself and for its special relevance to these critics. If it and its relevance were not overlooked, we would be more aware than we are of the unison with which these critics feel about subject and object, about the operation of will, and about the relation of will to the world of subjects and objects. This awareness, in turn, might take us a long way toward understanding the extent to which this critical tradition is akin, in its attitudes to self and world, to the recently flowering existentialist and personalist doctrines in its contemporaries on the Continent, with whom, in most obvious respects, it would seem to have little in common.

We learn much of what we have to learn about Coleridgean epistemology as we note his insistence that objects are dead rather than vital only insofar as they function for us *as* objects. Or would it not be more accurate to say only insofar as we permit them to function as *mere* objects, thanks to the failure of our imagination to give them their life, to create them as subjects? Here, of course, we reach the heart of the Coleridgean I AM.[1] As the "living power and prime agent of all human perception," the imagination is an act, a vitalizing act that inspirits the object with the subjective assertion of being, the I AM. The imagination, then, permits the object to

---

[1] In speaking of the I AM as Coleridgean, as earlier I spoke of his epistemology or his imagination, I of course do not mean to make any claims for the originality of these doctrines with him or to take sides in disputes about his sources in (or plagiarizing from) German idealistic philosophers and romantic theorists. These historical matters, however important, do not affect my somewhat different historical interests here.

be—if I may use the graceless coinage—I-AM-ized. It is thus transformed from object to subject. And we recall the Idealist's struggle to destroy the antinomy between subject and object, the unforgivably Germanic involutions which Coleridge borrowed to work the union of subject and object, the involutions which he claimed for the I AM in his Thesis VI of the twelfth chapter of the *Biographia:* In the I AM, he tells us,

and in this alone, object and subject, being and knowing, are identical, each involving and supposing the other. In other words, it is a subject which becomes a subject by the act of constructing itself objectively to itself; but which never is an object except for itself, and only so far as by the very same act it becomes a subject.

And when this "genial" power fails, the consequences are those we witness in "Dejection: An Ode":

I may not hope from outward forms to win
The passion and the life, whose fountains are within.

O Lady! we receive but what we give,
And in our life alone does Nature live:
Ours is her wedding garment, ours her shroud!
   And would we aught behold, of higher worth,
Than that inanimate cold world allowed
To the poor loveless ever-anxious crowd,
   Ah! from the soul itself must issue forth
A light, a glory, a fair luminous cloud
   Enveloping the Earth—
And from the soul itself must there be sent
   A sweet and potent voice, of its own birth,
Of all sweet sounds the life and element! . . .

But now afflictions bow me down to earth:
Nor care I that they rob me of my mirth;
   But oh! each visitation
Suspends what nature gave me at my birth,
   My shaping spirit of Imagination.

All objects are left mere objects and dead. The poem is full of the imagery of stasis, the hushed stilling of natural and human movement. The lifeless poet, the passive viewer of a lifeless world of objects, is in effect the ancient mariner becalmed, trapped by his own creative failures and, consequently, his destructive propensities, through the death he gives to objects by failing to create them as subjects. And he is similarly cursed.

    Ever since the formulations of Coleridge and the post-Kantian Germans behind him, the poet's act of imagination has thus been seen as a liberating act that establishes his creative humanity; it is a victory over passivity, over the oppressive materiality and necessity of the formless, other-than-human world outside him. For the forms of imagination, in constituting our world, free it for human occupancy, give it the life that guarantees our own proper life, our realized humanity. Of course, as a T. E. Hulme would angrily remind us, our humanity is thus being realized by our daring to play God, through a presumptuous imitation of Genesis.

This divine-human need, at once metaphysical and aesthetic, to merge with the object and thus to destroy its *object*ivity is inevitably allied to the need that modern critics, in the tradition of Schopenhauer and Bergson, find central to the poet's role: his need to reject the world as an instrument of willful practicality and to cherish it as a unique and terminal object. But this very act would convert the object to subject by infusing it with the creative vitality he then can find in it. This relaxation of the practical will returns the tradition to its source in the aesthetic disinterestedness called for by Immanuel Kant.

But I want to look ahead rather than back from Coleridge. Even a professed anti-transcendentalist, anti-Germanic, and anti-Coleridgean neoclassicist like T. E. Hulme finds a common front with Coleridge in his concern about the vitalistic impulse that moves the poet. It comes to Hulme, of course, from his discipleship to Bergson.[2] In the spirit of Bergson, Hulme urges the fluidity of experience that keeps all unique by destroying entityhood; he decries the stereotypes of thinghood that freeze organic vitality by imposing the mechanics of spatial fixity upon it. So we look upon a veil of dead universals instead of piercing through to the pulsing actualities beneath. But, he sadly acknowledges, we are all too often victims of this perceptual sloth, of this substitution of neatly stacked counters for our actual felt experience. And why? Because our will-driven need for action permits only those mechanical distortions of experience that its ruthless efficiency can make use of. So, as in Schopenhauer, the villain is still the will—or rather our propensity for action, and not for contemplation for its own sake, together with the will as the faculty summoned by action for its governance. The alternative is the suspension of will, which makes contemplation possible as an autotelic activity. Hulme's plea for us to rend the false veil of universals is of course, despite the differences between them, reminiscent of

[2] On Hulme and his relations to Coleridge and Bergson, see *The New Apologists for Poetry* (Minneapolis, 1956), pp. 31–45.

Coleridge's despair over "the film of familiarity and selfish solicitude," in consequence of which "we have eyes, yet see not, ears that hear not, and hearts that neither feel nor understand."[3]

This tendency to celebrate contemplation and denigrate action is an inevitable response of the aesthetic impulse to the modern world's pragmatism and the child of pragmatism, instrumentalism. It is the concentration on the world as instrument, on the converting of the world to one's use, that, we remember in Coleridge, kept the object a mere object and thus dead. The aesthetic need is for satisfaction that looks no further than the object, cherishes it as alive, so that the hostility of this need to the practical intent is inevitable. It is the purposiveness, the *objective*, the world of means and end, of means *to* end, that is the enemy of aesthetic experience. Thus it was that Coleridge's master and the modern world's, Kant, could distinguish the aesthetic experience—in terms of his teleological concerns—by speaking of its finality-without-end. To deny immediacy, to move through and beyond the object to what it can be made good for, is to bring death into our perceptual world.

In part the attack upon use is linked to an almost pantheistic cherishing of the object, a love for the thing in its unique thingness that defies even the generic naming tendencies of language (or at least of other-than-poetic language). And in the fear of giving death to the object by submitting it to our ruthless service, we see the desire to restore particularity to an unpoetic, anaesthetic generic world whose singulars have had to purge themselves of their singularity as they submit to the universal. It is a desire that would have been understood by Kierkegaard, aimed as it is against the over-unified, over-universalized world-view produced by the straining metaphysical ambitiousness of a Hegel.

This is the attitude that leads to John Crowe Ransom's metaphor about

[3] *Biographia Literaria* (New York, 1906), p. 161. See p. 210 for his rejection of a poem for being "a pure work of the *will*," a charge that sounds like Allen Tate's. Throughout this essay I am emphasizing and extending those tendencies toward particularity in Coleridge which are often overlooked by those who emphasize his Idealism and its consequent universalizing tendencies. But I do not mean to quarrel with his primary dedication to Idealism. Rather I fully acknowledge that his Platonic interest in universality normally predominates over his relatively minor interest which I am purposely inflating here. By pressing the consequences of his anti-objective definition of the I AM, I am trying to suggest some degree of union between metaphysical and anti-metaphysical—essentialist and existentialist—doctrines of reality. In Coleridge's "film of familiarity and selfish solicitude" and its similarity to Hulme's veil, we see the point at which these doctrines can join. Thus the higher metaphysics of transcendental Idealism can, strangely and perhaps unwillingly, end by feeding its anti-doctrine of Existentialism.

the world's body.⁴ Ransom takes the metaphor seriously—that is, literally—even suggesting, in the poet's love of this "body," a biological sanction for the poetic impulse. It seems, at times, a very little less than erotic love. The world's body, we are told, has been unfleshed by the modern habit of the loveless use which is the abuse of that world. It is the sin of the Hobbesian "naturalist":

> A naturalist is a person who studies nature not because he loves it but because he wants to use it, approaches it from the standpoint of common sense, and sees it thin and not thick.⁵

In our naturalistic world only the poet remains stubbornly to cherish the world's body by exploring its every particularity. He refuses to abandon any of those particularities "lurking" within the body, insisting on all that makes it endlessly contingent. He will not subdue the contingency for any universal that would absorb the particular to itself, thereby denying its particularity—hence Ransom's almost violent antipathy to what he calls Platonism, the universalizing force that furnishes a single archetype to account for a host of unfleshed particulars. Shifting his metaphor from love to politics, he treats Platonism as a predatory state at once loveless, totalitarian, and insatiable in its appetite for particulars. He sees it as ever on the prowl for new experiences that it must rob of the contingencies that make them unique—and the precious objects of our poetic devotion. In our day it leads to the "sciencing" of the world and its body.

Ransom's famous distinction between structure and texture in poetry follows accordingly. For him logical structure results from our predatory need to use the world and the world of language, to subdue them to our universalizing needs. We move *through* objects and *through* the words that will refer others to them. Texture results from our recalcitrant insistence, as lovers of the world and of the word—in short, as poets—on being inefficient, on lingering wastefully in order to cherish at leisure the richness of the body, those particularities which pragmatic urgency would lead us to ignore in our haste to make use of them. Ransom seems to be recalling us to Coleridge's plea against the pull of the end, of terminus and objective, in poetry:

> The reader should be carried forward, not merely or chiefly by the mechanical impulse of curiosity, or by a restless desire to arrive at the final solution; but by

---

⁴ This metaphor, the world's body, is the title of Ransom's 1938 collection of essays.
⁵ "Poetry: A Note in Ontology," *The World's Body* (New York, 1938), p. 134.

the pleasurable activity of mind excited by the attractions of the journey itself. Like the motion of a serpent, which the Egyptians made the emblem of intellectual power; or like the path of sound through the air; at every step he pauses and half recedes, and from the retrogressive movement collects the force which again carries him onward. "Praecipitandus est *liber* spiritus," says Petronius Arbiter most happily.[6]

The word *liber* makes Ransom's indebtedness to this passage unmistakable.

Structure for Ransom, then, consists of the determinacies that were there before the poet even began: the argument on the one hand and the meter on the other. Texture consists of the indeterminacies he discovers and pauses to cultivate along the winding way. They can be indeterminacies of meaning as he indulges the waywardness of anti-argument or indeterminacies of sound-pattern as he indulges the waywardness of words. We come to understand Ransom's curious justification of meter: it is the sop the poet throws to the aroused Platonism (the "Platonic censor") in his impatient reader, a sop that gives him some sort of order, of regularity, to hold onto while the poet maddeningly involutes the order of meaning.

A formal metre impresses us as a way of regulating very drastically the material, and we do not stop to remark (that is, as readers) that it has no particular aim except some nominal sort of regimentation. It symbolizes the predatory method, like a sawmill which intends to reduce all the trees to fixed unit timbers, and as business men we require some sign of our business. But to the Platonic censor in us it gives a false security, for so long as the poet appears to be working faithfully at his metrical engine he is left comparatively free to attend lovingly to the things that are being metered, and metering them need not really hurt them. Metre is the gentlest violence he can do them, if he is expected to do some violence.[7]

The metaphor of love is joined to the metaphor of politics: thanks to the waywardness of texture, the poem offers a democratic state of nearly autonomous elements (of objects and words) instead of the coldly marshaled totalitarian state of non-poetry. It offers this as a state of love, of a love that can cherish beyond utility value, indeed that can cherish as a gesture to non-utility, to positive irrelevance (to use one of Ransom's favorite terms). The poem becomes an affectionate tribute to reckless non-pursuit, to sampling everything in the Bower of Bliss, to lotus-

[6] *Biographia Literaria*, p. 165. I am grateful to Emerson R. Marks for reminding me that Coleridge, in borrowing the Latin phrase, gives a systematic seriousness to what was far more casually meant in the original. In this distortion I have followed him. It is reminiscent of *ut pictura poesis* and the weighty history that descends from the phrase Horace tossed off so lightly.

[7] *The World's Body*, pp. 130–31.

eating as a poetic, a moral, and a political necessity, the sole necessity in a world loosed from all structural moorings. The poet is to fight always against the specter of Spenser's austere knight, the unlurable, no-nonsense Platonist, who stands ready to force the poem back into the properly structural place of discourse.[8]

Allen Tate joins Ransom in the attack upon Platonism as the destroyer of poetry.[9] With one as with the other, it is always the quest for universality, for essence, for the abstract reason of propositional certainty, that forecloses the lowly but indispensable immediacy of experiential particularity. When Tate shifts from his attack on Platonism in his early "Three Types of Poetry" to his attack on the "angelic imagination" in his essay of that name and its companion essay, "The Symbolic Imagination," it is really the same attack. It is the bypassing of commonplace, particular reality, of the world of the senses and the sense of the word, "in the illusory pursuit of essence" that constitutes aesthetic as well as metaphysical failure. The poetic equivalent of the Gnostic heresy, it is the failure of most of us most of the time in our vision as in our language. The inherently generic tendency of our language must be subverted at every point by the poet who—as Hulme had taught—cannot but resist the counters, the fixed (and thus deadened) forms of the semantic and syntactic formulae that pre-existed his poem. Each poem struggles to create its own unique language system in order to prove its adequacy to experience by demonstrating the incapacities of generic systems.

We have been moving from the cherishing and cultivating of the world's body to the cherishing and cultivating of the body of language. The ruthlessness of Platonism, in its pursuit of universal ends, is said to ignore the one as it ignores the other. Just as it treats the individual object *as* object only, indifferently pressing its particular properties into the nearest universal, so it indifferently presses language into the counterservice of those concepts it is dedicated to "communicate." It is the use of language as tool, in the name of the god clarity, that finds its *reductio* in the absurd pleadings of

---

[8] It is no wonder that an austere moralist like Yvor Winters must attack Ransom for what Winters calls his hedonism. Of course, there is for Ransom also the crucial problem of restoring what is logically irrelevant or indeterminate to a place of relevance in a finally determined aesthetic order. This problem, which I have discussed elsewhere (see, for example, *The New Apologists for Poetry*, pp. 82–87), is not central to my discussion of the tradition I am tracing here.

[9] For the following, see especially "Three Types of Poetry," *On the Limits of Poetry* (New York, 1948), pp. 91–114, and "The Symbolic Imagination" and "The Angelic Imagination," *The Man of Letters in the Modern World* (New York, 1955), pp. 93–112 and 113–31.

the semanticists, the use of language as the neutral (neutered?) unclouded hustler of universalized things. It is only to be a bearer of meaning, but to fetch and carry and—no nonsense—nothing more. And—prohibited most of all—no play. Where poetry is pursued within the terms of this view of language, only that Platonic pseudo-poetry which Tate, after Yeats, termed poetry of the will can result. It is ideological, even propositional, poetry. To be sure, this pseudo-poetry can strongly—and persuasively—modify the rawness of the less disguised versions of this conceptual exploitation of language. But at every crucial point pressure is exerted from outside to overcome the internal pressure generated by the play of language within itself as it seeks vainly to become system. And the Platonic domination, the propositional structure, stands revealed: the skeleton that puritanically denies flesh, denies body—ultimately denies the singularity that permits love. Thus the sin of language is joined to the sin of metaphysics, or at least so the personalist, as well as the contextualist critic, must charge.

In the existentialist-personalist tradition—in Sartre, in Berdyaev, in Buber, in Simone Weil, in the *Personnalisme* of Emmanuel Mounier and the *Esprit* group, in Kierkegaard himself—the cardinal sin is the turning of person into thing, of subject into object, of unique into common, of end into means. It is the generic form of murder, the turning off of life. And this is precisely the failure of imagination we have seen critics speaking of from Coleridge on, whether a failure of one's visioning of objects or of one's creative relations to his medium.[10] And often it is both. The failure is, finally, a failure to break through the veil, through "the film of familiarity

---

[10] I am aware that, in pressing this similarity, I am overlooking an important difference between the existentialist-personalist tradition and the tradition descended from the German Idealistic attempt to overcome the subject-object antinomy. While the Coleridgean I AM, like Ransom's textural demands upon the poet, requires that all objects—natural and human—be transformed and vitalized by the assertive subject, the existentialist-personalist distinguishes sharply between nature and man, insisting that only the latter be preserved against objectification, be cherished as a precious and irreducible subject. The treatment of the subhuman, of the less-than-person, as object is hardly a matter for condemnation by the personalist, since things are things and only persons are to be kept from thingification. But the entire external world—all that is other-than-myself—is equally to be rescued from objectification by the Coleridgean bent on saving his imagination, on keeping his a living, breathing world. Clearly the Coleridgean seems to be making a metaphysical—or at least an epistemological—insistence, the personalist a moral one. But I am now trying to find moral elements in the epistemological claims. My point, despite the difference I am here mentioning, rests on a temperamental and methodological similarity between the two traditions: a common attack on the use that is abuse, through the assertiveness of the universalizing practical will, and a common reverence for the unique and for the notion of *process* with its indivisible multiplication of uniques.

and selfish solicitude" that Coleridge decried, that turns the poet of will into the counterpart of the cursed ancient mariner. The veil that Hulme saw the practical will cast upon reality to protect our action-ridden propensities is, after all, the veil that our slothful and insensitive language habits cast upon the symbolic potency of words. The world we see, conditioned by the vision our symbolic medium permits, must in turn affect our symbolic capacities. And the dulling, the veiling of one involves the dulling, the veiling of the other. Hulme's veil is the oriental and neo-Platonic veil of illusion; he takes it from Bergson who, in turn, follows the early Schopenhauerian Nietzsche and Schopenhauer himself. This genealogy reminds us of the profound epistemological implications of the hatred of the veil, of the claims against its universals as unreal superimpositions, of the oriental retreat to pure contemplation as the alternative to the ego's death through its too aggressive self-assertion.

The relaxation of will and the consequent transcendent disinterest can bring us beyond reason's pragmatic demarcations to the fluid, ever-changing reality that brooks no imposition of identifiable bounds, of classifiable property, indeed of the rational notion of class itself. It brings about a radical nominalism of unyielding particulars, none of which will give up any particle of its autonomy to band together with any other. There can be no adequate propositions, then, no knowledge, if by knowledge we mean more than knowledge of discrete particulars. The existential realm is, from the standpoint of propositional structures, a raging chaos.[11]

But such cognitive (or anti-cognitive) claims must have moral consequences. For our very viewing of reality and of language is made to be a moral act, calling for moral judgment: we look and speak either with the wasteful lingering that echoes our love for the object as subject or with the ruthless pursuit that moves beyond the object with a denial of its uniqueness that gives death to its vitality. What seems to be the contextualist attack on those who finally allow poems to yield propositional meaning now turns out to be the personalist attack on those who subsume persons and their actions within universal principles of an objective morality. The veil that the practical will must place between us and an infinitely varied mass of unique phenomena now turns out to be another veil as well: the veil of universal

[11] I must remind the reader that this extreme position is hardly one that would be countenanced by transcendental Idealists like Coleridge, with whom I began. But, as I tried to show in footnote 3, above, there are tendencies in Coleridge which, if pressed, can justify these extensions. To press them in this way, to find such consequences in them, is a major purpose of this essay.

principles that our anti-existential need for moral order, for sanity, must place between our judgment or decision and the contradictory mass of raging and resistant particulars that make up the raw edges of our moral experience—what I have elsewhere called the Manichaean face of reality. This is the veil that organized society or organized rebellion against society —that man in his social dimension—must hold before his vision if he is to permit himself to function, to believe in the legitimacy of this functioning. He must stalwartly stare at the veil and keep from looking beyond it—as if it constituted reality, all of reality. The veil may be rent in a thousand places by the violent clawings of the rumbling reality beneath, but moral man must fix on the non-holes, not daring to see through the static comfort of his illusory universals that permit action and the confident judgment that makes decision possible. The veil of a generic, a stock language, seen by Coleridge as a veil of an imaginatively blinded vision, becomes also the veil that saves us from confronting the unique and unresolvable crises among unique persons, saves us from the paralyzing, too aware contemplation that blocks action, muddies the cleanness of decision, blurs the trim lines on the chart of universal judgment. As the veil of language prevents our symbolizing our unique experience, as the veil of vision prevents our *having* any unique experience, so the veil of morally binding universals prevents our daring *not* to judge, prevents our acknowledgment that uniqueness, with its apparent contradictions that preclude judgment, involves only the principle of automatic secession, of utter autonomy—hence the existential consequences of the recent concern for paradox and tension as the basis of poetic structure.

From the standpoint of poetry, the formal particularities are echoed in thematic particularities, the contextualist critic echoing the existentialist-personalist philosopher. The Manichaean implications of the contextualist aesthetic should now be manifest. And the reasons behind W. K. Wimsatt's quarrel with these implications are now obvious.[12] One devoted to the rational nature of experience as a ground for universal moral judgments must have confidence in a universal language, too, in the adequacy of a discourse grounded in a propositional structure. His dogmatic metaphysic must be accompanied by his Platonic, his finally didactic, aesthetic. He must be affronted by the charge that his vision of experience is blinded by the veil of rational universals which, without ontological sanction, he has arbitrarily imposed for his comfort, so that his propositional claims for poetic language

---

[12] See the passages from Wimsatt in "Platonism, Manichaeism, and the Resolution of Tension: A Dialogue," above.

reduce it to the universalizing and blinding veil of non-poetic discourse. Affronted—and frightened by the dangerous consequences of what he must see as a radical nominalism. Experience, always unique, is never to be seen as common, is unapproachable except by poetry; and poetry, in order to keep itself eligible to approach, resists all non-poetic sense. Life in its phenomenological fullness is the reality behind the universals that as rationalists we insist upon, though these are the veil, only the construct of our social necessities, as poetry exists to remind us when we can afford to free our vision to look. Poetry breaks through because it alone dares construct itself in freedom from the equally false, equally comforting, veils of the stock forms of language. Poetry is the only object, fixed in a final form, that does not objectify and destroy—that embodies to preserve—the object as universal subject by refusing itself to be universal.

No wonder the rationalist recoils from this heretical arrogance, especially when, as with Wimsatt, he has himself been an ally of those who foster these anarchic claims. No wonder, after he gives ground in his theory to the forces of opposition, of tension, that prevent an open and easy didacticism, he must insist on stopping short of total opposition, must insist on the final moral—which is to say propositional, even Platonic—affirmation. There must for him be thematic, as well as aesthetic, resolution.[13] For him poetry must stop short of being finally subversive. And the contextualist, like the personalist, however he may sympathize with the order life demands if we are to live it sanely, still denies this order any existence, denies any authenticity even to assertions made most qualifiedly, to the veil applied most tentatively. For the reality of the unique is still lost to us, hidden from us, even if by the more insidious device of crypto-didacticism, what in the spirit of Ransom we could call crypto-authoritarianism.

When in the final chapter of *The Tragic Vision* I first pointed out the existentialist-personalist affinity of contextualist criticism, I was aware of no direct influence of the one tradition upon the other. Nor am I aware of any now, after several more years of looking for it. On the contrary, many of the key critics, who in their philosophical conservatism mean to be clearly anti-existentialist, may perhaps be shocked, and annoyed, by having me

[13] In the spirit of the tensional aspect of contextualism (in *The Tragic Vision* [New York, 1960], pp. 241–57), I argue for a distinction between thematic and aesthetic resolutions, claiming the need only for the latter since the former would run the risk of Platonism. And again I call attention to the dialogue with Wimsatt, above, this time to my passages.

claim such a relation. But this relation cannot be avoided, shouts to be observed. As a dominant motive for their contextualist method and claims, the existentialist-personalist impulse of these critics turns the complaint of aesthetic formalism that is often made against them into an especially inappropriate one. The existence of such an affinity may be expressive of a bizarre intellectual unity in our dreadfully splintered conceptual atmosphere, or—more likely—it may be the consequence of common romantic sources that persist in showing themselves among very different temperaments that have made use of them.

It would seem, then, that in their professed classical allegiances and their sometime conservative affiliations with philosophical realism, these critics are properly doubted by more staunchly orthodox colleagues like Wimsatt or Yvor Winters. For the apologists for poetry who have contributed to the contextualist poetic may be seen also as embattled warriors in the romantic quest to rediscover—or recreate—imagination in spite of the dulling, leveling, and automatizing hand of technological science. Symbolists all, they are with Wallace Stevens in tracing "The Course of a Particular" (". . . the cry of leaves that do not transcend themselves"), in settling for a "supreme fiction" whose rich and full mythology turns reason's universals into empty myth and poetry into the caressing of the hopelessly real. In spite of the enormous and important differences in poetic theory, these critics in their daring objectives may in their special way be members after all of the company of visionary critics who seem to have superseded them.[14]

It is fitting that, in one of his most exploratory essays, Robert Penn Warren, student of John Crowe Ransom, should find "The Ancient Mariner" to be a poem about the hopes and failures of imagination. The contextualist tradition, like the personalist tradition, sees in the exercise of will, in the indifferent use of objects, the grand objective of the "sciencing" modern world as universalizing machine, the turning away from particularity, from imagination, from love. Our imagination, like the faithful albatross, was once free-flowing but is now dead, killed by ourselves, by the ruthless world of use. That deadened imagination is our albatross still, the curse that we, like the ancient mariner, have created out of our failure to love. We, too, must wear it around our necks "instead of the cross" we have foresworn; and we, too, must stay afloat in a world nightmarishly

---

[14] By using the words of Hart Crane as adapted by Harold Bloom, I mean, of course, to suggest the recent restoration of romantic studies and, through these, the growing ascendancy of a mythic, apocalyptic, even utopist criticism.

becalmed by our failure to keep imagination alive, by the lack of that inspiring breeze from within which gives movement to all that is outside—the failure and the lack that Coleridge traces for us in "Dejection" as well as in "The Ancient Mariner" ("I had killed the bird/That made the breeze to blow").

Like the mariner we must earn a newly sacramental world with the surge of a revitalized imagination, a vision born of "a spring of love," of the abjuring of that ruthless use which is abuse. We must manage to take our albatross from our necks. And as poets or critics, we must tell and retell our tales. Earlier we saw Coleridge coming out of Kant's notion of disinterested interest, of finality-without-end. In a related way Schiller came away from Kant with his play-theory of aesthetics. In their anti-Platonic celebration of luxurious waste over lean efficiency, in the leisurely victory over the practical will, we have seen recent critics plead for the playful freedom of the poets—at times even using political terminology to constitute the mythology of an endlessly contingent state of love. The poet explores his freedom in his affectionate toying, his love-play with the world's body. The critic must follow in a similar spirit, disdaining the ideological adaptation, the propositional use of poems; he rather must play with them as converted objects of *his* love that deserve no less than his unwillful, sportive resting among them. A not-quite-poet who has been given the charter for the freedom of his imagination by the poem, the critic, like the wedding guest, is never again the same; and the freedom, the playfulness, of his vision of the world and response to it are his tributes to the poem for what it has given him. He undertakes the labor of love, joining the anti-willful crusade without a Jerusalem or rather with indiscriminate and ubiquitous Jerusalems. So this volume closes as it began: if the contextualist poet is an existentialist-personalist whose expressive act is an imitation of the creative act of an existentialist-personalist God, the contextualist critic, from his lesser place, follows the poet in the free—yet imitative—play that makes his activity creative as well. After all, as the poet, confronting the world, must transform it into an object that has become his subject, so that critic, confronting the poem, must create *it* as an object that has become *his* subject.

Index

Addison, Joseph, 174–75
Anatomy of Criticism (Frye), 221–37
Apology for Poetry, An (Sidney), 192, 230, 231–33
Aristotle, 124, 137, 141, 159, 169, 176, 181, 187–88, 217, 233n, 236
Arnold, Matthew: 187n, 235; "Dover Beach," 69–77
Ault, Norman, 175n

Bachelard, Gaston, 106n
Bateson, F. W., 217
Beach, Joseph Warren, 132, 149–52
Berdyaev, Nicolas, 246
Bergson, Henri, 69, 127, 241, 247
Biographia Literaria (Coleridge), 238–40, 242n, 243–44
Blackmur, R. P., 167
Blake, William: 207, 211, 214, 217, 220n, 234, 236; "London," 209–10, 217
Blanchot, Maurice, 127
Bloom, Harold, 250n
Boiardo, Matteo Maria: *Orlando Innamorato*, 12–13
Bolingbroke, Henry St. John, 65
Brooks, Cleanth: 131, 135, 177–93, 196, 198; *Literary Criticism: A Short History* (with W. K. Wimsatt), 177–93, 195–97, 234; *The Well Wrought Urn*, 55, 110, 112, 115
Brothers Karamazov, The (Dostoevsky), 206
Browne, Sir Thomas: *Urne Buriall*, 110, 113–16, 125
Buber, Martin, 246
Burckhardt, Sigurd, 107–8, 125
Burke, Edmund, 125
"Burnt Norton" (Eliot), 106
Butt, John, 168n, 175n

"Canonization, The" (Donne), 110n, 112
Cassirer, Ernst, 187, 190
Castelvetro, Lodovico, 160
Chase, Richard, 179
Cicero, 181, 187
Coleridge, Samuel Taylor: 124, 143, 184–88, 190–91, 240–42, 246–48;

Biographia Literaria, 238–40, 242n, 243–44; "Dejection: An Ode," 123, 240, 251; "The Rime of the Ancient Mariner," 122–23, 250–51
Colie, Rosalie L.: *Paradoxia Epidemica*, 109n
Congreve, William, 174n
Conrad, Joseph: 72, 91–104, 162; *Heart of Darkness*, 99n, 100n, 101; *Lord Jim*, 92, 94, 96, 98–104; *The Nigger of the "Narcissus,"* 101; *Youth*, 92–101
"Corinna's Going A-Maying" (Herrick), 122–23
Crane, Hart, 250n
Crane, R. S., 133
Critique of Judgment (Kant), 209
Croce, Benedetto, 15, 141, 184, 185n, 188, 190

"Dejection: An Ode" (Coleridge), 123, 240, 251
Dewey, John: *Art as Experience*, 106
Donne, John: 20; "The Canonization," 110n, 112
Dostoevsky, Feodor Mikhailovich: 91, 104; *The Brothers Karamazov*, 206
"Dover Beach" (Arnold), 69–77
Dryden, John, 183
Dunciad, The (Pope), 53–54, 58, 64–68, 175–76, 183
Dunn, Michael W., 73n

Educated Imagination, The (Frye), 232
Eliot, T. S.: 20, 107, 109, 114, 119, 126–28, 145, 205, 207, 213, 221–22, 225; "Burnt Norton," 106; *Murder in the Cathedral*, 106, 112
Elliott, Robert C.: *The Power of Satire*, 168n
"Eloisa to Abelard" (Pope), 111, 116–18
Emerson, Ralph Waldo, 191
Empson, William, 55
"Epistle to Dr. Arbuthnot" (Pope), 168–76
Essay on Criticism, An (Pope), 109n
Essay on Man, An (Pope), 54, 62–64

253

INDEX

Essays on English and American Literature (Spitzer), 3–7, 109n, 110

Fables of Identity (Frye), 232n, 233n
Faerie Queene (Spenser), 208, 211, 244–45
Faulkner, William: *The Bear*, 112n; *A Fable*, 207; *Light in August*, 112–14, 116
Feidelson, Charles, 177
Fiedler, Leslie, 179
Fisher, John H., 131n
Fletcher, Angus, 221n, 222, 227
Foerster, Norman, 133
Frank, Joseph: *The Widening Gyre*, 106n
Freud, Sigmund, 20, 37, 228, 233
Frye, Northrop: 119n, 124n, 220n, 221–37; *Anatomy of Criticism*, 221–37; *The Educated Imagination*, 232; *Fables of Identity*, 232n, 233n; *A Natural Perspective*, 237n; *The Well-Tempered Critic*, 224n, 232, 235

Gerber, John C., 131n
Grant, John E., 230n
Gulliver's Travels (Swift), 168

Hagstrum, Jean: *The Sister Arts*, 108
Hartman, Geoffrey H., 120n, 221n, 222, 223n, 227
Hateful Contraries (Wimsatt), 196, 205–9
Hausman, Carl R.: "Art and Symbol," 159n
Hawthorne, Nathaniel: 232n; *Italian Notebooks*, 80–86; *The Marble Faun*, 79–90; *The Scarlet Letter*, 84–85
Hazlitt, William, 54, 179
Heart of Darkness (Conrad), 99n, 100n, 101
Hegel, Georg Wilhelm Friedrich, 204, 242
Heilman, Robert B., 196, 212–13
Herbert, George, 110
Herrick, Robert: "Corinna's Going A-Maying," 122–23
History of Modern Criticism 1750–1950, A (Wellek), 178, 185
Holloway, John: *The Colours of Clarity*, 230n
Holman, C. Hugh, 112n
Homer, 62, 108–9, 222
Horace, 118, 168, 183, 192, 214, 244n

Hulme, T. E., 186, 222, 225–26, 230–31, 235, 241, 242n, 245, 247

Ion (Plato), 2–3, 12
Isocrates, 181
Italian Notebooks (Hawthorne), 80–86

James, D. G.: *Skepticism and Poetry*, 186
James, Henry, 58, 65, 79, 81, 84, 90–93, 104, 232
Johnson, Samuel, 184, 220, 225
Jonson, Ben, 183
Jung, Carl Gustav, 233–34

Kant, Immanuel: 63, 118, 210, 241–42, 251; *Critique of Judgment*, 209
Keats, John: 75, 109–10, 112, 116–19, 124–25, 225; "Ode on a Grecian Urn," 15, 110, 116, 124–25, 127; "Ode to a Nightingale," 73n, 120–21
Kierkegaard, Sören, 204, 242, 246
Koestler, Arthur, 179
Krieger, Murray: "After the New Criticism," 147n; *The New Apologists for Poetry*, 53, 153, 163, 186n, 201, 205, 241n, 245n; *The Tragic Vision*, 99n, 100n, 155n, 196, 201–5, 211–12, 249; *A Window to Criticism*, 7n, 8n, 19, 224n

Langer, Susanne, 188, 190–91
"Laokoön" (Lessing), 105–7, 118, 125
Lessing, Gotthold Ephraim: "Laokoön," 105–7, 118, 125
Lewis, Clive Staples, 21, 200
Light in August (Faulkner), 112–14, 116
Literary Criticism: A Short History (Wimsatt and Brooks), 177–93, 195–97, 234
"London" (Blake), 209–10, 217
Longinus, 141, 184
Lord Jim (Conrad), 92, 94, 96, 98–104
Lowes, John Livingston, 133

McLuhan, Marshall, 207
Marble Faun, The (Hawthorne), 79–90
Maritain, Jacques, 189
Marks, Emerson R., 244n
Marlowe, Christopher, 37, 39, 43, 45, 52
Marvell, Andrew: 190; "To His Coy Mistress," 122

254

Melville, Herman: 72; *Moby Dick*, 202, 204
Merivale, Patricia, 126*n*
Milton, John: *Paradise Lost*, 56, 58, 202, 211
Moby Dick (Melville), 202, 204
More, Paul Elmer, 207
Mörike, Eduard Friedrich, 110
Mounier, Emmanuel, 246
Murder in the Cathedral (Eliot), 106, 112

Natural Perspective, A (Frye), 237*n*
Nietzsche, Friedrich Wilhelm, 70*n*, 204, 247
Nigger of the "Narcissus," The (Conrad), 101

Obsessive Images (Beach), 149–52
O'Connor, William Van, 149*n*, 152
"Ode on a Grecian Urn" (Keats), 15, 110, 116, 124–25, 127
"Ode to a Nightingale" (Keats), 73*n*, 120–21
Oedipus (Sophocles), 124
Olson, Elder: "Rhetoric and the Appreciation of Pope," 168*n*, 169–70
Orlando Innamorato (Boiardo), 12–13

Paradise Lost (Milton), 56, 58, 202, 211
Pearce, Roy Harvey: "Historicism Once More," 53*n*
Pearson, Norman H., 112*n*
Percival, M. O.: *A Reading of "Moby Dick,"* 202
Plato: 14, 141, 181–82, 187–88, 208, 215, 230, 233–34; *Ion*, 2–3, 12
Plotinus, 74, 184, 187–88, 190, 206
Poe, Edgar Allan: 154–56, 160; "Letter to B———," 220
Pope, Alexander: 143, 182–84, 186, 188, 236; *The Dunciad*, 53–54, 58, 64–68, 175–76, 183; "Eloisa to Abelard," 111, 116–18; "Epistle to Dr. Arbuthnot," 168–76; *An Essay on Criticism*, 109*n*; *An Essay on Man*, 54, 62–64; "The First Satire of the Second Book of Horace Imitated," 168*n*; "The Rape of The Lock," 53–68, 114–17, 119, 126
Poulet, Georges, 106*n*, 127
Power of Satire, The (Elliott), 168*n*
"Prelude, The" (Wordsworth), 120

Problems of Aesthetics, The (ed. Vivas and Krieger), 167*n*
"Pure and Impure Poetry" (Warren), 12–13, 215

Ramus, Petrus, 188
Ransom, John Crowe: 21, 133, 214*n*, 226, 233, 242–45, 246*n*, 249–50; *The World's Body*, 20–21, 243, 244*n*
"Rape of the Lock, The" (Pope), 53–68, 114–17, 119, 126
Reynolds, Sir Joshua, 120*n*
Richards, I. A., 154, 187, 205, 235
"Rime of the Ancient Mariner, The" (Coleridge), 122–23, 250–51
Ruskin, John, 186

St. Augustine, 190, 200
St. John of the Cross, 5
Saintsbury, George, 143–45
Sartre, Jean Paul, 246
Scaliger, Julius Caesar, 233
Scarlet Letter, The (Hawthorne), 84–85
Schelling, Friedrich Wilhelm Joseph von, 189
Schiller, Johann Christoph Friedrich von, 251
Schlegel, Friedrich, 189
Schopenhauer, Arthur, 241, 247
Shakespeare, William: *Hamlet*, 124, 160–61; *Henry IV, Part, I*, 46, 49*n*; *Henry VI, Part III*, 37–40, 47–48, 51; *King Lear*, 124, 232*n*; *A Midsummer Night's Dream*, 36; *Much Ado About Nothing*, 46; *The Phoenix and the Turtle*, 110*n*, 112; *Richard II*, 48, 51; *Richard III*, 37–52; *Sonnets*, 7*n*, 8*n*, 19–36; *The Tempest*, 36, 237; *Troilus and Cressida*, 49; *Venus and Adonis*, 49
Shapiro, Karl: "A Farewell to Criticism," 4–5, 11
Shelley, Percy Bysshe: 230; "To a Skylark," 122, 126
Sidney, Sir Philip: *An Apology for Poetry*, 192, 230, 231–33
Sister Arts, The (Hagstrum), 108
Skepticism and Poetry (James), 186
Sophocles, 73–75
Spenser, Edmund: *Faerie Queene*, 208, 211, 244–45
Spitzer, Leo: *Essays on English and American Literature*, 3–7, 109*n*, 110

255

INDEX

Stevens, Wallace: 250; "Anecdote of the Jar," 126–27
Sutton, Walter, 153–64
Swift, Jonathan: 65–66; *Gulliver's Travels*, 168

Tate, Allen: 55, 57, 145, 226, 233, 242n, 245–46; "The Angelic Imagination," 245n; "The Symbolic Imagination," 245; "Tension in Poetry," 154n; "Three Types of Poetry," 165, 245
Theory of Literature (Wellek and Warren), 131–32, 135
Tillotson, Geoffrey, 54, 61n
"To a Skylark" (Shelley), 122, 126
"To His Coy Mistress" (Marvell), 122
"To the Cuckoo" (Wordsworth), 73n, 119–20

Unger, Leonard: *The Man in the Name*, 20–21, 49n
Urne Buriall (Browne), 110, 113–16, 125

Van Nostrand, Albert, 136, 138
Vivas, Eliseo: 156–57, 160, 226; "Contextualism Reconsidered," 153; *The Problems of Aesthetics* (ed.), 167n

Waggoner, Hyatt H.: "A Poem is Just a Part," 196, 211–12
Warren, Austin: *Theory of Literature* (with René Wellek), 131–32, 135

Warren, Robert Penn: 135, 250; "Pure and Impure Poetry," 12–13, 215
Weil, Simone, 246
Wellek, René: 135, 177–78; *A History of Modern Criticism 1750–1950*, 178, 185; *Theory of Literature* (with Austin Warren), 131–32, 135
Well-Tempered Critic, The (Frye), 224n, 232, 235
Well Wrought Urn, The (Brooks), 55, 110, 112, 115
Wimsatt, William K.: 170, 172, 195, 198, 200, 214, 215–16, 221n, 224–25, 231, 234, 236, 248–50; *Hateful Contraries*, 196, 205–9; "Poetic Tension," 155n; "Responsio Scribleri," 196, 212–14, 216–18; review of *The Tragic Vision*, 196, 201–5; "What to Say About a Poem," 196, 209–11; *Literary Criticism: A Short History* (with Cleanth Brooks), 177–93, 195–97, 234
Winckelmann, Johann Joachim, 106
Winters, Yvor, 76, 132, 191, 198, 207, 245n, 250
Wordsworth, William: 119–21, 124; "The Prelude," 120; "To the Cuckoo," 73n, 119–20
World's Body, The (Ransom), 20–21, 243, 244n

Yeats, William Butler, 57, 118–19, 124, 127, 165, 190–91, 246
Youth (Conrad), 92–101

Zimansky, Curt A., 131n

The Play and Place of Criticism
by Murray Krieger

Designer: Gerard Valerio
Typesetter: Kingsport Press, Inc.
Typeface: Garamond #3